# An Introduction to Text Mining

Sara Miller McCune founded SAGE Publishing in 1965 to support the dissemination of usable knowledge and educate a global community. SAGE publishes more than 1000 journals and over 800 new books each year, spanning a wide range of subject areas. Our growing selection of library products includes archives, data, case studies and video. SAGE remains majority owned by our founder and after her lifetime will become owned by a charitable trust that secures the company's continued independence.

Los Angeles | London | New Delhi | Singapore | Washington DC | Melbourne

# An Introduction to Text Mining

## Research Design, Data Collection, and Analysis

Gabe Ignatow

*University of North Texas*

Rada Mihalcea

*University of Michigan*

Los Angeles | London | New Delhi
Singapore | Washington DC | Melbourne

FOR INFORMATION:

SAGE Publications, Inc.
2455 Teller Road
Thousand Oaks, California 91320
E-mail: order@sagepub.com

SAGE Publications Ltd.
1 Oliver's Yard
55 City Road
London EC1Y 1SP
United Kingdom

SAGE Publications India Pvt. Ltd.
B 1/I 1 Mohan Cooperative Industrial Area
Mathura Road, New Delhi 110 044
India

SAGE Publications Asia-Pacific Pte. Ltd.
3 Church Street
#10-04 Samsung Hub
Singapore 049483

Acquisitions Editor:   Helen Salmon
Editorial Assistant:   Megan O'Heffernan
eLearning Editor:   Chelsea Neve
Production Editor:   Kelly DeRosa
Copy Editor:   Megan Markanich
Typesetter:   C&M Digitals (P) Ltd.
Proofreader:   Wendy Jo Dymond
Indexer:   Joan Shapiro
Cover Designer:   Michael Dubowe
Marketing Manager:   Shari Countryman

Printed in the United States of America

*Library of Congress Cataloging-in-Publication Data*

Names: Ignatow, Gabe, author. | Mihalcea, Rada, 1974- author.

Title: An introduction to text mining : research design, data collection, and analysis / Gabe Ignatow, University of North Texas, Rada Mihalcea, University of Michigan.

Description: Thousand Oaks : SAGE Publications, [2018] | Includes bibliographical references and index.

Identifiers: LCCN 2017038203 | ISBN 9781506337005 (pbk. : alk. paper)

Subjects: LCSH: Data mining. | Social sciences—Research.

Classification: LCC QA76.9.D343 I425 2017 | DDC 006.3/12—dc23
LC record available at https://lccn.loc.gov/2017038203

This book is printed on acid-free paper.

Certified Sourcing
www.sfiprogram.org
SFI-00453

SFI label applies to text stock

17 18 19 20 21 10 9 8 7 6 5 4 3 2 1

# BRIEF CONTENTS

# DETAILED CONTENTS

# ACKNOWLEDGMENTS

*An Introduction to Text Mining* has been a long time in the making, and there are too many people to count who deserve our thanks for helping to bring this book to publication. First and foremost, we must thank our undergraduate and graduate students who have shown so much enthusiasm for learning about online communities. It was their energy and questions that convinced us of the need for this book. Helen Salmon, Katie Ancheta, and the entire editorial and production staff at SAGE deserve our special thanks. In truth, it was Helen who got this project off the ground, and she and the entire SAGE staff, including SAGE's team of expert reviewers, provided support and guidance throughout the writing and production process. SAGE's reviewers played an especially critical role by providing invaluable feedback based on their research and teaching experiences in their home disciplines. A textbook as interdisciplinary as this one requires absolutely top-flight reviewers, and we were fortunate to have many of them. A special thank-you goes to Roger Clark, Kate de Medeiros, Carol Ann MacGregor, Kenneth C. C. Yang, A. Victor Ferreros, and Jennifer Bachner.

Last but by no means least we thank our spouses and children Neva, Alex, and Sara, and Mihai, Zara, and Caius, for their patience with us and their encouragement over the many years of research, writing, and editing that went into this textbook.

GI and RM

# PREFACE

---

Students are accustomed to participating in all sorts of online communities. While interacting on platforms such as Facebook, Twitter, Snapchat, and Instagram as well as on blogs, forums, and many other apps and sites, some students taking courses in the social sciences and computer science want to take things a step further and perform their own research on the social interactions that occur in these communities. We have written this book for those students, including especially undergraduate and graduate students in anthropology, communications, computer science, education, linguistics, marketing, political science, psychology, and sociology courses who want to do research using online tools and data sets. Whether they are writing a term paper or honors thesis, or working on an independent research project or a project with a faculty adviser, students who want to use text mining tools for social research need a place to start.

Online communities offer no end of interesting linguistic and social material to study, from emojis and abbreviations to forms of address, themes, metaphors, and all sorts of interpersonal conversational dynamics. The volume of data available for research, and the many research tools available to students, are simply overwhelming. *An Introduction to Text Mining* is here to help. The book is organized to guide students through major ethical, philosophical, and logical issues that should be considered in the earliest stages of a research project (see Part I) and then to survey the landscape of text mining and text analysis tools and methodologies that have been developed across the social sciences and computational linguistics. Appendices A through G on data and software resources are a key to the book, and readers should consider reviewing these early and returning to them often as they work their way through the early chapters and begin to design their own research projects (see Chapter 5).

If you think of your text mining research project as a house, then the chapters in Part I are instructions for building the foundation. Just as a house with a flaw in its foundation will not last long, a research project with a shaky logical foundation or questionable ethics may look good at the start, but it is inevitable that at some point its flaws will be exposed. Chapter 5 on research design provides architectural instruction for building the framework of your house. Designing a research project that can address, and perhaps conclusively answer, a research question or questions is a challenging task, and it is useful to know the kinds of research designs that have a track record of success in research using text mining tools and methodologies. Parts III through V survey text mining and analysis methodologies, the equivalent of proven house-building methods. Appendix A provides a partial survey of online sources of textual data, which is the raw material of your research project. Appendices B through G provide, as it were, a survey of the practical tools that are available for house construction, from hand tools to heavy-duty machinery. While setting the foundation, designing the house, and choosing a construction method, it is a good idea to be aware of the types of practical tools that are available and within budget so that your project can reach a successful conclusion. Appendices H and I, as well as the Glossary, provide handy summaries of web resources, statistical tools, and key terms.

Additional resources for instructors using *An Introduction to Text Mining* are also provided. Editable, chapter-specific Microsoft® PowerPoint® slides, as well as assignments and activities created by the authors, are available for download at: **http:/study.sagepub.com/ introtextmining**.

# NOTE TO THE READER

*A*n *Introduction to Text Mining* grew out of our earlier SAGE methods guidebook *Text Mining*, which is a shorter volume intended to serve as a practical guidebook for graduate students and professional researchers. The two books share both a core mission and structure. Their mission is to enable readers to make better informed decisions about research projects that use text mining and text analysis methodologies. And they both survey text mining tools developed in multiple disciplines within the social sciences, humanities, and computer science.

Where *Text Mining* was intended for advanced students and researchers, the current volume is a dedicated undergraduate or first-year graduate textbook intended for use in social science and data science courses. This book is thus longer than *Text Mining*, as it includes new material related to ethical and epistemological considerations in text-based research. There is a new chapter on how to write text-based social science research papers. And there are appendices that list and review data sources and software for preparing, cleaning, organizing, analyzing, and visualizing patterns in texts. Although these appendices were intended for students in undergraduate courses we suspect that they will prove valuable for experienced researchers as well.

GI and RM

# ABOUT THE AUTHORS

**Gabe Ignatow** is an associate professor of sociology at the University of North Texas (UNT), where he has taught since 2007. His research interests are in the areas of sociological theory, text mining and analysis methods, new media, and information policy.

Gabe's current research involves working with computer scientists and statisticians to adapt text mining and topic modeling techniques for social science applications. Gabe has been working with mixed methods of text analysis since the 1990s and has published this work in the following journals: *Social Forces*, *Sociological Forum*, *Poetics*, the *Journal for the Theory of Social Behaviour*, and the *Journal of Computer-Mediated Communication*. He is the author of over 30 peer-reviewed articles and book chapters and serves on the editorial boards of the journals *Sociological Forum*, the *Journal for the Theory of Social Behaviour*, and *Studies in Media and Communication*. He has served as the UNT Department of Sociology's graduate program codirector and undergraduate program director and has been selected as a faculty fellow at the Center for Cultural Sociology at Yale University. He is also a cofounder and the CEO of GradTrek, a graduate degree search engine company.

**Rada Mihalcea** is a professor of computer science and engineering at the University of Michigan. Her research interests are in computational linguistics, with a focus on lexical semantics, multilingual natural language processing, and computational social sciences. She serves or has served on the editorial boards of the following journals: *Computational Linguistics*, *Language Resources and Evaluation*, *Natural Language Engineering*, *Research on Language and Computation*, *IEEE Transactions on Affective Computing*, and *Transactions of the Association for Computational Linguistics*. She was a general chair for the Conference of the North American Chapter of the Association for Computational Linguistics (NAACL, 2015) and a program cochair for the Conference of the Association for Computational Linguistics (2011) and the Conference on Empirical

Methods in Natural Language Processing (2009). She is the recipient of a National Science Foundation CAREER award (2008) and a Presidential Early Career Award for Scientists and Engineers (2009). In 2013, she was made an honorary citizen of her hometown of Cluj-Napoca, Romania.

# Foundations

# TEXT MINING AND TEXT ANALYSIS

## INTRODUCTION

Text mining is an exciting field that encompasses new research methods and software tools that are being used across academia as well as by companies and government agencies. Researchers today are using text mining tools in ambitious projects to attempt to predict everything from the direction of stock markets (Bollen, Mao, & Zeng, 2011) to the occurrence of political protests (Kallus, 2014). Text mining is also commonly used in marketing research and many other business applications as well as in government and defense work.

Over the past few years, text mining has started to catch on in the social sciences, in academic disciplines as diverse as anthropology (Acerbi, Lampos, Garnett, & Bentley, 2013; Marwick, 2013), communications (Lazard, Scheinfeld, Bernhardt, Wilcox, & Suran, 2015), economics (Levenberg, Pulman, Moilanen, Simpson, & Roberts, 2014), education (Evison, 2013), political science (Eshbaugh-Soha, 2010; Grimmer & Stewart, 2013), psychology (Colley & Neal, 2012; Schmitt, 2005), and sociology (Bail, 2012; Heritage & Raymond, 2005; Mische, 2014). Before social scientists began to adapt text mining tools to use in their research, they spent decades studying transcribed interviews, newspaper articles, speeches, and other forms of textual data, and they developed sophisticated text analysis methods that we review in the chapters in Part IV. So while text mining is a relatively new interdisciplinary field based in computer science, text analysis methods have a long history in the social sciences (see Roberts, 1997).

Text mining processes typically include information retrieval (methods for acquiring texts) and applications of advanced statistical methods and **natural language processing (NLP)** such as part-of-speech tagging and syntactic parsing. Text mining also often involves named entity recognition (NER), which is the use of statistical techniques to identify named text features such as people, organizations, and place names; **disambiguation**, which is the use of contextual clues to decide where words refer to one or another of their multiple meanings; and **sentiment analysis**, which involves discerning subjective material and extracting attitudinal information such as sentiment, opinion, mood, and emotion. These techniques are covered in Parts III and V of this book. Text mining also involves more basic techniques for acquiring and processing data. These techniques include tools for **web scraping** and **web crawling**, for making use of dictionaries and other lexical resources, and for processing texts and relating words to texts. These techniques are covered in Parts II and III.

## RESEARCH IN THE SPOTLIGHT
### Predicting the Stock Market With Twitter

Bollen, J., Mao, H., & Zeng, X.-J. (2011). Twitter mood predicts the stock market. *Journal of Computational Science, 2*(1), 1–8.

The computer scientists Bollen, Mao, and Zeng asked whether societies can experience mood states that affect their collective decision making, and by extension whether the public mood is correlated

or even predictive of economic indicators. Applying sentiment analysis (see Chapter 14) to large-scale Twitter feeds, Bollen and colleagues investigated whether measurements of collective mood states are correlated to the value of the Dow Jones Industrial Average over time. They analyzed the text content of daily Twitter feeds using OpinionFinder, which measures positive versus negative mood and Google Profile of Mood States to measure mood in terms of six dimensions (calm, alert, sure, vital, kind, and happy). They also investigated the hypothesis that public mood states are predictive of changes in Dow Jones Industrial Average closing values, finding that the accuracy of stock market predictions can be significantly improved by the inclusion of some specific public mood dimensions but not others.

Specialized software used:

OpinionFinder

http://mpqa.cs.pitt.edu/opinionfinder

Text analysis involves systematic analysis of word use patterns in texts and typically combines formal statistical methods and less formal, more humanistic interpretive techniques. Text analysis arguably originated as early as the 1200s with the Dominican friar Hugh of Saint-Cher and his team of several hundred fellow friars who created the first biblical **concordance**, or cross-listing of terms and concepts in the Bible. There is also evidence of European inquisitorial church studies of newspapers in the late 1600s, and the first well-documented quantitative text analysis was performed in Sweden in the 1700s when the Swedish state church analyzed the symbology and ideological content of popular hymns that appeared to challenge church orthodoxy (Krippendorff, 2013, pp. 10–11). The field of text analysis expanded rapidly in the 20th century as researchers in the social sciences and humanities developed a broad spectrum of techniques for analyzing texts, including methods that relied heavily on human interpretation of texts as well as formal statistical methods. Systematic quantitative analysis of newspapers was performed in the late 1800s and early 1900s by researchers including Speed (1893), who showed that in the late 1800s New York newspapers had decreased their coverage of literary, scientific, and religious matters in favor of sports, gossip, and scandals. Similar text analysis studies were performed by Wilcox (1900), Fenton (1911), and White (1924), all of whom quantified newspaper space devoted to different categories of news. In the 1920s through 1940s, Lasswell and his colleagues conducted breakthrough **content analysis** studies of political messages and propaganda (e.g., Lasswell, 1927). Lasswell's work inspired large-scale content analysis projects including the **General Inquirer project** at Harvard, which is a lexicon attaching syntactic, semantic, and pragmatic information to part-of-speech tagged words (Stone, Dunphry, Smith, & Ogilvie, 1966).

While text mining's roots are in computer science and the roots of text analysis are in the social sciences and humanities, today, as we will see throughout this textbook, the two fields are converging. Social scientists and humanities scholars are adapting text mining tools for their research projects, while text mining specialists are investigating the kinds of social phenomena (e.g., political protests and other forms of collective behavior) that have traditionally been studied within the social sciences.

# SIX APPROACHES TO TEXT ANALYSIS

The field of text mining is divided mainly in terms of different methodologies, while the field of text analysis can be divided into several different approaches that are each based on a different way of theorizing language use. Before discussing some of the special challenges associated with using online data for social science research, next we review six of the most prominent approaches to text analysis. As we will see, many researchers who work with these approaches are finding ways to make use of the new text mining methodologies and tools that are covered in Parts II, III, and V. These approaches include **conversation analysis**, analysis of **discourse positions**, **critical discourse analysis (CDA)**, content analysis, **Foucauldian analysis**, and analysis of texts as social information. These approaches use different logical strategies and are based on different theoretical foundations and philosophical assumptions (discussed in Chapter 4). They also operate at different levels of analysis (micro, meso, and macro) and employ different selection and sampling strategies (see Chapter 5).

## Conversation Analysis

Conversation analysts study everyday conversations in terms of how people negotiate the meaning of the conversation in which they are participating and the larger discourse of which the conversation is a part. Conversation analysts focus not only on what is said in daily conversations but also on how people use language pragmatically to define the situations in which they find themselves. These processes go mostly unnoticed until there is disagreement as to the meaning of a particular situation. An example of conversation analysis is the educational researcher Evison's (2013) study of "academic talk," which used corpus linguistic techniques (see Appendix F) on both a corpus of 250,000 words of spoken academic discourse and a benchmark corpus of casual conversation to explore conversational turn openings. The corpus of academic discourse included 13,337 turns taken by tutors and students in a range of social interactions. In seeking to better understand the unique language of academia and of specific academic disciplines, Evison identified six items that have a particularly strong affinity with the turn-opening position (*mhm, mm, yes, laughter, oh, no*) as key characteristics of academic talk.

Further examples of conversation analysis research include studies of conversation in educational settings by O'Keefe and Walsh (2012); in health care settings by Heath and Luff (2000), Heritage and Raymond (2005), and Silverman (2016); and in online environments among Wikipedia editors by Danescu-Niculescu-Mizil, Lee, Pang, and Kleinberg (2012). O'Keefe and Walsh's 2012 study combined corpus linguistics and conversation analysis methodologies to analyze higher education small-group teaching sessions. Their data are from a 1-million-word corpus, the Limerick–Belfast Corpus of Academic Spoken English (LIBEL CASE). Danescu-Niculescu-Mizil and colleagues (2012) analyzed signals manifested in language in order to learn about roles, status, and other aspects of groups' interactional dynamics. In their study of Wikipedians and of arguments before the U.S. Supreme Court, they showed that in group discussions, power differentials between participants are subtly revealed by the degree to which one individual immediately echoes the linguistic style of the person to whom they are responding. They proposed an analysis framework based on linguistic coordination that can be used to shed light on power relationships and that works consistently across multiple types of power, including more static forms of power based on status differences and more situational forms in which one individual experiences a type of dependence on another.

Hakimnia and her colleagues' (2015) conversation analysis of transcripts of calls to a telenursing site in Sweden used a comparative research design (see Chapter 5). The study's goal was to analyze callers' reasons for calling and the outcome of the calls in terms of whether men and women received different kinds of referrals. The researchers chose to randomly sample 800 calls from a corpus of over 5,000 total calls that had been recorded at a telenursing site in Sweden over a period of 11 months. Callers were informed about the study in a prerecorded message and consented to participate, while the nurses were informed verbally about the study. The first step in the analysis of the final sample of 800 calls was to create a matrix (see Chapter 5 and Appendices C and D), including information on each caller's gender, age, fluency or nonfluency in Swedish as well as the outcome of the call (whether callers were referred to a general practitioner). The researchers found that men, and especially fathers, received more referrals to general practitioners than did women. The most common caller was a woman fluent in Swedish (64%), and the least likely caller was a man nonfluent in Swedish (3%). All in all, 70% of the callers were women. When the calls concerned children, 78% of the callers were female. Based on these results, the researchers concluded that it is important that telenursing not become a "feminine" activity, only suitable for young callers fluent in Swedish. Given the telenurses' gatekeeping role, there is a risk that differences on this first level of health care could be reproduced throughout the whole health care system.

## Analysis of Discourse Positions

Analyzing discourse positions is an approach to text analysis that allows researchers to reconstruct communicative interactions through which texts are produced and in this way gain a better understanding of their meaning from their author's viewpoint. Discourse positions are understood as typical discursive roles that people adopt in their everyday communication practices, and the analysis of discourse positions is a way of linking texts to the social spaces in which they have emerged. An example of contemporary discourse position research is Bamberg's (2004) study of the "small stories" told by adolescents and postadolescents about their identities. Bamberg's 2004 study is informed by theories of human development and of narrative (see Chapter 10). His texts are excerpts of transcriptions from a group discussion among five 15-year-old boys telling a story about a female student they all know. The group discussion was conducted in the presence of an adult moderator, but the data were collected as part of a larger project in which Bamberg and his colleagues collected journal entries and transcribed oral accounts from 10-, 12-, and 15-year-old boys in one-on-one interviews and group discussions. Although the interviews and groups discussions were open-ended, they all focused on the same list of topics, including friends and friendships, girls, the boys' feelings and sense of self, and their ideas about adulthood and future orientation. Bamberg and his team analyzed the transcripts line by line, coding instances of the boys positioning themselves relative to each other and to characters in their stories.

Edley and Wetherell's (1997, 2001; Wetherell & Edley, 1999) studies of masculine identity formation are similar to Bamberg's study in that they also focus on stories people tell themselves and others in ordinary everyday conversations. Edley and Wetherell studied a corpus of men's talk on feminism and feminists to identify patterns and regularities in their accounts of feminism and in the organization of their rhetoric. Their samples of men included a sample of white, middle-class 17- to 18-year-old school students and a sample of 60 interviews with a more diverse sample of older men aged 20 to 64. The researchers identified two "interpretative repertoires of feminism and feminists," which set up a "Jekyll and Hyde" binary and "positioned feminism along with feminists very differently as reasonable versus extreme" (Edley & Wetherell, 2001, p. 439).

In the end, analysis of discourse positions is for the most part a qualitative approach to text analysis that relies almost entirely on human interpretation of texts (see Hewson, 2014). Appendix D includes a list of contemporary qualitative data analysis software (QDAS) packages that can be used to organize and code the kinds of text corpora analyzed by Bamberg, Edley, Wetherell, and other researchers working in this tradition.

## Critical Discourse Analysis

CDA involves seeking the presence of features from other discourses in the text or discourse to be analyzed. CDA is based on Fairclough's (1995) concept of "intertextuality," which is the idea that people appropriate from discourses circulating in their social space whenever they speak or write. In CDA, ordinary everyday speaking and writing are understood to involve selecting and combining elements from dominant discourses.

While the term *discourse* generally refers to all practices of writing and talking, in CDA discourses are understood as ways of writing and talking that "rule out" and "rule in" ways of constructing knowledge about topics. In other words, discourses "do not just describe things; they do things" (Potter & Wetherell, 1987, p. 6) through the way they make sense of the world for its inhabitants (Fairclough, 1992; van Dijk, 1993).

Discourses cannot be studied directly but can be explored by examining the texts that constitute them (Fairclough, 1992; Parker, 1992). In this way, texts can be analyzed as fragments of discourses that reflect and project ideological domination by powerful groups in society. But texts can also be considered a potential mechanism of liberation when they are produced by the critical analyst who reveals mechanisms of ideological domination in them in an attempt to overcome or eliminate them.

Although CDA has generally employed strictly interpretive methods, use of quantitative and statistical techniques is not a novel practice (Krishnamurthy, 1996; Stubbs, 1994), and the use of software to create, manage, and analyze large collections of texts appears to be increasingly popular (Baker et al., 2008; Koller & Mautner, 2004; O'Halloran & Coffin, 2004).

A 2014 study by Bednarek and Caple exemplifies the use of statistical techniques in CDA. Bednarek and Caple introduced the concept of "news values" to CDA of news media and illustrated their approach with two case studies using the same collection of British news discourse. Their texts included 100 news stories (about 70,000 words total) from 2003 covering 10 topics from 10 different national newspapers, including five quality papers and five tabloids. The analysis proceeded through analysis of word frequency of the top 100 most frequently used words and two-word clusters (bigrams), focusing on words that represent news values such as *eliteness, superlativeness, proximity, negativity, timeliness, personalization*, and *novelty*. The authors concluded that their case studies demonstrated that corpus linguistic techniques (see Appendix F) can identify discursive devices that are repeatedly used in news discourse to construct and perpetuate an ideology of newsworthiness.

In another CDA study, Baker and his colleagues (2008) analyzed a 140-million-word corpus of British news articles about refugees, asylum seekers, immigrants, and migrants. They used collocation and concordance analysis (see Appendix F) to identify common categories of representation of refugees, asylum seekers, immigrants, and migrants. They also discussed how collocation and concordance analysis can be used to direct researchers to representative texts in order to carry out qualitative analysis.

## RESEARCH IN THE SPOTLIGHT
### Combining Critical Discourse Analysis and Corpus Linguistics

Baker, P., Gabrielatos, C., Khosravinik, M., Krzyzanowski, M., Mcenery, T., & Wodak, R. (2008). A useful methodological synergy? Combining critical discourse analysis and corpus linguistics to examine discourses of refugees and asylum seekers in the UK press. *Discourse & Society, 19*(3), 273–306.

In this critical discourse analysis (CDA) study, the linguist Baker and his colleagues analyzed a 140-million-word corpus of British news articles about refugees, asylum seekers, immigrants, and migrants. The authors used collocation and concordance analysis (see Appendix F) to identify common categories of representations of the four groups. The authors also discuss how collocation and concordance analysis can be used to direct researchers to representative texts in order to carry out qualitative analysis.

Specialized software used:

WordSmith
www.lexically.net/wordsmith

## Content Analysis

Content analysis adopts a quantitative, scientific approach to text analysis. Unlike CDA, content analysis is generally focused on texts themselves rather than texts' relations to their social and historical contexts. One of the classic definitions of content analysis defines it as "a research technique for the objective, systematic-quantitative description of the manifest content of communication" (Berelson, 1952, p. 18). At a practical level, content analysis involves the development of a coding frame that is applied to textual data. It mainly consists of breaking down texts into pertinent units of information in order to permit subsequent coding and categorization.

Krippendorff's (2013) classic textbook *Content Analysis* is the standard reference for work in this area. Many of the research design principles and sampling techniques covered in Chapter 5 of this textbook are shared with content analysis, although Krippendorff's book goes into much greater detail on statistical sampling of texts and units of texts, as well as on statistical tests of interrater reliability.

## Foucauldian Analysis

The philosopher and historian Foucault (1973) developed an influential conceptualization of intertextuality that differs significantly from Fairclough's conceptualization in CDA. Rather than identifying the influence of external discourses within a text, for Foucault the meaning of a text emerges in reference to discourses with which it engages in dialogue. These engagements may be explicit or, more often, implicit. In Foucauldian intertextual analysis, the analyst must ask each text about its presuppositions and with which discourses it dialogues. The meaning of a text therefore derives from its similarities and differences with respect to other texts and discourses and from implicit presuppositions within the text that can be recognized by historically informed close reading.

Foucauldian analysis of texts is performed in many theoretical and applied research fields. For instance, a number of studies have used Foucauldian intertextual analysis to analyze forestry policy (see Winkel, 2012, for an overview). Researchers working in Europe (e.g., Berglund, 2001; Franklin, 2002; Van Herzele, 2006), North America, and developing countries (e.g., Asher & Ojeda, 2009; Mathews, 2005) have used Foucauldian analysis to study policy discourses regarding forest management, forest fires, and corporate responsibility.

Another example of Foucauldian intertextual analysis is a sophisticated study of the professional identities of nurses by Bell, Campbell, and Goldberg (2015). Bell and colleagues argued that nurses' professional identities should be understood in relation to the identities of other occupational categories within the health care field. The authors collected their data from PubMed, a medical research database. Using PubMed's own user interface, the authors acquired the abstracts for research papers that used the terms *service* or *services* in the abstract or key words for a period from 1986 to 2013. The downloaded abstracts were added to an SQLite database, which was used to generate comma-separated values (CSV) files with abstracts organized into 3-year periods. The authors then spent approximately 6 weeks of full-time work, manually checking the data for duplicates and other errors. The final sample included over 230,000 abstracts. Bell and colleagues then used the text analysis package Leximancer (see Appendix C) to calculate frequency and co-occurrence statistics for all concepts in the abstracts (see also Appendix F). Leximancer also produced concept maps (see Appendix G) to visually represent the relationships between concepts. The authors further cleaned their data after viewing these initial concept maps and finding a number of irrelevant terms and then used Leximancer to analyze the concept of nursing in terms of its co-occurrence with other concepts.

## Analysis of Texts as Social Information

Another category of text analysis treats texts as reflections of the practical knowledge of their authors. This type of analysis is prevalent in grounded theory studies (see Chapter 4) as well as in applied studies of expert discourses. Interest in the informative analysis of texts is due in part to its practical value, because user-generated texts can potentially provide analysts with reliable information about social reality. Naturally, the quality of information about social reality that is contained in texts varies according to the level of knowledge of each individual who has participated in the creation of the text, and the information that subjects provide is partial insofar as it is filtered by their own particular point of view.

An example of analysis of texts as social information is a 2012 psychological study by Colley and Neal on the topic of organizational safety. Starting with small representative samples of upper managers, supervisors, and workers in an Australian freight and passenger rail company, Colley and Neal conducted open-ended interviews with members of the three groups. These were transcribed and analyzed using Leximancer (see Appendix C) for map analysis (see also Appendix G). Comparing the concept maps produced for the three groups revealed significant differences between the "safety climate schema" of upper managers, supervisors, and workers.

## CHALLENGES AND LIMITATIONS OF USING ONLINE DATA

Having introduced text mining and text analysis, in this section we review some lessons that have been learned from other fields about how best to adapt social science research methods to data from online environments. This section is short but critically important for students who plan to perform research with data taken from social media platforms and websites.

Methodologies such as text mining that analyze data from digital environments offer potential cost- and time-efficiency advantages over older methods (Hewson & Laurent, 2012; Hewson, Yule, Laurent, & Vogel, 2003), as the Internet provides ready access to a potentially vast, geographically diverse participant pool. The speed and global reach of the Internet can facilitate cross-cultural research projects that would otherwise be prohibitively expensive. It also allows for the emergence of patterns of social interactions, which are elaborate in terms of their richness of communication exchange but where levels of anonymity and privacy can be high. The Internet's unique combination of digital archiving technologies and users' perceptions of anonymity and privacy may reduce social desirability effects (where research participants knowingly or unknowingly attempt to provide researchers with socially acceptable and desirable, rather than accurate, information). The unique attributes of Internet-based technologies may also reduce biases resulting from the perception of attributes such as race, ethnicity, and sex or gender, promoting greater candor. The convenience of these technologies can also empower research participants by allowing them to take part in study procedures that fit their schedules and can be performed within their own spaces such as at home or in a familiar work environment.

While Internet-based research has many advantages (see Hewson, Vogel, & Laurent, 2015), Internet-based data have a number of serious drawbacks for social science research. One major disadvantage is the potentially biased nature of Internet-accessed data samples. **Sample bias** is one of the most fundamental and difficult to manage challenges associated with Internet-mediated research (see Chapter 5). Second, as compared to offline methods, Internet-based data are often characterized by reduced levels of researcher control. This lack of control arises mainly from technical issues, such as users' different hardware and software configurations and network traffic performance. Research participants working with different hardware platforms, operating systems, and browsers may experience social media services and online surveys very differently, and it is often extremely difficult for researchers to fully appreciate differences in participants' experiences. In addition, hardware and software failures may lead to unpredicted effects, which may cause problems. Because of the lack of researcher presence, in Internet-based research there is often a lack of researcher control over and knowledge of variations in participants' behaviors and the participation context. This may cause problems related to the extent to which researchers can gauge participants' intentions and levels of sincerity and honesty during a study, as researchers lack nonverbal cues to evaluate participants compared with face-to-face communication.

Despite these weaknesses, scholars have long recognized digital technologies' potential as research tools. While social researchers have occasionally developed brand-new Internet-based methodologies, they have also adapted preexisting research methods for use with evolving digital technology. Because a number of broadly applicable lessons have been learned from these adaptation processes, in the remainder of this chapter we briefly review some of the most widely used social science research methods that have been adapted to Internet-related communication technologies and some of the lessons learned from each. We discuss offline and online approaches to *social surveys*, *ethnography*, and *archival research* but do not cover online focus groups (Krueger & Casey, 2014) or experiments (Birnbaum, 2000). While focus groups and experiments are both important and widely used research methods, we have found that the lessons learned from developing online versions of these methods are less applicable to text mining than lessons learned from the former three.

## Social Surveys

Social surveys are one of the most commonly used methods in the social sciences, and researchers have been working with online versions of surveys since the 1990s. Traditional telephone and paper surveys tend to be costly, even when using relatively small samples, and the costs of a traditional large-scale survey using mailed questionnaires can be enormous. Although the costs of online survey creation software and web survey services vary widely, by eliminating the need for paper, postage, and data entry costs, online surveys are generally less expensive than their paper- and telephone-based equivalents (Couper, 2000; Ilieva, Baron, & Healey, 2002; Yun & Trumbo, 2000). Online surveys can also save researchers time by allowing them to quickly reach thousands of people despite possibly being separated by great geographic distances (Garton, Haythornthwaite, & Wellman, 2007). With an online survey, a researcher can quickly gain access to large populations by posting invitations to participate in the survey to newsgroups, chat rooms, and message boards. In addition to their cost and time savings and overall convenience, another advantage of online surveys is that they exploit the ability of the Internet to provide access to groups and individuals who would be difficult, if not impossible, to reach otherwise (Garton et al., 1997).

While online surveys have significant advantages over paper- and phone-based surveys, they bring with them new challenges in terms of applying traditional survey research methods to the study of online behavior. Online survey researchers often encounter problems regarding sampling, because relatively little may be known about the characteristics of people in online communities aside from some basic demographic variables, and even this information may be questionable (Walejko, 2009). While attractive, features of online surveys themselves, such as multimedia, and of online survey services, such as use of company e-mail lists to generate samples, can affect the quality of the data they produce in a variety of ways.

The process of adapting social surveys to online environments offers a cautionary lesson for text mining researchers. The issue of user demographics casts a shadow over online survey research just as it does for text mining, because in online environments it is very difficult for researchers to make valid inferences about their populations of interest. The best practice for both methodologies is for researchers to carefully plan and then explain in precise detail their sampling strategies (see Chapter 5).

## Ethnography

In the 1990s, researchers began to adapt ethnographic methods designed to study geographically situated communities to online environments which are characterized by relationships that are technologically mediated rather than immediate (Salmons, 2014). The result is **virtual ethnography** (Hine, 2000) or **netnography** (Kozinets, 2009), which is the ethnographic study of people interacting in a wide range of online environments. Kozinets, a netnography pioneer, argues that successful netnography requires researchers to acknowledge the unique characteristics of these environments and to effect a "radical shift" from offline ethnography, which observes people, to a mode of analysis that involves recontextualizing conversational acts (Kozinets, 2002, p. 64). Because netnography provides more limited access to fixed demographic markers than does ethnography, the identities of discussants are much more difficult to discern. Yet netnographers must learn as much as possible about the forums, groups, and individuals they seek to understand. Unlike in traditional ethnographies, in the identification of relevant communities, online search engines have proven invaluable to the task of learning about research populations (Kozinets, 2002, p. 63).

Just as the quality of social survey research depends on sampling, netnography requires careful case selection (see Chapter 5). Netnographers must begin with specific research questions and then identify online forums appropriate to these questions (Kozinets, 2009, p. 89).

Netnography's lessons for text mining and analysis are straightforward. Leading researchers have shown that for netnography to be successful, researchers must acknowledge the unique characteristics of online environments, recognize the importance of developing and explaining their data selection strategy, and learn as much as they possibly can about their populations of interest. All three lessons apply to text mining research that analyzes user-generated data mined from online sources.

## Historical Research Methods

Archival research methods are among the oldest methods in the social sciences. The founding fathers of sociology—Marx, Weber, and Durkheim—all did historical scholarship based on archival research, and today, archival research methods are widely used by historians, political scientists, and sociologists.

Historical researchers have adapted digital technology to archival research in two waves. The first occurred in the 1950s and 1960s when, in the early years of accessible computers, historians taught themselves statistical methods and programming languages. Adopting quantitative methods developed in sociology and political science, during this period historians made lasting contributions in the areas of "social mobility, political identification, family formation, patterns of crime, economic growth, and the consequences of ethnic identity" (Ayers, 1999). Unfortunately, however, that quantitative social science history collapsed suddenly, the victim of its own inflated claims, limited method and machinery, and changing academic fashion. By the mid-80s, history, along with many of the humanities and social sciences, had taken the linguistic turn. Rather than SPSS guides and codebooks, innovative historians carried books of French philosophy and German literary interpretation. The social science of choice shifted from sociology to anthropology; texts replaced tables. A new generation defined itself in opposition to social scientific methods just as energetically as an earlier generation had seen in those methods the best means of writing a truly democratic history. The first computer revolution largely failed (Ayers, 1999).

Beginning in the 1980s, historians and historically minded social scientists began to reengage with digital technologies. While today historical researchers use digital technologies at every stage of the research process, from professional communication to multimedia presentations, **digital archives** have had perhaps the most profound influence on the practice of historical research. Universities, research institutes, and private companies have digitized and created accessible archives of massive volumes of historical documents.

Historians recognize that these archives offer tremendous advantages in terms of the capacity, flexibility, accessibility, flexibility, diversity, manipulability, and interactivity of research (Cohen & Rosenzweig, 2005). However, digital research archives also pose dangers in terms of the quality, durability, and readability of stored data. There is also a potential for inaccessibility and monopoly and also for digital archives to encourage researcher passivity (Cohen & Rosenzweig, 2005).

There are lessons to be learned from digital history for text mining and text analysis, particularly from the sudden collapse of the digital history movement of the 1950s and 1960s. In light of the failure of that movement, it is imperative that social scientists working with text mining tools recognize the limitations of their chosen methods and not make imperious or inflated claims about these tools' revolutionary potential. Like all social science methods, text mining methods have benefits and drawbacks that must be recognized from the start and given consideration in every phase of the research process. And text mining researchers should be aware of historians' concerns about the quality of data stored in digital archives and the possibility for digital archives to encourage researcher passivity in the data gathering phase of research.

## Conclusion

This chapter has introduced text mining and text analysis methodologies, provided an overview of the major approaches to text analysis, and discussed some of the risks associated with analyzing data from online sources. Despite these risks, social and computer scientists are developing new text mining and text analysis tools to address a broad spectrum of applied and theoretical research questions, in academia as well as in the private and public sectors.

In the chapters that follow, you will learn how to find data online (Chapters 2 and 6), and you will learn about some of the ethical (Chapter 3) and philosophical and logical (Chapter 4) dimensions of text mining research. In Chapter 5, you will learn how to design your own social science research project. Parts II, IV, and V review specific text mining techniques for collecting and analyzing data, and Chapter 17 in Part VI provides guidance for writing and reporting your own research.

## Key Terms (see Glossary)

| | | |
|---|---|---|
| Concordance   5 | Critical discourse analysis | Disambiguation   4 |
| Content analysis   5 | (CDA)   6 | Discourse positions   6 |
| Conversation analysis   6 | Digital archives   15 | Foucauldian analysis   6 |

## Highlights

- Text mining processes include methods for acquiring digital texts and analyzing them with NLP and advanced statistical methods.

- Text mining is used in many academic and applied fields to analyze and predict public opinion and collective behavior.

- Text analysis began with analysis of religious texts in the Middle Ages and was developed by social scientists starting in the early 20th century.

- Text analysis in the social sciences involves analyzing transcribed interviews, newspapers, historical and legal documents, and online data.

- Major approaches to text analysis include analysis of discourse positions, conversation analysis, CDA, content analysis, intertextual analysis, and analysis of texts as social information.

- Advantages of Internet-based data and social science research methods include their low cost, unobtrusiveness, and use of unprompted data from research participants.

- Risks and limitations of Internet-based data and research methods include limited researcher control, possible sample bias, and the risk of researcher passivity in data collection.

## Review Questions

- What are the differences between text mining and text analysis methodologies?

- What are the main research processes involved in text mining?

- How is analysis of discourse positions different from conversation analysis?

- What kinds of software can be used for analysis of discourse positions and conversation analysis?

## Discussion Questions

- If you were interested in conducting a CDA of a contemporary discourse, what discourse would you study? Where would you find data for your analysis?

- How do researchers choose between collecting data from offline sources, such as in-person interviews, and online sources, such as social media platforms?

- What are the most critical problems with using data from online sources?

- If you already have an idea for a research project, what are likely to be the most critical advantages and disadvantages of using online data for your project?

- What are some ways text mining research be used to benefit science and society?

## Developing a Research Proposal

Select a social issue that interests you. How might you analyze how people talk about this issue? Are there differences between people from different communities and backgrounds in terms of how they think about this issue? Where (e.g., offline, online) do people talk about this issue, and how could you collect data from them?

## Further Reading

Ayers, E. L. (1999). *The pasts and futures of digital history*. Retrieved June 17, 2015, from http://www.vcdh.virginia.edu/PastsFutures.html

Bauer, M. W., Bicquelet, A., & Suerdem, A. K. (Eds.), *Textual analysis. SAGE benchmarks in social research methods* (Vol. 1). Thousand Oaks, CA: Sage.

Krippendorff, K. (2013). *Content analysis: An introduction to its methodology*. Thousand Oaks, CA: Sage.

Kuckartz, U. (2014). *Qualitative text analysis: A guide to methods, practice, and using software*. Thousand Oaks, CA: Sage.

Roberts, C. W. (1997). *Text analysis for the social sciences: Methods for drawing statistical inferences from texts and transcripts*. Mahwah, NJ: Lawrence Erlbaum.

# ACQUIRING DATA

## LEARNING OBJECTIVES

The goals of Chapter 2 are to help you to do the following:

1. Recognize the role data plays in text mining and the characteristics of ideal data sets for text mining applications.

2. Identify a variety of different data sources used to compile text mining data sets.

3. Assess the advantages and limitations of using social media to acquire data.

4. Analyze examples of social science research using data sets drawn from different sources.

## INTRODUCTION

While social scientists have for decades made use of data from attitude surveys, today researchers are attempting to leverage the growing volume of naturally occurring **unstructured data** generated by people, such as text or images. Some of these unstructured data are referred to as "big data," although that term has become a bit of a faddish buzzword. Naturally, there are questions that arise from the use of textual data sets as a way to learn about social groups and communities. There are, of course, advantages and disadvantages to each, and there are also ways to leverage both surveys and big data.

Surveys are the traditional mechanisms for gathering information on people, and there are entire fields that have developed around these data collection instruments. Surveys can collect clear, targeted information, and as such, the information obtained from surveys is significantly "cleaner" and significantly easier to process as compared to the information extracted from unstructured data sources. Surveys also have the advantage that they can be run in controlled settings, with complete information on the survey takers. These controlled settings can however also be a disadvantage. It has been argued, for instance, that survey research is often biased because of the typical places where surveys are run—for example, large student populations from Introduction to Psychology courses. Another challenge associated with surveys is that it excludes those people who do not like to provide information, and there is an entire body of research around methodologies to remove such participation bias. Above all, the main difficulty associated with survey instruments is the fact that they are expensive to run, both in terms of time and in terms of financial costs.

The alternative to surveys that has been extensively explored in recent years is the extraction of information from unstructured sources. For instance, rather than surveying a group of people on whether they are optimistic or pessimistic, alongside with asking for their location, as a way to create maps of "optimism," one could achieve the same goal by collecting Twitter or blog data, extracting the location of the writers from their profile, and using automatic text classification tools to infer their level of optimism (Ruan, Wilson, & Mihalcea, 2016). The main advantage of gathering people information from such data sources is their "always on" property, which allows one to collect information continuously and inexpensively. These digital resources also eliminate some of the biases that come with the survey instruments, but they nonetheless introduce other kinds of biases. For instance, most of these data-driven collections of information on people rely on social media or on crowdsourcing platforms such as Amazon Mechanical Turk, but these sources cover only a certain type of population who is open to posting on social media or participating in online crowdsourcing experiments. Even more important, another major difficulty associated with the use of unstructured data sources is the lack of exactness during the process of extracting information. This process often consists of automatic tools for text mining and classification, which even if they are generally very good, they are not perfect. This effect can, however, be counteracted with the use of large data quantities: If the data that one can get from surveys are often limited by the number of participants (which in turn is limited by time and cost reasons), that limit is much higher when it comes to the information that one can gather from digital data sources. Thus, if cleverly used, the richness of the information obtained from unstructured data can rival, if not exceed, the one obtained with surveys.

## ONLINE DATA SOURCES

Researchers often prefer to use ready-made data rather than, or often in addition to, constructing their own data sets using crawling and scraping tools. While many sources of data are in the public domain, some require access through a university subscription. For example, sources of news data include the websites of local and regional news outlets as well as private databases such as EBSCO, Factiva, and LexisNexis, which provide access to tens of thousands of global news sources, including blogs, television and radio transcripts, and traditional print news. One example of the use of such databases is a study of academic research on international entrepreneurship by the management researchers Jones, Coviello, and Tang (2011). Jones and colleagues used EBSCO and ABI/INFORM search tools to select their final data set of 323 journal articles on international entrepreneurship published between 1989 and 2009. They then used thematic analysis (see Chapter 11) to identify themes and subthemes in their data.

In addition to being able to access digitized news sources, researchers have access to writing produced by organizations including political statements, organizational calendars, and event reports. These data include recent online writing as well as digitized historical archives. Unfortunately, many online data sources are not simple to access. Most news databases allow access to a few articles but generally do not allow access to their entire database, as the subscriptions universities pay for are based on the assumption that researchers want to read a few articles on a subject rather than use large numbers of articles as primary data. Yet despite these limitations, a large and growing number of digital text collections are available for text mining researchers to use (see Appendix A). Among the most useful of these collections is the Corpus of Contemporary American English (COCA; http://corpus.byu.edu/coca), the largest public access corpus of English. Created by Davies of Brigham Young University, the corpus contains more than 520 million words of text and is equally divided among spoken, fiction, popular magazines, newspapers, and academic texts. It includes 20 million words each year from 1990 to 2015 and is updated regularly. The interface allows you to search for exact words or phrases, wildcards, lemmas, part of speech, or any combinations of these. COCA and related corpora are often used by social scientists as secondary data sources in order to compare word frequencies between their main data source and "standard" English (e.g., Baker et al., 2008).

Another major source of digital data is represented by social media platforms, many of which provide their own application programming interfaces (APIs) for programmatic access to their data. The Twitter APIs (http://dev.twitter.com), for instance, allow one to access a small set of random tweets every day, or larger keyword-based collections of tweets (e.g., all the recent tweets with the hashtag #amused). If larger collections are necessary, they can be obtained through third-party vendors such as Gnip or others, which cover several social media sites and often partly curate the data. Twitter also provides limited demographic information on their users, such as location and self-maintained free-text profiles that sometime can include gender, age, industry, interests, and others.

Blogs can also be accessed through an API—for instance, the Blogger platform offers programmatic access to the blogs and the profile of the bloggers, which includes a rich set of fields covering location, gender, age, industry, favorite books and movies, interests, and so on. Other blog sites, such as LiveJournal, also include additional information on the bloggers, for instance, their mood when writing a blog post.

Facebook is another very large platform for social media, although less available for public access. The main way for developers to access Facebook data is via their Graph API, but the access is nonetheless limited to the content of those profiles that are either publicly available, or are "friends" (in Facebook terms) of the developers. An interesting data set for social science research is the myPersonality[1] data set: It was compiled using a Facebook application, and it includes the profiles and updates of a large number of Facebook users who have also completed taken a battery of psychological surveys (e.g., personality, values).

In addition, there are several other social media websites, with different target audiences, such as Instagram (where users upload mainly images they take), Pinterest (with "pins" of interesting things, covering a variety of domains from DIY to fashion to design and decoration), and many review platforms such as Amazon, Yelp, and others.

If you are interested in assembling your own data set, Chapter 6 provides an overview of software tools for scraping and crawling websites to collect your own data, and Chapter 5 provides instruction related to data selection and sampling.

## ADVANTAGES AND LIMITATIONS OF ONLINE DIGITAL RESOURCES FOR SOCIAL SCIENCE RESEARCH

The use of online digital resources, and in particular of social media, comes with its plusses and minuses. Salganik (in press) provided a good summary of the characteristics of big data in general, many of which apply to social media in particular. He grouped characteristics into those that are good for research and those that are not good for research.

Among the characteristics that make big data good for research are (a) its size, which can allow for the observation of rare events, for causal inferences, and generally for more advanced statistical processing that is not otherwise possible when the data are small; (b) its "always-on" property, which provides a time dimension to the data and makes it suitable to study unexpected events and produce real time measurements (e.g., capture people's reactions during a tornado, by analyzing the tweets from the affected area); and (c) its nonreactive nature, which implies that the respondents behave more naturally due to the fact that they are not aware of their data being captured (as it is the case with surveys).

---

[1]Available upon request from http://mypersonality.org.

Then there are also characteristics that make big data less appealing to research, such as (a) its incompleteness—that is, often digital data collections lack demographics or other information that is important for social studies; (b) its inherent bias, in that the contributors to such online resources are not a random sample of the people—consider, for instance, the people who tweet many tweets a day versus those who choose to never tweet; they represent different types of populations with different interests, personalities, and values, and even the largest collection of tweets will not capture the behaviors of those who are not users of Twitter; (c) its change over time, in terms of users (who generates social media data and how it generates it) and platforms (how is the social media data being captured), which makes it difficult to conduct longitudinal studies; and (d) finally its susceptibility to algorithmic confounds, which are properties that seem to belong to the data being studied which in fact are caused by the underlying system used to collect the data—as in the seemingly magic number of 20 friends that many people seem to have on Facebook, which turns out to be an effect of the Facebook platform that actively encourages people to make friends until they reach 20 friends (Salganik, in press). In addition, some types of digital data are inaccessible—for example, e-mails, queries sent to search engines, phone calls, and so forth, which makes it difficult to conduct research on behaviors associated with those data types.

# EXAMPLES OF SOCIAL SCIENCE RESEARCH USING DIGITAL DATA

There are examples of social science research studies that use social media data in most of the chapters of this textbook. If you are interested in using Facebook data for your own project, it is important to review the studies discussed in Chapter 3 on the Facebook ethics controversy. In addition, research by the sociologist Hanna (2013) on using Facebook to study social movements may be a useful starting point. Hanna reviewed procedures for analyzing social movements such as the Arab Spring and Occupy movements by applying text mining methods to Facebook data. Hanna uses the Natural Language Toolkit (NLTK; www.nltk.org) and the R package ReadMe (http://gking.harvard.edu/readme) to analyze mobilization patterns of Egypt's April 6 youth movement. He corroborated results from his text mining methods with in-depth interviews with movement participants.

If you are interested in using Twitter data, two Twitter-based thematic analysis (see Chapter 11) studies are good places to start. The first is a study of the live Twitter chat of the Centers for Disease Control and Prevention conducted by Lazard, Scheinfeld, Bernhardt, Wilcox, and Suran (2015). Lazard's team collected, sorted, and analyzed users' tweets to reveal major themes of public concern with the symptoms and life span of the virus, disease transfer and contraction, safe travel, and protection of one's body. Lazard and her team used SAS Text Miner (www.sas.com/en_us/software/analytics/text-miner .html) to organize and analyze the Twitter data.

A second thematic analysis study that uses Twitter data is by the mental health researchers Shepherd, Sanders, Doyle, and Shaw (2015). The researchers assessed how Twitter is used by individuals with experience of mental health problems by following the hashtag #dearmentalhealthprofessionals and conducting a thematic analysis to identify common themes of discussion. They found 515 unique communications that were related to the specified conversation. The majority of the material related to four overarching themes: (1) the impact of diagnosis on personal identity and as a facilitator for accessing care, (2) balance of power between professional and service user, (3) therapeutic relationship and developing professional communication, and (4) support provision through medication, crisis planning, service provision, and the wider society.

## Conclusion

This chapter has addressed the role played by data in social science research and provided an overview of the advantages and limitations of digital data as a way to collect information from people in support of such human-centered research projects. The chapter has overviewed a number of online data sources, with forward pointers to Chapters 5 and 6, which specifically address aspects relevant to data collection and data sampling. Examples of social science research projects that make use of information obtained from digital resources were also provided, mainly as an illustration of the kind of research questions that can be answered with this kind of data; more such examples are provided in the following chapters (specifically in Chapters 10 through 12).

## Key Term

Unstructured data    19

## Highlights

- Social science research has been traditionally conducted based on surveys, but new computational approaches have enabled the use of unstructured data sources as a way to learn information about people.

- Surveys are structured data sets that include clear, targeted information collected in controlled settings. They have the disadvantage of being expensive to run, which limits the frequency and number of surveys that can be collected for a study.

- Unstructured data sets are very large, "always on" naturally occurring digital resources, which can be used to extract or infer information on people. They have their own disadvantages, which include the fact that the information that can be obtained from these resources is often inexact and incomplete as well as subject to the biases associated with the groups of people who generate these data sources.

- Digital resources can be accessed either as collections available through institutional memberships (e.g., LexisNexis), via APIs provided by various platforms (e.g., Twitter API), or otherwise through scraping and crawling as described in Chapter 6.

## Discussion Questions

- Describe a social science research project that you know of, which has been based on survey data, and discuss how that same research project could be conducted using digital data resources. What kind of resources would you use? What kind of challenges do you expect to run into?

- While digital resources have their own advantages, as discussed in this chapter, there are certain types of information that cannot be collected from such unstructured data. Give examples of such types of information that can be collected only through surveys.

- Now consider a research project in which you would need to combine the benefits of unstructured data (e.g., Twitter) and structured data (e.g., surveys). In other words, your project requires that every subject in your data set provides both their Twitter data as well as responses to a set of surveys. How would you go about collecting such a mixed data set for your project?

# RESEARCH ETHICS

## INTRODUCTION

In early January 2012, for over a week the news feeds of almost 700,000 Facebook users subtly changed. Researchers were manipulating the content in these users' news feeds without notifying them. To learn how friends' emotions affect each other, a team of researchers from Cornell University and Facebook had removed content that contained positive words for one group of users and removed content that contained negative words for another group. The researchers found that users who saw more positive posts tended to write slightly more positive status updates and that users who had been exposed to more negative posts wrote slightly more negative updates.

The Cornell–Facebook study was published in the *Proceedings of the National Academy of Sciences* in 2014 (Kramer, Guillory, & Hancock, 2014). It sparked outrage after a blogger claimed the study had used Facebook users as "lab rats." Following the early criticism from bloggers, the study came in for harsh criticism from both individual researchers and professional research associations. Unlike the advertising that Facebook shows, which aims to alter people's behavior by encouraging them to buy products and services from Facebook advertisers, the changes to users' news feeds were made without the users' knowledge or explicit consent. And yet the question of whether the study was unethical is debatable. While there are no black-and-white answers, understanding the ethical dimensions of the Facebook emotion study can help you to plan your own study so that it will meet the highest possible ethical standards.

Gorski, a surgeon, researcher, and editor of the blog Science-Based Medicine (https://www.sciencebasedmedicine.org), wrote on his blog in 2014 that the reaction to the Cornell–Facebook study showed a "real culture gap" between social science researchers on the one side and technology companies on the other. At a minimum, he argued, users should have been given the choice to not participate in the study, because it is "absolutely ridiculous to suggest that clicking a box on a website constitutes informed consent" (see the Informed Consent section). Moreno, a professor of medical ethics and health policy at the University of Pennsylvania, also criticized the study for "sending people whose emotional state you don't know anything about communications that they might find disturbing" (Albergotti & Dwoskin, 2014). Broaddus (2014), a social psychologist at the Medical College of Wisconsin, noted a lack of transparency as an issue in the study. Grimmelmann, a law professor at the University of Maryland, pointed out the following in a May 2015 *Slate* article:

> If it had been carried out in a university lab by university faculty on volunteers they recruited, the researchers would almost certainly have drawn up a detailed description of the experiment and submitted it to their school's institutional review board. The IRB would have gone through the proposal in detail, making sure that the participants gave a level of informed consent appropriate to the design of the study and the risks of the research. What's more, the researchers and their colleagues would share a sense of professional ethics, taking into account respect for participants, balancing risks and benefits, and the integrity of the research process itself. The process is slow but careful; it is deliberately, explicitly, extensively public-spirited.

There were also legal concerns. It is unclear whether the population sample used in the study contained people under 18 years of age or people from outside the United States who may be subject to different levels of scrutiny in a research study than are U.S. citizens.

Many researchers have defended the study, pointing out that Facebook and other Internet companies routinely perform such studies for their own benefit or as part of social experiments. For instance, *Newsweek* reported that the popular online dating site OkCupid has engaged in manipulation of user-generated site content for years. The president of OkCupid observed that "if you use the Internet, you're the subject of hundreds of experiments at any given time, on every site" (Wofford, 2014). Also defending the study, the bioethicist Meyer (2014) argued that the sort of research done on the Facebook data were scientifically important and that the scientific community should not respond to it in such a way as to drive such research underground or discourage companies from joining forces with social scientists in the future.

Facebook claims to have revised its ethics guidelines since the emotion study was conducted and has proposed that studies now undergo three internal reviews, including one centered on privacy for user data. Regardless of its ultimate effects on social science research, the Facebook study certainly provides an opportunity to carefully consider the ethics of text mining research. In the remainder of this chapter, we consider the most critical ethical issues that were brought to the fore in the Cornell–Facebook study and that must be addressed in any text mining study, including the cornerstones of humans subjects research—respect for persons, beneficence, and justice; ethical guidelines; IRBs; privacy; **informed consent**; and manipulation. We also review ethical issues involved in authorship and publishing.

## RESPECT FOR PERSONS, BENEFICENCE, AND JUSTICE

One cornerstone of modern research ethics is the Belmont Report, which was commissioned by the U.S. government in response to ethical failures in medical research and published in 1979. Written by a panel of experts, the Belmont Report has three principles that should underlie the ethical conduct of research involving human subjects: *respect for persons*, *beneficence*, and *justice*. These principles were later operationalized into the rules and procedures of the Common Rule, which governs research at U.S. universities (www.hhs.gov/ohrp/regulations-and-policy/regulations/common-rule). In the Belmont Report, respect for persons consists of two principles: that individuals should be treated as autonomous and that individuals with diminished autonomy are entitled to additional protections. This is interpreted to mean that researchers should, if possible, receive informed consent from participants (informed consent is discussed later in the chapter). Beneficence can be understood to mean having the interests of research participants in mind. This principle requires that researchers minimize risks to participants and maximize benefits to participants and society. The principle of justice addresses the distribution of the costs and benefits of research so that one group in society does not bear the costs of research while another group benefits. Issues of justice tend to relate to questions about the selection of participants.

Today, the Belmont Report continues as an essential reference for IRBs that review research proposals involving human subjects, in order to ensure that the research meets the ethical foundations of the regulations (IRBs are discussed later in this chapter). It also serves as a reference for ethical guidelines developed by professional associations, including associations whose members work with Internet data.

# ETHICAL GUIDELINES

Influenced by the Belmont Report, but also by the special challenges of performing research on human subjects online, many professional associations have published guidelines for ethical decision making in online research. One influential set of guidelines was published by the Association of Internet Researchers (AoIR) in 2002 and again in 2012 (http://aoir.org/ethics). The original 2002 AoIR guidelines discuss issues pertaining to informed consent and the ethical expectations of online users. The group's more recent 2012 guidelines draw particular attention to three areas that need to be negotiated by researchers using user-generated online data: the concept of human subjects, public versus private online spaces, and data or persons. The 2012 guidelines do not prescribe a set of dos and don'ts but instead recommend a series of questions for researchers to consider when thinking about the ethical dimensions of their study.

For human subjects, the AoIR guidelines state as a key guiding principle that because "all digital information at some point involves individual persons, consideration of principles related to research on human subjects may be necessary even if it is not immediately apparent how and where persons are involved in the research data." However, while the term *human subject* persists as a guiding concept for ethical social research, in Internet research this gets a bit tricky:

> "Human subject" has never been a good fit for describing many internet-based research environments. Ongoing debates among our community of scholars illustrate a diverse, educated range of standpoints on the answers to the question of what constitutes a "human subject." We agree with other regulatory bodies that the term no longer enjoys the relatively straightforward definitional status it once did. As a community of scholars, we maintain the stance that when considered outside a regulatory framework, the concept of "human subject" may not be as relevant as other terms such as harm, vulnerability, personally identifiable information, and so

forth. We encourage researchers to continue vigorous and critical discussion of the concept of "human subject," both as it might be further specified in internet related research or as it might be supplant by terms that more appropriately define the boundaries for what constitutes inquiry that might be ethically challenging. (p. 6)

A second major consideration in the AoIR ethics guidelines is the idea of public versus private data. While privacy is a concept that must include a consideration of expectations and consensus, a "clearly recognizable boundary" between public and private does not exist:

> Individual and cultural definitions and expectations of privacy are ambiguous, contested, and changing. People may operate in public spaces but maintain strong perceptions or expectations of privacy. Or, they may acknowledge that the substance of their communication is public, but that the specific context in which it appears implies restrictions on how that information is—or ought to be—used by other parties. Data aggregators or search tools make information accessible to a wider public than what might have been originally intended. (p. 7)

The third consideration or tension in the AoIR guidelines is that between data and persons. The report's authors noted the following:

> The internet complicates the fundamental research ethics question of personhood. Is an avatar a person? Is one's digital information an extension of the self? In the U.S. regulatory system, the primary question has generally been: Are we working with human subjects or not? If information is collected directly from individuals, such as an email exchange, instant message, or an interview in a virtual world, we are likely to naturally define the research scenario as one that involves a person.

For example, if you are working with a data set that contains thousands of tweets or Facebook posts, it may appear that your data are far removed from the people who did the actual tweeting or posting. While it may be hard to believe that the people who produced your data could be directly or indirectly impacted by the research, there is considerable evidence that even "anonymized" data sets contain personal information that allows the individuals who produced it to be identified. Researchers continue to debate how to adequately protect individuals when working with such data sets (e.g., Narayanan & Shmatikov, 2008, 2009; Sweeney, 2003). These debates are important because they are concerned with the fundamental ethical principle of minimizing harm; the connection between a person's online data and his or her physical person could possibly lead to psychological, economic, or even physical, harm. Thus, as a researcher, you must consider whether your data can possibly be linked back to the people who produced it and whether there are scenarios in which this link could cause them harm.

Professional research associations such as the British Psychological Society (www.bps .org.uk/system/files/Public%20files/inf206-guidelines-for-internet-mediated-research .pdf) and American Psychological Association (APA; www.apa.org/science/leadership/ bsa/internet/internet-report.aspx) have developed their own reports and ethical guidelines for online research. But because not all professional research associations have developed their own guidelines, it is critical that you submit your research proposal to your IRB for review before collecting or analyzing data.

## INSTITUTIONAL REVIEW BOARDS

IRBs are university committees that approve, monitor, and review behavioral and biomedical research involving humans. Within higher education institutions ethical approval is required from a university-level ethics committee for any research involving human participants. IRBs and other university ethics committees continue to develop and revise standards to keep up with evolving social media and big data technologies.

Since the 1990s, a consensus has emerged that the study of computer-mediated and Internet-based communication often requires that IRBs modify their human subjects principles and research ethics policies. Such modifications are necessary because in online environments it is often impossible to gain the consent of research participants (Sveningsson, 2003), and there is often an expectation of public exposure by users. Researchers and ethics professionals who write and revise university research ethics policies continue to grapple with several issues that we address next, including privacy, informed consent, manipulation of human subjects, and publishing ethics.

## PRIVACY

In 1996, the Internet researchers Sudweeks and Rafaeli argued that social scientists should treat "public discourse on computer-mediated communication as just that: public" and that, therefore, "such study is more akin to the study of tombstone epitaphs, graffiti, or letters to the editor. Personal? Yes. Private? No" (p. 121). Sudweeks and Rafaeli's position may be convenient for the practice of research, but it has proved not to always be sufficient for research using data from contemporary social media platforms. In many cases there is a lack of consensus about whether people who have posted messages on the Internet should be considered "participants" in research or whether research that uses their messages as data should be viewed as involving the analysis of secondary data that already existed in the **public domain**.

Some researchers have argued that publicly available data carry no expectation of privacy, while many researchers who have carried out studies of online messages (e.g., Attard & Coulson, 2012; Coulson, Buchanan, & Aubeeluck, 2007) have deemed the data to be in the public domain yet have sought IRB approval from within their own institutions anyway.

A number of Internet researchers have concluded that where data can be accessed without site membership, such data can be considered as public domain (Attard & Coulson, 2012; Haigh & Jones, 2005, 2007). Therefore, if data can be accessed by anyone, without website **registration**, it would be reasonable to consider the data to be within the public domain of the Internet.

There appears to be agreement that websites that require registration and **password-protected data** should be considered private domain (Haigh & Jones, 2005) because users posting in password-protected websites are likely to have expectations of privacy. Websites that require registration are often copyrighted, which raises a legal issue of ownership of the data and whether posts and messages can be legally and ethically used for research purposes.

The Cornell–Facebook study is widely seen as having invaded the privacy of Facebook users. Some websites and social media platforms have privacy policies that set expectations for users' privacy, and these can be used by researchers as guidelines for whether it is ethical to treat the site's data as in the public domain or else whether informed consent may be required. But in most cases, such guidelines are insufficient and at best provide minimum standards that may not meet the standards set by universities' IRBs. For example, the European Union has stringent privacy laws that may have been violated by the Facebook study. Adding to the difficulties for researchers attempting to follow privacy laws, it is unclear whether laws governing data protection are the laws in the jurisdiction where research participants reside, the jurisdiction where the researchers reside, the jurisdiction of the IRB, the location of the server, the location where the data are analyzed, or some combination of these.

Because acquiring users' textual data from online sources is a passive method of information gathering that generally involves no interaction with the individual about whom data are being collected, for the most part text mining research is not as ethically challenging as experiments and other methods that involve recruiting participants and that may involve deception. Nevertheless, universities' IRBs are increasingly requiring participant consent (see the next section) in cases where users can reasonably expect that their online discussions will remain private. At the very least, in almost all cases social scientists are required to **anonymize** (use pseudonyms for) users' user names and full names.

It has also been suggested that although publicly available online interactions exist within the public domain, site members may view their online interactions as private.

Hair and Clark (2007) have warned researchers that members of online communities often have no expectation that their discussions are being observed and may not be accepting of being observed.

In order for text mining research using user-generated data to progress, researchers must make several determinations. First, they must use all available evidence to determine whether the data should be considered to be in the public or private domain. Second, if data are in the public domain, the researcher must determine whether users have a reasonable expectation of privacy. In order to make these determinations, researchers should note whether websites, apps, and other platforms require member registration and whether they include privacy policies that specify users' privacy expectations.

## INFORMED CONSENT

Informed consent refers to the process by which individuals explicitly agree to be participants in a research project based on a comprehensive understanding of what will be required of them. The Belmont Report (discussed previously) identified three elements of informed consent: information, comprehension, and voluntariness. The principle of respect for persons implies that participants should be presented with relevant information in a comprehensible format and then should voluntarily agree to participate. Participants in research projects who have given their informed consent are not expected to be informed of a study's theories or hypotheses, but they are expected to be informed of what data the researcher will be collecting and what will happen to that data as well as of their rights to withdraw from the research.

Informed consent is a core principle of human research ethics established in the aftermath of the Second World War. In important cases where the question is deemed vital and consent isn't possible (or would prevent a fair test), it can be legally bypassed. But this is rare, and it is clear that the researchers in the Cornell–Facebook study failed to obtain consent from the thousands of Facebook users who were subjected to the manipulation of their news feeds. Instead, the researchers took advantage of the fine print in Facebook's data use policy to conduct an experiment without users' informed consent. Even though the academic researchers collaborated with Facebook in designing the study, it appears that they obtained ethical approval only after the data collection was finished (Chambers, 2014).

Researchers have argued that informed consent is not required for research in online contexts in which the data can be considered to be in the public domain (Eysenbach & Till, 2001; Sudweeks & Rafaeli, 1996). And professional research associations occasionally deem informed consent unnecessary in cases where the scientific value of a research project can justify undisclosed observation. However, in cases where it cannot be legitimately argued that data are in the public domain or where data are in the public domain but are protected by copyright laws, participants' informed consent to use such data must be sought.

Because the process of seeking informed consent is onerous and requires the creation and administration of an IRB-approved informed consent form, text mining researchers typically prefer to use data that are clearly in the public domain.

## MANIPULATION

So far, we have assumed that the researcher is collecting unprompted user conversations (rather than **prompted data**, such as from interviews or questionnaires), but social scientists are beginning to collect users' textual data after actively manipulating the online environment as a stimulus intended to assess reactions or responses. The Cornell–Facebook emotion study is an example of such research. Researchers could also prime users by, for example, introducing sexist, racist, or homophobic language into the online environment and then recording the responses of members of different communities. From an ethical standpoint, for this kind of experimental online research it is not sufficient for the researcher to anonymize participants' names after the experiment has been conducted.

As always, in the case of manipulation, the best practice is for university researchers who plan to manipulate the social media environment in any way to consult with their IRB and for researchers in the industry to follow the regulations and guidelines of their respective professional associations.

## PUBLISHING ETHICS

If you are thinking about graduate school or a career in research and teaching, you have many outlets available for publishing your research papers. You can publish your own work in specialized undergraduate research journals, present your work in undergraduate poster sessions at national and international academic conferences, and possibly upload your undergraduate honors thesis to your university's digital research archives. You may also publish collaboratively, as research assistants or perhaps occasionally coauthors, with faculty members in research journals and conference proceedings. Whatever your specific goals, it is important to be aware of the many ethical pitfalls involved in scholarly publishing. In this section, we borrow liberally from research ethics scenarios (http://ethicist .aom.org/2013/02/ethics-in-research-scenarios-what-would-you-do) that were developed by management researchers Davis and Madsen in 2007. The following scenarios presented all represent ethics violations related to authorship and publishing, and they all represent patterns of behavior that occur quite often.

## Scenario 1

In the first scenario, you have recently begun to work with a professor who is a productive scholar who has published in major journals for many years. But you have discovered that he has an unusual approach to research. He begins by gathering and analyzing data, which may include using a student's data set, to see if the data have anything interesting to say. You have found that the professor often manipulates the data and changes the dependent variable to ensure a statistically significant result and increase the probability of a major publication.

*Is this professor's approach to research ethical? Why or why not?*

*Is there anything you could or should do as a student in this situation?*

## Scenario 2

In the second scenario, a professor has a long and impressive resume, but upon closer examination, you realize that many of her publications seem to be quite similar. One day you met with this professor and commented on her impressive body of work. She said that she never writes anything that doesn't get as much ink and attention as possible. Among other things, she said that she may change the name of some of her papers to get them into conferences. She also claimed that she spends so much time gathering data that to be as productive as possible she must use the same data and theory in multiple published studies.

*Can one plagiarize oneself?*

*How often can data be used ethically?*

*Can the same paper be submitted to a conference and for publication in a journal?*

## Scenario 3

In the third scenario, three graduate students were chatting one evening about their frustrations. Student A said that she had written a final paper for a course taught by her adviser. When she asked him if the paper was worthy of submitting to a conference, her adviser said that it is worth submitting and suggested the insertion of a few references. He then requested that he be listed as the paper's coauthor. Student B then shared the story of his adviser's request. He explained that as he wrote his dissertation he received wonderful support from his adviser, but once the dissertation was completed his adviser insisted on being first author on all publications coming out of the dissertation research. Student C trumped all three by saying that her adviser told her that he owns the data and all **intellectual property (IP)** coming from the dissertation because he consented to supervise her research.

*How is authorship resulting from your research determined?*

*Who owns the IP and data from your research?*

Scenarios 1, 2, and 3 all represent ethics violations related to authorship and publishing, and they all represent patterns of faculty behavior that occur quite more often than we might prefer to believe. What would you do in each scenario? In each of the scenarios, the faculty adviser has immense power over the student's future academic career. An adviser who refuses to write a letter of recommendation for a student for a job or graduate school or who writes an unflattering letter can cause permanent damage to the student's career. Davis and Madsen considered these and other ethical scenarios on their blog post, which is a very useful resource (http://ethicist.aom.org/2013/02/ethics-in-research-scenarios-what-would-you-do). You can also refer to the research ethics sites in the Web Resources and Further Reading sections toward the end of the chapter.

## Conclusion

Choosing appropriate guidelines for text mining research can pose a serious challenge. Watson, Jones, and Burns (2007) suggested that it is impractical to suppose any single set of guidelines could address all issues concerning online research due to the diversity of online platforms and communities. Hair and Clark (2007) made the point that what might be considered ethical research conduct in one community might be considered unethical in others. In light of this uncertainty, it is critically important that you pay close attention to what is considered ethical conduct within the online community or communities you choose to study. And you should consider multiple sets of guidelines for your text mining research project rather than a single set. If a review of literature from within your academic discipline does not provide clear ethical guidelines for text mining research or other forms of research using user-generated online data, you should consult literature from closely related fields.

Research involving the collection of data about people through social media and networking sites involves many of the same considerations as any other research with human participants, including determining appropriate informed consent processes, assuring that participation is voluntary whenever possible, protecting the privacy of individuals and the confidentiality of data collected, and minimizing risks to participants. Clearly, if you are working within a university you must consult with your IRB before collecting or analyzing any user-generated textual data.

## Key Terms

Anonymize   33
Ethical guidelines   27
Informed consent   29
Institutional review board
   (IRB)   27

Intellectual property
   (IP)   37
Password-protected
   data   33
Plagiarism   40

Privacy   27
Prompted data   35
Public domain   32
Registration   33

## Highlights

- IRBs are university committees that approve, monitor, and review behavioral and biomedical research involving humans.

- Consult AoIR and other professional research associations' guidelines before collecting data that involves humans.

- You must use all available evidence to determine whether data you are considering using should be considered to be in the public or private domain.

- If data are in the public domain, you must determine whether users have a reasonable expectation of privacy.

- In order to make determinations about users' expectation of privacy, note whether the websites, apps, or other platforms you are using to collect data require member registration and whether they include privacy policies that specify users' privacy expectations.

- In your research papers, always use pseudonyms for users' user names and full names.

- Because the process of seeking informed consent is onerous and requires the creation and administration of an IRB-approved informed consent form, text mining researchers often prefer to use data that are clearly in the public domain.

- Authorship and publishing present ethical challenges due to power dynamics within universities (see O'Leary, 2014, Chapter 4). In case you are concerned about authorship and publication of your own work or the work of a friend or colleague, you should consult the Davis–Madsen ethical scenarios and other web resources listed at the end of the chapter.

## Review Questions

- Under what circumstances can a social scientist gather data without gaining informed consent?

- How can text mining research be used to benefit science and society?

- How should data collected under unethical conditions be treated? Should it be used just like data collected under ethically rigorous conditions?

## Discussion Questions

- Closely read the privacy policies of three social media websites or apps. Is it reasonable to consider the comments and posts on these platforms to be in the public domain? Why or why not?

- What impact will your research project have on the community from which participants are drawn?

- How would you apply the concept of informed consent to your own research?

## Web Resources

- 2012 AoIR report "Ethical Decision-Making and Internet Research: Recommendations from the AoIR Ethics Working Committee" (http://aoir.org/reports/ethics2.pdf)

- The APA's report "Psychological Research Online: Opportunities and Challenges" (www.apa.org/science/leadership/bsa/internet/internet-report.aspx)

- The British Psychological Society's "Ethics Guidelines for Internet-Mediated Research" (www.bps.org.uk/system/files/Public%20files/inf206-guidelines-for-internet-mediated-research.pdf)

- The Ethicist Blog from the Academy of Management (http://ethicist.aom.org)

*(Continued)*

(Continued)

- The Office of Research Integrity, U.S. Department of Health & Human Services (http://ori.hhs .gov). This federal government website provides not only federal policies and regulations but also training resources on what is and how to handle research misconduct, case summaries involving research misconduct that make for sobering reading, and free tools for detecting **plagiarism**.

- The Davis–Madsen ethics scenarios on the Ethicist Blog from the Academy of Management: "Ethics in Research Scenarios: What Would YOU Do?" (http://ethicist.aom.org/2013/02/ethics- in-research-scenarios-what-would-you-do)

## Developing a Research Proposal

Consider the ethical dimensions of the research proposal or proposals you are developing. Does it make use of human subjects? Is the data in the public or private domain? And does your data contain information that can be used to identify individual research participants?

## Further Reading

Israel, M. (2014). *Research ethics and integrity for social scientists: Beyond regulatory compliance.* Thousand Oaks, CA: Sage.

O'Leary, Z. (2014). *The essential guide to doing your research project.* Thousand Oaks, CA: Sage.

# THE PHILOSOPHY AND LOGIC OF TEXT MINING

## INTRODUCTION

You may be tempted to skim over or even skip this chapter entirely, and it is certainly possible to make use of the more technical later chapters of this textbook without giving much thought to **epistemology**, **ontology**, **metatheory**, or inferential logic. But if you are in the early stages of a text mining research project, you would do well to read this chapter carefully. As we discussed in the Preface to this textbook, just as the foundations of a house must be properly designed and built if the house is to last, the philosophical foundations of your research project should be as solidly constructed as possible. Text mining research often involves making strong inferences about groups of people based on the texts they produce. Researchers working with these tools frequently claim to know something about the language people use that those same people do not themselves know; justifying such claims is not a simple matter. Several academic fields are relevant to questions about when researchers are justified in using digital texts to make inferences about social groups. These fields include the philosophy of science (Curd, Cover, & Pincock, 2013), the philosophy of technology (Kaplan, 2009), and science and technology studies (STS; Kleinman & Moore, 2014).

A historical example may be in order. Like text mining technologies today, a century ago the lie detector (polygraph machine) was a revolutionary technology with social implications that could not have been predicted. As with text mining technologies, it was claimed that lie detector technology would allow scientists to extend their powers of perception and even know what people were thinking. As a lie detector can potentially reveal things about individuals that they themselves do not know or would prefer not to reveal, text mining tools can potentially reveal what members of a group or community are thinking and feeling. But is it true that lie detectors can reveal whether people are attempting to deceive? What do data produced by lie detectors mean? How should these data be used? Lie detector technology itself does not provide answers to these questions. Instead, it took decades for individual scientists and scientific, legal, and criminal justice institutions to sort out what lie detectors can and cannot accomplish and how the data they produce could be used ethically (see Alder, 2007; Bunn, 2012). And even today there is often disagreement about the results of polygraph tests. In the same way, scientific institutions and public and private sector organizations are still in the early stages of sorting out what kinds of conclusions can be drawn from text mining research. This sorting-out process involves technical discussions but also philosophical discussions about knowledge, facts, and language.

The philosophy of social science is one of the main fields in which researchers debate how socially sensitive research technologies such as polygraphs and text mining tools can and should be used. The philosophy of social science is an academic research area that lies at the intersection of philosophy and contemporary social science. Philosophers of social science develop and critique concepts that are foundational to the practice of social science research (Howell, 2013). They critically analyze epistemological assumptions in social research, which are assumptions about the nature of knowledge. They also analyze ontological assumptions, which are assumptions about the nature of reality, and metatheoretical assumptions, which are assumptions about the capacities and limitations of scientific theories. Social scientists often make claims about the validity and generalizability of their findings, the adequacy of their research designs, and why one theory is superior to another. Such claims are grounded in epistemological, ontological, and metatheoretical positions that are generally implicit (Woodwell, 2014). The philosophy of social science allows us to bring these positions to light and to help us understand why different approaches to social science research can, or cannot, make use of each other's findings. In this section we briefly review what we have found to be the most critical philosophical issues that arise in text mining research, and we discuss some of the practical implications of different philosophical positions.

# ONTOLOGICAL AND EPISTEMOLOGICAL POSITIONS

When are we justified in reaching a conclusion about some person or group of people based on the texts they produce? Does text mining research produce findings that are merely interesting, or can it produce findings that are true and accurate reflections of reality?

Every approach to social science research addresses these kinds of questions based on one or another philosophical position. But the philosophical foundations of text mining research are uniquely unsettled because text mining methods are, for the most part, "mixed methods" (Creswell, 2014; Teddlie & Tashakkori, 2008) that are positioned at the intersection of the "two cultures" of the sciences and the humanities (Snow, 1959/2013). The "two cultures" was part of a 1959 lecture and subsequent book by the British novelist and scientist Snow. Snow was referring to the loss in Western society of a common culture as a result of the division between the sciences and humanities, a division that he saw as an impediment to solving social problems.

Although the idea of two cultures may seem simplistic, within the social sciences there continues to be a divide between more scientific and more humanistic forms of knowledge. These are sometimes referred to as *idiographic* and *nomothetic* knowledge (see Chapter 5), although social scientists themselves more often refer to *scientific positivism* and *postpositivism*. Positivism is a paradigm of inquiry that prioritizes quantification, hypothesis testing, and statistical analysis; postpositivism is a more interpretive paradigm that values close reading and multiple interpretations of texts. In practice, text mining and text analysis research is usually performed as a pragmatic combination of these two paradigms. Because positivism and postpositivism are premised on different epistemological and ontological positions, they often produce research findings that are "incommensurable," meaning that they cannot build upon one another. Positivism and postpositivism are based on epistemological and ontological orientations that can be sorted into the following five philosophical positions (Howell, 2013).

## Correspondence Theory

The first philosophical position that provides a foundation for social research, **correspondence theory**, is a traditional model of knowledge and truth associated with scientific positivism. This position considers that there exists a correspondence between truth and reality and that notions of truth and reality correspond with things that actually exist in the world, be they earthworms, comets, chemical reactions, or people's thoughts and ideas. It is understood that there are relationships between things that exist in the world and the concepts we use to describe and understand them, and the truth of concepts is gauged by how they relate to an objective reality that exists independent of how people think and talk about it. Thus, truth and knowledge are universal and absolute, and the goal of theories, be they from the social, natural, or physical sciences, is to accurately reflect objective reality through the precise use of thoughts, words, and symbols.

An implication of correspondence theory for text analysis research projects is that the goal of such projects should be to learn objective facts about online groups and communities based on the documents they produce. If text mining and analysis methods are properly applied, they ought to be able to uncover facts about social groups that are objective and therefore incontrovertible.

## Coherence Theory

In the second major philosophical position that has influenced social science, **coherence theory**, truth, knowledge, and theory must fit within a coherent system of propositions. Such a system of propositions may be applied to specific cases only in accordance with properties of the general system (Hempel & Oppenheim, 1948). There may be one true knowledge system, or there may be many such systems, but in either case, coherency exists between specific facts and general propositions. Like correspondence theory, coherence theory is a traditional model of truth and knowledge that is closely associated with scientific positivism.

For text mining research, coherence theory implies that while there may be multiple ways to analyze online groups and communities, to be considered true the specific facts uncovered by text mining and analysis methods must fit within a coherent system of theoretical and empirical propositions.

## Pragmatism

In pragmatist approaches to the philosophy of social science, truth is defined as those tenets that prove useful to the believer or user, and truth and knowledge are verified through experience and practice (James, 1907/1975, 1909/1975). In a pragmatist ontology, objective truth cannot exist because truth needs to relate to groups' practices, and truth, therefore, always has both subjective and objective dimensions (Howell, 2013, p. 132).

A pragmatist approach to text mining treats as true and valid those specific facts uncovered by text mining methods that relate not only to objective reality or to a theoretical system but to the practices and interests of researchers themselves, be they members of academic communities, government agencies, or for-profit companies.

## Constructionism

The constructionist position in philosophy of social science is generally traced to Berger and Luckmann's 1966 sociological classic *The Social Construction of Reality*. **Constructionism** considers that no external objective reality or system exists; therefore, truth is not a matter of concepts' correspondence to objective reality or coherence between specific cases and a system of propositions. Instead, truth and knowledge are produced when communities and groups reach consensus about what is or is not true. The core assumption of the constructionist paradigm is thus that socially constructed realities are not independent of the observer but are constructed by people under the influence of a variety of social and cultural factors that lead to intersubjective agreement about what is real (Howell, 2013, p. 90).

As in **pragmatism**, constructionism implies that text mining methods cannot eliminate subjectivity. But constructionism goes further in implying that objectivity is not a realistic goal of social research. Instead, researchers should aim to provide new interpretations of social phenomena that are edifying or enlightening. But they are not justified in claiming that their methods give them privileged access to an objective reality that cannot be otherwise apprehended. Accordingly, constructionism is a foundational philosophical position in postpositivist social science.

## Critical Realism

**Critical realism**, as pioneered by Bhaskar (1975/2008), combines the realism of correspondence theory with the sociocultural reflexivity required by constructionism. Critical realism involves a distinction between the production of knowledge by human beings and knowledge that is of things or grounded within things. In critical realism, some objects are understood to be *more* socially constructed (or more "transitive") than others. The critical realist ontology perceives reality as external to humanity but "considers our intellectual capacities to be unable to fully understand opaque and confounding truth" (Howell, 2013, pp. 50–51).

For text mining research, critical realism implies that because documents produced by social groups and communities are forms of knowledge produced by human beings, they are socially constructed and our understanding of them is always partial and limited at best. Yet unlike constructionism, critical realism also implies that there are elements of texts that are "intransitive," meaning they can be treated as objective facts that are measurable and amenable to scientific research.

# METATHEORY

Along with epistemology and ontology, metatheory is an area of philosophy that has special relevance to the practice of social science research. Metatheory involves searching for answers to questions about the role of theory within social science research projects. Different approaches to social science research are generally based on one or another of the epistemological and ontological positions outlined previously. Partly stemming from their particular philosophical premises, these approaches to research end up using theory in strikingly different ways. Put another way, we can say that different approaches to text mining and text analysis are based on different *metatheoretical* premises, which are premises about the uses, capacities, and limitations of theory within empirical research. Howell (2013) provided the following list of metatheoretical positions commonly found in social science methodologies, ordered from the most abstract to the most concrete types of theorizing.

## Grand Theory and Philosophical Positions

**Grand theory** refers to sweeping abstract explanations of social phenomena and human existence (e.g., Marxian historical materialism). Regardless of the method used, individual research projects can rarely directly test the claims of grand theories and philosophical positions. But over time, the findings from large numbers of empirical research projects can generally support or weaken the standing of such theories and positions.

## Meso Theory

**Meso theory** is less sweeping and abstract than grand theory and is more closely connected to the practice of empirical research. The term refers to theories of the "middle range" (Merton, 1949) that draw on empirically supported substantive theories and models. Meso theory is common in psychology and sociology, where researchers develop, test, and refine relatively narrow theories related to specific psychological and sociological phenomena, such as theories of cognitive biases or of gender discrimination in hiring.

## Models

**Theoretical models** are simplified, often schematic representations of complex social phenomena. They are used in almost all empirical research, particularly in research that is done in a positivist mode of inquiry.

## Substantive Theory

**Substantive theory** is theory derived from data analysis that involves rich conceptualizations of specific social and historical situations. While theorists and empirical researchers understand that the more parsimonious the theory, the easier it is to identify relations of cause and effect between independent and dependent variables, greater simplification often makes it more difficult to reach a full understanding or explanation of a phenomenon. Where theoretical models may at times be oversimplified, substantive theories are more complex and arrived at inductively through interpretive methods (e.g., archival research and ethnography).

# MAKING INFERENCES

Social science research involves making inferences (drawing conclusions) about theories; about patterns in data and about the individuals and communities that are, ultimately, the source of the data used in research. Inferential logic involves thinking about how and why it is warranted to make inferences from data. Based on their analysis of collected data, researchers use specific forms of logic to make inferences about relationships among social phenomena and between social phenomena and theoretical propositions and generalizations. In the early stages of a project, a researcher may not know the sorts of inferences they will make or conclusions they will draw. But in the end, they inevitably use one or more of the following forms of inferential logic, and it is beneficial for you as a researcher to be aware of these well-established forms of inferential logic as early as possible.

## Inductive Logic

Inductive logic involves making inferences that take data as their starting point and then working upward to theoretical generalizations and propositions. Researchers begin by analyzing empirical data with their preferred tools and then allow general conclusions to emerge organically from their analysis (see Figure 4.1). The first ethical scenario in Chapter 3 is an example of a researcher relying exclusively on **induction**.

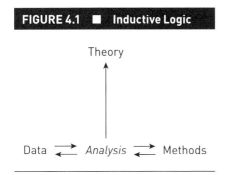

**FIGURE 4.1   ■   Inductive Logic**

Theory

Data ⇄ *Analysis* ⇄ Methods

When qualitatively oriented researchers use inductive logic, they often position their research as **grounded theory** (Glaser & Strauss, 1967), while more quantitatively oriented researchers refer to **data mining**. Both grounded theory and data mining are used extensively in text mining research.

The use of inductive **inference** is attractive to social scientists for several reasons. First, it allows them to work with data sets and specialized tools quickly without having to invest time mastering abstruse philosophical debates and theories or setting up complex research designs. It also allows for great flexibility and adaptability, as analysts can allow their data to speak to them and adjust their conclusions accordingly rather than imposing a priori categories and concepts onto data in an artificial manner. And inductive research designs allow quantitatively oriented researchers, in particular, to immediately make use of the very large data sets and powerful software and programming languages that are at their disposal.

In its purer forms, induction has some serious drawbacks. First, it encourages analysts to begin research projects without first formulating a research question. Researchers simply assume that the project's purpose will become evident during its analysis phase. But there is a very real risk that this simply will not happen, and the researcher will have invested significant time and resources in a directionless and perhaps purposeless project.

Another drawback of purely inductive research is that it can encourage researcher passivity with regard to mastering the research literatures in their areas of interest. Rather than mastering the work that has been done by others so as to identify gaps in knowledge, unsolved puzzles, or critical disagreements and then designing a study to address one or several of these, induction encourages researchers to skip straight to data collection and analysis and then work backward from their findings to the pertinent gaps in the literature, puzzles, and disagreements. In practice, this is often a high-risk strategy.

Although relying exclusively on inductive inferential logic is a risky and sometimes dangerous strategy, induction does end up playing a role in most text mining research projects. The complexity of natural language data demands that researchers allow their data to alter their theoretical models and frameworks rather than forcing data to conform to their preferred theories.

An example of a text mining study with a research design based on inductive logic is Frith and Gleeson's 2004 thematic analysis of male undergraduate students' responses to open-ended survey items related to clothing and body image. The undergraduates in the study were recruited through snowball sampling (see Chapter 5). In order to better understand how men's feelings about their bodies influence their clothing practices, Frith and Gleeson analyzed written answers to four questions about clothing practices and body

## SPOTLIGHT ON THE RESEARCH
### An Inductive Approach to Media Framing

Bastin, G., & Bouchet-Valat, M. (2014). Media corpora, text mining, and the sociological imagination: A free software text mining approach to the framing of Julian Assange by three news agencies. *Bulletin de Méthodologie Sociologique, 122,* 5–25.

In this paper, the sociologists Bastin and Bouchet-Valat introduced R.TeMiS (http://rtemis.hypotheses .org), a free text mining software package designed for media framing analysis. Unique among R text mining tools, R.TeMiS features a graphical user interface (GUI) to help in the automation of corpus construction and management procedures based on the use of large media content databases and to facilitate the use of a range of statistical tools such as one- and two-way tables, time series,

hierarchical clustering, correspondence analysis, and geographical mapping. Bastin and Bouchet-Valat presented a case study on the media framing of Julian Assange from January 2010 to December 2011 based on an analysis of a corpus of 667 news dispatches published in English by the international news agencies Agence France-Presse, Reuters, and the Associated Press. Bastin and Bouchet-Valat's inductive approach to their data incorporates correspondence analysis (see Appendix G) as well as geographic tagging and mapping based on country names in the texts.

Specialized software used:

R.TeMiS

http://rtemis.hypotheses.org

image and discovered four main themes relevant to their research question, including *men value practicality, men should not care how they look, clothes are used to conceal or reveal,* and *clothes are used to fit a cultural ideal.*

A second example of an inductive text mining study is Jones, Coviello, and Tang's (2011) study of academic research on the academic field of international entrepreneurship research. Jones, Coviello, and Tang constructed a corpus from 323 journal articles on international entrepreneurship published between 1989 and 2009 and then inductively synthesized and categorized themes and subthemes in their data.

## Deductive Logic

Deductive logic is the form of inferential logic most closely associated with the **scientific method**. Deductive research designs start with theoretical abstractions (see Figure 4.2), derive **hypotheses** from those theories, and then set up research projects that test the hypotheses on empirical data. The purest form of a deductive research design is the laboratory experiment, which in principle allows the researcher to control all variables except for those of theoretical interest and then to determine unequivocally whether hypotheses derived from a theory are supported or not.

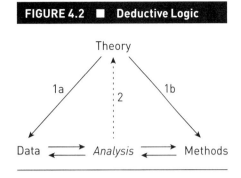

**FIGURE 4.2 ■ Deductive Logic**

Deductive inferential logic has been applied in many text mining studies. An early example is Hirschman's (1987) study "People as Products," which tested an established theory of resource exchange on male- and female-placed personal advertisements. In total, Hirschman derived 16 hypotheses from this theory and tested these hypotheses on a year's worth of personal dating advertisements collected from *New York* and *Washingtonian* magazines. Hirschman selected at random 100 male-placed and 100 female-placed advertisements, as well as 20 additional advertisements that she used to establish content categories for the analysis. One male and one female coder coded the advertisements in terms of the categories derived from the 20 additional advertisements. The data were transformed to represent the proportionate weight of each resource category coded (e.g., money, physical status, occupational status) for each sample, and the data were analyzed with a 2 × 2 **analysis of variance (ANOVA)** procedure. As is discussed in Appendix I, ANOVA is a collection of statistical models used to analyze variation between groups. In Hirschman's 1987 study, gender of advertiser (male or female) and city (New York or Washington) were the factors analyzed in the ANOVA procedure, while Cunningham, Sagas, Sartore, Amsden, and Schellhase (2004) used ANOVAs to compare news coverage of women's and men's athletic teams.

Management researchers Gibson and Zellmer-Bruhn's 2001 study of concepts of team-work across national organizational cultures is another example of the use of deductive inferential logic in a text mining project. This study's goal was to test an established theory of the influence of national culture on employees' attitudes. Gibson and Zellmer-Bruhn tested this theory on data from four organizations in four different countries (France, the Philippines, Puerto Rico, and the United States), conducting interviews that they transcribed to form their corpora. They used QSR NUD*IST (which subsequently evolved into NVivo; see Appendix D) and TACT (Popping, 1997) to organize qualitative coding of five frequently used teamwork metaphors (see Chapter 12), which were then used to create dependent variables for hypothesis testing using multinomial logit and logistic **regression (multiple regression)**.

Cunningham and colleagues' (2004) analysis of coverage of women's and men's sports in the newsletter *NCAA* (National Collegiate Athletic Association) *News* is another example of a deductive research design. Cunningham and his colleagues tested theories of organizational resource dependence on data from 24 randomly selected issues of the *NCAA News*. One issue of the magazine was selected from each month of the year from the years 1999 and 2001 (see Chapter 5 on *systematic sampling*). From these issues, the authors chose to analyze only articles specifically focused on athletics, coaches, or their teams, excluding articles focused on committees, facilities and other topics (see Chapter 5 on *relevance sampling*). Two researchers independently coded each of 5,745 paragraphs in the sample for gender and for the paragraph's location within the magazine and content. Reliability coefficients including Cohen's kappa and the Pearson product-moment coefficient were calculated. As is discussed in Appendix I, reliability coefficients are used to measure the degree of agreement among raters. Interrater reliability is useful for determining if a particular scale is appropriate for measuring a particular variable. If the raters do not agree, either the scale is defective or the raters need retraining.

Cunningham and his colleagues also calculated word use frequencies, ANOVA, and chi-square statistics. The chi-square statistic, also discussed in Appendix I, is a very useful statistic in text mining research. It allows for comparisons of observed versus expected word frequencies across documents or groups of documents that may differ in size.

The extreme complexity of user-generated textual data poses challenges for the use of deductive logic in social science research. One cannot perform laboratory experiments on the texts that result from interactions among members of large online communities, and it is difficult, and often unethical, to use manipulation to perform field experiments in online communities (see Chapter 3). And even researchers who are immersed in the relevant literatures in their field may not know precisely what they want to look for when they begin their analysis. For this reason, many researchers who work with text mining tools advocate for *abductive inferential logic*, a more forensic logic that is commonly use in social science research but also in natural science fields such as geology and astronomy where experiments are rarely performed.

## Abductive Logic

A weakness of both induction and **deduction** are that they do not provide guidance about how theories, whether grand theories, middle-range theories, or theoretical models, are discovered in the first place (Hoffman, 1999). The inferential logic that best accounts for theoretical innovation is **abduction**, also known, approximately, as "**inference to the best explanation**" (Lipton, 2003). Abduction differs from induction and deduction in that abduction involves an inference in which the conclusion is a hypothesis that can then be tested with a new or modified research design. The term was originally defined by the philosopher Peirce (1901), who claimed that for science to progress it was necessary for scientists to adopt hypotheses "as being suggested by the facts":

> Accepting the conclusion that an explanation is needed when facts contrary to what we should expect emerge, it follows that the explanation must be such a proposition as would lead to the prediction of the observed facts, either as necessary

consequences or at least as very probable under the circumstances. A hypothesis, then, has to be adopted, which is likely in itself, and renders the facts likely. This step of adopting a hypothesis as being suggested by the facts, is what I call abduction. (pp. 202–203)

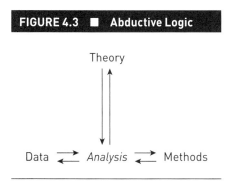

FIGURE 4.3 ■ Abductive Logic

Theory

Data ⇄ Analysis ⇄ Methods

Abduction "seeks no algorithm, but is a heuristic for luckily finding new things and creating insights" (Bauer, Bicquelet, & Suerdem, 2014). Abductive logic does not replace deduction and induction but bridges them iteratively (through a process that repeats itself many times). It is a "forensic" form of reasoning in that it resembles the reasoning of detectives who interpret clues that permit a course of events to be reconstructed or of doctors who make inferences about the presence of illness based on patients' symptoms.

A number of researchers who work with text mining and text analysis tools advocate for abduction as the optimal inferential logic for their research, including Bauer and colleagues (2014) and Ruiz Ruiz (2009). Bauer and colleagues (2014) argued that with abduction, text mining researchers need not do the following:

. . . face a dilemma between the Scylla of deduction on the one hand, and Charybdis of induction on the other. We suggest abductive logic as the middle way out of this forced choice: the logic of inference to the most plausible explanation of the given evidence, considering less plausible alternatives. As it entails both machine inference and human intuition, it can maintain the human-machine-text trialogue.

One of the main problems of abductive inference is how to formulate an abduction. Peirce was not especially clear on this point when he referred to a "flash of understanding" or when attributing abductive capacity to an adaptive human need to explain surprising or unexpected facts. Although Peirce did not establish formal procedures to generate abductive inferences, he did propose criteria to distinguish between good and bad abduction. These include the need for abduction to propose truly *new ideas or explanations*, the need to derive *empirically contrastable predictions* from the hypotheses, and the need for the hypotheses to fit in with or *give an adequate account of the social and historical context* in which they emerge (Peirce, 1901).

The sheer complexity of language as compared with the kinds of phenomena studied in the natural and physical sciences makes it difficult to implement text mining research designs that are entirely inductive or deductive. Even the most carefully planned text mining projects that are presented as though they were products of pure deductive reasoning generally result from long periods in which research teams use abductive logic to refine and reformulate their hypotheses and, at times, even their research questions.

Abductive inferential logic is compatible with the use of any number of sophisticated research tools and is used in the early stages of many deductive research designs. One example is Ruiz Ruiz's (2009) text analysis of transcriptions of discussions with Spanish manual workers. In the transcripts, the workers are seen as criticizing the chauvinism and submissiveness of Moorish immigrants from Morocco. Ruiz Ruiz described his use of abductive, as well as inductive and deductive, logics of inference in his 2009 survey of discourse analysis methods.

## Conclusion

In this chapter, we have reviewed the most critical philosophy of social science concepts that are relevant to the practice of text mining. We hope to have convinced you that philosophical assumptions and decisions about methodology are interdependent and to have given you the tools to allow you to position your own research project in terms of debates over positivist and postpositivist social science. You should also now be well equipped to recognize the types of logical inferences that are possible in different approaches to text mining and text analysis research.

## Key Terms

Abduction   51

analysis of variance
   (ANOVA)   50

Coherence theory   44

Constructionism   45

Correspondence theory   44

Critical realism   45

Data mining   48

Deduction   51

Epistemology   41

Grand theory   46

Grounded theory   48

Hypotheses   49

Induction   47

Inference   48

Inference to the best
   explanation   51

Meso theory   46

Metatheory   41

Ontology   41

Philosophy of social
   science   41

Pragmatism   45

Regression (multiple
   regression)   50

Scientific method   49

Substantive theory   47

Theoretical models   47

## Highlights

- Different approaches to text mining and text analysis research are premised on different epistemological and ontological positions.

- Theory plays fundamentally different roles in different approaches to social science research.

- Text mining and text analysis research involves making inductive, deductive, and/or abductive inferences.

## Discussion Questions

- What do social scientists mean by "constructionism"?

- What is inferential logic, and why do social scientists spend time thinking about it?

- What are limitations of deductive reasoning in social science research?

- What are problems with abductive reasoning in social science research?

- What risks are associated with purely inductive approaches to social science research?

- What is the definition of *ontology*? Can you give examples of contexts in which epistemology would be important in social science research?

- In what ways can metatheory stimulate problem solving by researchers?

- What is the definition of *epistemology*? Can you give examples of contexts in which epistemology would be important in social science research?

## Internet Resources

The journal *Philosophy of the Social Sciences* (http://pos.sagepub.com)

## Developing a Research Proposal

Do you favor positivism or postpositivism as a guide for your research? Explain your position.

What types of theories will you use in your research project? Consider the role of theory in your research in light of how theory is used in published research in your area.

## Further Reading

Reed, I. (2011). *Interpretation and social knowledge*. Chicago, IL: University of Chicago Press.

Rosenberg, A. (2012). *Philosophy of social science*. Boulder, CO: Westview Press.

Snow, C. P. (2013). *The two cultures and the scientific revolution*. London, England: Martino Fine Books. (Original work published 1959)

# Research Design
# and Basic Tools

## PART II

# 5

# DESIGNING YOUR RESEARCH PROJECT

## LEARNING OBJECTIVES

The goals of Chapter 5 are to help you to do the following:

1. Strategize your **research design** from the earliest stages of your project.
2. Determine where the most critical decisions are made in text mining research.
3. Compare various research designs for qualitative, quantitative, and **mixed methods** research.
4. Reference influential text mining studies that employ a variety of research designs.

## INTRODUCTION

Research design is one of the most critically important but also most difficult topics in the social sciences (Creswell, 2014; Gorard, 2013). Research design is essentially concerned with the basic architecture of research projects, with designing projects as systems that allow theory, data, and research methods to interface in such a way as to maximize a project's ability to achieve its goals (see Figure 5.1). Research design involves a sequence of decisions that have to be taken in a project's early stages, when one oversight or poor decision can lead to results that are ultimately trivial or untrustworthy. Thus, it is critically

**FIGURE 5.1 ■ The Research Design Triad**

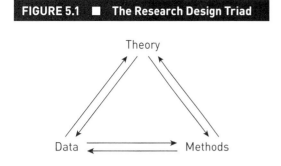

important to think carefully and systematically about research design before committing time and resources to acquiring texts or mastering software packages or programming languages for your text mining project.

We begin this chapter with a review of the major principles of social science research design that are applicable to text mining research projects. We discuss the differences between **idiographic approaches** and **nomothetic approaches** to research (see Chapter 4), between research performed at different **levels of analysis**, and among qualitative, quantitative, and mixed methods designs. We cover data selection strategies and then review exemplary text analysis projects that use various qualitative, quantitative, and mixed methods approaches in combination with various **case selection** and **data sampling** strategies.

## CRITICAL DECISIONS

Research design is concerned with the basic architecture of research projects, with how a research project systematically brings together theory, data, and a method or methods of analysis. The research design process generally starts with a research question regarding the social world (Ravitch & Riggan, 2016). As is discussed in detail in the next section, to attempt to contribute to the understanding of a social phenomenon, social scientists strive to generate two main forms of evidence-based knowledge: idiographic and nomothetic knowledge. Researchers working with text mining methods design projects that operate at a **textual level** of analysis or at a **contextual level**, or else that attempt to identify sociological relationships between texts and the social contexts in which they are produced and received (Ruiz Ruiz, 2009). Research designs are often classified as using either qualitative, quantitative, or mixed methods, as using either single- or multiple-document collection research designs, as employing one or more specific case selection and/or data sampling methods, and as employing inductive, deductive, and/or abductive inferential logic (see Chapter 4).

Figure 5.2 is a stylized representation of the research design decisions that are generally made within social science text mining projects. The most fundamental and abstract decisions are at the top of the figure, and the decisions become more data-driven as one proceeds from 1 through 5. But, in fact, the order of the decisions presented in Figure 5.2 is not critical because the figure is a simplification that hides various relations of compatibility, incompatibility, and interdependency between decisions made.

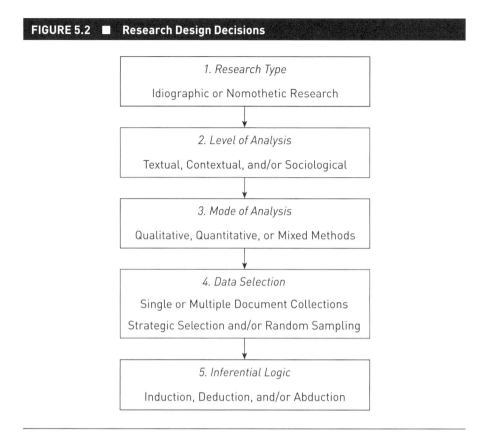

**FIGURE 5.2 ■ Research Design Decisions**

1. *Research Type*

Idiographic or Nomothetic Research

2. *Level of Analysis*

Textual, Contextual, and/or Sociological

3. *Mode of Analysis*

Qualitative, Quantitative, or Mixed Methods

4. *Data Selection*

Single or Multiple Document Collections

Strategic Selection and/or Random Sampling

5. *Inferential Logic*

Induction, Deduction, and/or Abduction

Still, while the order in which you make these decisions may be unpredictable and while you may have to revise some of your figures several times, each decision in Figure 5.2 is critically important if your research project is to achieve its goals.

# IDIOGRAPHIC AND NOMOTHETIC RESEARCH

In the late 19th century, the German philosopher Windelband (1894/1998) coined the terms *idiographic* and *nomothetic* to refer to different forms of evidence-based knowledge. For Windelband (1901/2001), idiographic knowledge involved description and explanation of particular phenomena, while nomothetic knowledge involved finding generalities that are common to a class of phenomena and deriving theories or laws to account for these generalities.

Idiographic and nomothetic forms of knowledge are not necessarily mutually exclusive. And yet, over the past century, highly specialized, sometimes mutually antagonistic research methodologies have developed to produce knowledge of the two forms. Nomothetic (or positivist) social science methods seek to analyze large data sets using inferential statistics, while idiographic (postpositivist; see Chapter 4) methods such as ethnography focus in on the details of cases or events.

Text mining methods have been used effectively for both idiographic (e.g., Kuckartz, 2014) and nomothetic forms of research, although there are specific text mining methods, software packages, and programming languages that are somewhat better suited for one or the other.

# LEVELS OF ANALYSIS

While text mining methods can be challenging to use even in basic applications, their use in social science research projects necessarily brings with it new sources of complexity. Some of this added complexity derives from the multiple levels of analysis that are endemic to social science research. Ruiz Ruiz (2009) usefully proposed three main levels of analysis at which text-based research can potentially operate: the level of the text itself, the level of the immediate social and intertextual context, and a **sociological level** that attempts to identify causal relations between texts and the social contexts in which they are produced and received. Text mining research conducted in various disciplines generally operates at one or another of these three levels, and awareness of these levels allows you to more readily comprehend similarities and differences between such approaches to research.

## The Textual Level

Social science text analysis at the textual level "involves characterizing or determining the composition and structure of the discourse" (Ruiz Ruiz, 2009). Most of the methods introduced in Parts IV and V of this book are concerned with analyzing texts at the textual level in terms of narrative structures (see Chapter 10) and texts' themes (see Chapter 11), metaphors (see Chapter 12), topics (see Chapter 16), and other aspects of the composition and structure of texts themselves.

## The Contextual Level

In addition to revealing patterns in texts themselves, text mining can also reveal elements of the social context in which texts are produced and received, including situational contexts in which the discourse has been produced and the characteristics of the texts' authors. Social scientists have developed several methods of situational text analysis, including analysis of discourse positions and conversation analysis (see Chapter 1).

## The Sociological Level

Analyzing texts at a sociological level involves making connections between the texts analyzed and the social spaces in which they are produced and received. Texts can be analyzed sociologically only if they are first analyzed at both textual and contextual levels. While connections between texts and their social spaces can be very diverse depending on the analyst's research questions and theoretical orientation, they can be roughly sorted into two categories: research that analyzes texts as *social information* and research that analyzes texts as reflections of the *ideology* of their authors and audience (for more detail, see Ruiz Ruiz, 2009).

### Texts as Social Information

The first form of sociological text mining treats texts as reflections of the practical knowledge of their authors. It is a common practice to interpret texts as information, and this can be very useful for both applied and academic research projects. This type of analysis is prevalent in grounded theory studies (see Chapter 4 on induction) and in applied studies of expert discourses. The widespread interest in the informative analysis of texts is due in part to its practical value, because user-generated texts can provide researchers with valid and relevant information about social reality. Recent examples of informational text analysis include studies by Trappey, Wu, and their colleagues on mining user data from Facebook pages (Trappey, Wu, Liu, & Lin, 2013; Wu, Liu, & Trappey, 2014).

### Texts as Ideological Products

In addition to their informative components, texts include ideological components. In ideologically oriented text mining, what is of interest to the researcher is the author's particular viewpoint, which is generally understood as an indication of popular ideology. Ideological analysis of texts is a characteristic feature of critical discourse analysis (CDA; Van Dijk, 1993), which aims to demonstrate how social discourses are shaped by dominant discourses projected from powerful groups and institutions (see Chapter 1). Examples of recent CDA studies include work on telenurses and callers by Hakimnia, Holmström, Carlsson, and Höglund (2014) and on corporate communications by Merkl-Davies and Koller (2012).

Another program of ideologically oriented text mining is centered on Bourdieu and Thompson's (1991) analysis of what they called **linguistic markets**. Bourdieu analyzes texts as social products resulting from their author's position in society. According to Bourdieu, texts reflect the *habitus* of their authors, where habitus is understood in this context as the linguistic competence of the author, which derives from inhabiting a specific position in society and from the social experiences that are entailed by this position. Different ways of communicating have different social value on linguistic markets. The diversity of styles of communication involving accents, diction, grammar, and vocabulary is seen as both a reflection of social inequality and a means to preserve and reproduce social inequality. Examples of Bourdieusian text mining research include studies of status production on user-generated content platforms by Levina and Arriaga (2012) and of online overeaters support groups by Ignatow (2009).

# QUALITATIVE, QUANTITATIVE, AND MIXED METHODS RESEARCH

In all text mining projects, the choice of methodological tools is closely related to the kind of evidence-based knowledge the researcher hopes to produce. Social scientists who wish to write richly detailed accounts of specific social phenomena rely almost exclusively on qualitative research methods such as ethnography. Researchers interested in producing knowledge that is generalizable to phenomena other than those under investigation typically make use of quantitative and mixed methods research (Creswell, 2014; Tashakkori & Teddlie, 2010) designs that include both interpretive and quantitative elements. Within the social sciences, the major text analysis research traditions divide rather neatly along the qualitative–quantitative divide. **Discourse analysis** is generally considered to be the most influential qualitative text analysis research tradition, while *content analysis* is the major text-based research tradition that uses quantitative and mixed methods (see Herrera & Braumoeller, 2004).

## Discourse Analysis

Discourse analysis is a methodology for analyzing social phenomena that is qualitative, idiographic, and constructionist (see Chapter 4). Discourse analysis differs from other qualitative methodologies that try to understand processes of meaning construction in that it attempts to uncover the social processes that contribute to the construction of shared meaning (Hardy, 2001; Phillips & Hardy, 2002). Discourse analysis presupposes that discourses have no inherent meaning in themselves and that to understand their constructive effects researchers must locate them socially and historically (Fairclough, 1995; see Chapter 1 on CDA). Thus, discourse analysis grows out of the belief that meaning, and, hence, social reality, arises out of interrelated collections of texts that bring new ideas, objects, and practices into the world. From this perspective, social science becomes the qualitative study of the development of discourses that make social reality meaningful.

Recent examples of published discourse analysis research include studies of the postwar discourse of human rights, which has brought about the contemporary idea of a refugee with rights to asylum (Phillips & Hardy, 2002), and the discourse of AIDS, which has empowered groups of patient–activists (Maguire, Hardy, & Lawrence, 2004).

## Content Analysis

Where discourse analysis uses qualitative methods to understand the relations between texts and their social and historical contexts, content analysis adopts a more quantitatively oriented, positivistic approach (see Chapters 1 and 4) involving hypothesis testing and statistical analysis (Schwandt, 2001). Accordingly, content analysis is generally focused on texts themselves rather than their relations to their social and historical contexts. One of the classic definitions of content analysis defines it as "a research technique for the objective, systematic-quantitative description of the manifest content of communication" (Berelson 1952, p. 18). This quantitative orientation has accompanied content analysis to the present day, although the statistical methods used have become much more sophisticated. Content analysis is characterized by a concern with being objective, systematic, and quantitative (Kassarjian, 1977). Underlying this concern is the belief that the meaning of a text is constant and can be known precisely and consistently by different researchers as long as they utilize rigorous and correct analytical procedures (Silverman, 2016). At a practical level, content analysis involves the development of analytical categories that are used to construct a coding frame that is then applied to textual data. It mainly consists of breaking down texts into pertinent units of information in order to permit subsequent coding and categorization. Where discourse analysis is highly theoretical, content analysis is often considered an inductive method (see Chapter 4).

Roberts (1997) has categorized content analysis techniques in the social sciences as **thematic techniques**, **network techniques**, or **semantic techniques**. Thematic content analysis techniques focus on manifest meanings in texts and include methods commonly used in business as well as social science, such as topic modeling (see Chapter 16). Network text analysis methods model statistical associations between words to infer the existence of mental models shared by members of a community. Semantic text analysis methods, sometimes termed *hermeneutic* or *hermeneutic structuralist* techniques, include a variety of methods designed to recognize latent meanings in texts (see Chapters 10 and 11).

## Mixed Methods

If discourse analysis involves **qualitative analysis** of how social contexts condition the production of texts and content analysis is **quantitative analysis** of texts themselves without much consideration of context (Bauer, Bicquelet, & Suerdem, 2014; Ruiz Ruiz,

2009), most social science research that uses text mining tools does not fit neatly into either of these categories. Many quantitative projects operate at contextual and sociological levels of analysis, while many scholars argue that *all* quantitative text mining research is suffused with qualitative evaluations:

> The purported dichotomy between qualitative and quantitative is spurious because, firstly, no quantification is possible without a priori qualification and, secondly, no quantifiable explanation is possible without a posteriori qualitative analysis. From the outset any social research project requires a notion of qualitative distinctions between social (or, in textual analysis, semantic) categories before the researcher can measure how many words belong to one or another category. Similarly, in the final and perhaps crucial stage of any analysis, it is the interpretation of outputs that is the key to making sense out of it all—and here, the more complex a statistical model, the more difficult the interpretation of the results. (Bauer, Gaskell, & Allum, 2000)

Bauer and colleagues (2000) are clearly correct here, and they went even further in problematizing the qualitative–quantitative distinction in a 2014 publication, suggesting that this distinction is superficial (see also Ruiz Ruiz, 2009) and only has value for pedagogical uses:

> It allows course syllabi and textbooks to precisely demarcate numerous highly specific qualitative and quantitative skills and techniques for dealing with various types of data and research questions. A student faced with a problem is thereby expected to resolve it through simply knowing and applying the right quantitative or qualitative technique; and the expectation is that this will work, like magic.

Complex research projects are often labeled as either *qualitative* or *quantitative* to claim the putative superiority of one approach over the other. But these labels are misleading in so far as they assume that the two approaches to research are incompatible. While particular text mining methods rely on quantification to greater or lesser degrees, most text mining methods are best understood as mixed methods (Creswell, 2014; Teddlie & Tashakkori, 2008). The qualitative–quantitative distinction has its place in textbooks and syllabi and as a shorthand way to categorize research, but researchers with experience working with text mining and text analysis tools know that this distinction can be misleading.

## CHOOSING DATA

In the next chapter (see Chapter 6), we survey the techniques that are available for acquiring textual data (see also Appendices A and B on data sources and software for preparing and cleaning your data). But before acquiring data, in most text mining research (with the exception of strictly inductive approaches; see Chapter 4), the analyst must make carefully considered decisions regarding choice of data. Choosing data requires consideration of practical concerns involving time and cost, as well as more theoretical concerns.

Where ethnographers and historical researchers have developed procedures for *strategic case selection* to help them to choose data, and more quantitatively oriented researchers use *statistical sampling methods*, most text mining and text analysis research projects require a mix of strategic selection procedures and **sampling** methods.

In practice, many text mining projects do not begin with a clearly formulated research question but rather with a data set. Researchers often come across interesting or unique collections of documents that they want to use for a research project, and they may not be concerned with "the potential problem of having to undo or compensate for the biases in such data" (Krippendorff, 2013, p. 122). The technical term for this practice is *convenience sampling*. In convenience sampling, data selection as discussed next is not applicable, the researcher will use inductive or abductive inferential logic (see Chapter 4), and data sampling is the critical next step. Conversely, researchers whose projects start with a research question, be it a theoretical or a substantive question, must carefully consider data selection strategies in order to set up a research design that can potentially answer the research question or questions before moving on to choosing a data sampling strategy (or perhaps multiple strategies).

## Data Selection

Data selection and data sampling are of central importance in connecting theory and data in any empirical research project. In this context, the term *case selection* is used in qualitative and mixed methods research projects involving small numbers of cases where the generalizability of the findings from such projects can be increased by the strategic selection of cases. In this section, we borrow the language of case selection from qualitative and mixed methods research to discuss data selection (sometimes referred to as document selection).

Text mining always involves data selection, and the more strategically texts are selected, the more likely it is that a research project will achieve its goals. When the objective of a project is to achieve the greatest possible amount of information about a phenomenon, selecting a **representative case** (data that are representative of a larger population) or a **random sample** may not be the optimal strategy because the typical or average case is often not the richest in information. An atypical or **extreme case** often reveals more information because it activates more actors and more basic mechanisms in the situation studied. The extreme case can be well suited for getting a point across in an especially dramatic way, which is the case in well-known studies such as Freud's (1918/2011) "Wolf-Man" and Foucault's (1975) "Panopticon." Examples of the use of extreme cases in text-based social science research include a 2004 study of five teenage boys telling a story about a female student they all know by Bamberg (2004; see Chapter 1) and a 2003 study of animal and death metaphors in high technology jargon by Ignatow (see Chapter 12). The texts analyzed in these studies are not necessarily statistically representative of the social groups that produce them, and the groups themselves are not representative of a larger population. Instead, the texts were selected because their language was seen as extreme or unusual in a way that appeared relevant to theoretical debates.

A **critical case** can be defined as having strategic importance in relation to the general problem:

> For example, an occupational medicine clinic wanted to investigate whether people working with organic solvents suffered brain damage. Instead of choosing a representative sample among all those enterprises in the clinic's area that used organic solvents, the clinic strategically located a single workplace where all safety regulations on cleanliness, air quality, and the like, had been fulfilled. This model enterprise became a critical case: if brain damage related to organic solvents could be found at this particular facility, then it was likely that the same problem would exist at other enterprises which were less careful with safety regulations for organic solvents. (Flyvbjerg, 2001)

Selecting critical cases allows social scientists to save time and money in studying a given topic by formulating a generalization of the form, "'If it is valid for this case, it is valid for all (or many) cases.' In its negative form, the generalization would be, 'If it is not valid for this case, then it is not valid for any (or only few) cases'" (Denzin & Lincoln, 2011, p. 307). An example of the use of critical cases in text mining research is Gibson and Zellmer-Bruhn's 2001 mixed method metaphor analysis of employee attitudes in four countries (see Chapter 4). The four countries in this study were strategically selected for comparison in order to maximize geographical and cultural variation so that the findings could be generalized.

## Data Sampling

Once you have strategically selected data sources for your research project, it may be necessary to implement a data sampling strategy. Unless you can mine all of a data source's data (e.g., every article in a newspaper archive, or every comment from a social media site), a sampling strategy of one kind or another will be needed.

Sampling is often performed for the purpose of creating *representative samples*, which are samples that are representative of the broader population from which they are drawn. Representative sampling allows findings to be generalized from the sample to this broader population. The ideal representative sample is a **probability sample**, which allows researchers to generalize their findings to the larger population through statistical inferences. However, in text mining research there are significant barriers to obtaining representative probability samples. Krippendorff (2013) went so far as to argue that the challenge faced by researchers of sampling from one population in view of another "differs radically from the problems addressed by statistical sampling theory" (p. 114). For example, a researcher can sample users' comments on a social media platform such as Facebook or Twitter, but it is almost impossible to sample in such a way as to be able to generalize from the sample to the entire universe of Facebook or Twitter users. There are also some fundamental differences between textual data and the sort of individual-level data that is typically used in large-scale social science research projects such as social surveys. First, for social surveys the unit of analysis is the indivisible, independent individual. But for texts, the unit of analysis can be conceived in many ways, including the following:

> . . . in terms of hierarchies in which one level includes the next (film genre, movie, scene, episode, encounter, shot, assertion/action, frame, and so on . . .). They could be read as sequentially ordered events, jointly constituting narratives whose integrity would be lost if the components were permuted, or as networks of inter-textualities (co-occurring, making reference to, building on, or erasing each other). There is no single "natural" way of counting texts. (Krippendorff, 2013, p. 113)

In addition, in text mining research the units sampled are rarely the units counted. For example, a researcher may *sample* newspaper articles from an archive, but *count* words or word co-occurrences (rather than articles). Even when the researcher does settle on **units of analysis** for sampling and counting and adopts probability sampling techniques, biases can occur. Certain groups may be systematically excluded from data collection or may be underrepresented due to self-selection biases. Collecting representative samples using the Internet has been considered highly problematic for some time (see Hewson & Laurent, 2012).

Representative probability samples are rare in text mining research, but analysts have other sampling strategies available to them. A first element in any sampling is strategy is **enumeration**, or assigning numbers to or comprehensively listing the units within a population. Some digital archives have documents that are already enumerated, but it is often left to the analyst to arrange units into ordered lists that can be enumerated.

Once you have an enumerated population of units, you may sample from the population using *random sampling* with a randomization device such as software or an online random number generator. Alternatively, or sometimes in addition, you may use **systematic sampling**, which involves sampling every *k*th unit from an enumerated list. However, as the interval *k* is a constant, systematic sampling may create a kind of rhythm to the sampling that leads to bias. For example, by sampling YouTube user comments starting on a Saturday, and then every 7 days you would risk biasing the sample toward comments about videos that are more popular on weekends, which may systematically differ from videos that are watched on weekdays.

You may also use **stratified sampling**, which involves sampling from within subunits, or strata, of a population. For instance, a researcher interested in readers' comments on newspaper articles could create a stratified sample from the most popular newspaper sections (e.g., world news, business, arts and entertainment, sports) and then randomly or systematically sample from each of these strata. Of course, the selection of strata would depend on the research questions guiding the project. You may also use **varying probability sampling** to sample proportionately from data sources with different sizes or levels of importance, such as newspapers with different circulation levels (see Krippendorff, 2013, p. 117).

A widely used sampling technique in qualitative research is **snowball sampling**, which is an iterative procedure in which a researcher starts with a small sample and then repeatedly applies a sampling criterion until a sample size limit is reached. For instance, you could record and transcribe interviews with each member of a close-knit group, then request that each member provide contact information for three friends and interview each of these, and then repeat the process with each friend until the sample size limit is reached and you have acquired enough data to begin analysis. **Relevance sampling** or **purposive sampling** is a more research question-driven, nonprobabilistic sampling technique in which the researcher learns about a population of interest and then gradually reduces the number of texts to be analyzed based on the texts' relevance to the research question. Relevance sampling is "so natural that it is rarely discussed as a category of its own" (Krippendorff, 2013, p. 121). As you design your research project, it is only natural that you will eliminate data that are not directly relevant to the research question. For instance, if you were interested in women's groups or pages on Facebook you could purposively sample women's groups and eliminate groups and pages that focus on men's issues. Such purposive sampling restricts the representativeness of the sample and the generalizability of the results, but in many projects, these will be secondary concerns.

## FORMATTING YOUR DATA

Once you have acquired your final data set, it is very likely that you will need to represent it in tabular (spreadsheet) form for statistical analysis. This step is often performed with a common spreadsheet software such as Microsoft Excel or Google Sheets. The rows represent cases, divided in terms of your unit of analysis, such as by paragraph, comment, message, or tweet. The columns represent your variables, which include two main types: *categorical variables* and *numerical variables*, such as frequency counts and scores. An example of a categorical variable used in text mining research is author *gender*. To ease computation later on, gender could be represented as 0 for men, 1 for women, and 2 for unknown. It is a good practice to maintain a document with your variable coding scheme so that there is no confusion if you are working with others or there are extended periods of time between working with your data. Examples of numerical variables include frequency counts (e.g., counts of metaphors, themes, or key words) and sentiment scores.

Once your data are formatted as a table, you can use descriptive statistics (frequencies, means, and medians) and simple crosstab commands to get a sense of how the data in your documents relates to your research questions. Then you can go on to apply analyses of variance (ANOVAs), chi-square tests, regressions (see Appendix I), and other statistical tests and procedures that will allow you to test your hypotheses in deductive research designs (see Chapter 4).

## Conclusion

Social science research design is much like architecture. Just as extensive planning is required before construction work begins on a building, in the same way it is important to think carefully and strategically about the design of your research project from its earliest stages. We hope that this chapter has helped you to recognize where the most critical decisions are made in text mining research and to gain familiarity with various research designs for qualitative, quantitative, and mixed methods research. But it would be a mistake to rely exclusively on this chapter as you design and carry out your own project. A better strategy would be to use published research as a methodological template rather than trying to reinvent the wheel. An advantage of knowing well the literature to which your study may potentially contribute is that you can learn the most innovative and successful research designs employed by professional researchers working in your area.

## Key Terms

| | | |
|---|---|---|
| Case selection   60 | Extreme case   67 | Nomothetic approaches   60 |
| Contextual level   60 | Idiographic approaches   60 | Probability sample   69 |
| Critical case   68 | Levels of analysis   60 | Purposive sampling (see |
| Data sampling   60 | Linguistic markets 63 | Relevance sampling)   70 |
| Discourse analysis   64 | Mixed methods   59 | Qualitative analysis   65 |
| Enumeration   69 | Network techniques 65 | Quantitative analysis   65 |

*(Continued)*

## Highlights

- Research design is concerned with designing projects as systems that allow theory, data, and methods to interface in such a way as to maximize your project's ability to achieve its goals.

- There are different research designs for idiographic and nomothetic approaches to research.

- There are also different research designs for projects that operate at textual, contextual, and sociological levels of analysis.

- Research designs differ depending on whether a project is primarily qualitative or quantitative or whether it uses mixed methods.

- Research designs can be further classified as either single- or multiple-document collection research designs as employing one or more specific case selection and/or data sampling methods and as employing inductive, deductive, and/or abductive inferential logic.

- Statistical sampling with textual data is in some ways fundamentally different from sampling with survey data.

- Because statistical sampling with textual data is very challenging, strategic data selection is critically important for social science text mining.

## Review Questions

- Social scientists often use statistical sampling techniques when collecting data. What are potential problems with these techniques of which researchers need to be aware? What steps can text mining researchers take to ensure that the data they are collecting are of good quality?

- What are some examples of data selection strategies that can be used in text mining research?

## Discussion Questions

- What is the primary level of analysis of the research project you are designing?

- What will be your project's unit of analysis?

## Developing a Research Proposal

Think about a topic of contemporary relevance in which you may be interested. Using what you learned in this chapter, create a simple research question about the topic. Match your research question to an appropriate research method and source of data. Share your ideas with your classmates, and consider carefully both their positive and negative feedback.

## Further Reading

Bauer, M. W., Bicquelet, A., & Suerdem, A. K. (2014). Text analysis: An introductory manifesto. In M. W. Bauer, A. Bicquelet, & A. K. Suerdem (Eds.), *Textual analysis (SAGE benchmarks in social research methods)* (Vol. 1, xxi–xvii). Thousand Oaks, CA: Sage.

Creswell, J. D. (2014). *Research design: Qualitative, quantitative, and mixed methods approaches.* Thousand Oaks, CA: Sage.

Gorard, S. (2013). *Research design: Creating robust approaches for the social sciences.* Thousand Oaks, CA: Sage

Hewson, C., & Laurent, D. (2012). Research design and tools for Internet research. In J. Hughes (Ed.), *SAGE Internet research methods: Volume 1,* 58–78. Thousand Oaks, CA: Sage.

Roberts, C. W. (1997). *Text analysis for the social sciences: Methods for drawing statistical inferences from texts and transcripts.* Mahwah, NJ: Lawrence Erlbaum.

Ruiz Ruiz, J. (2009). Sociological discourse analysis: Methods and logic. *Forum: Qualitative Social Research, 10*(2). Retrieved June 27, 2015, from qualitative-research.net/index.php/fqs/article/view/1298/2882

# WEB SCRAPING AND CRAWLING

## INTRODUCTION

In this chapter, we survey two categories of tools that are critically important for acquiring large amounts of digital textual data: web scraping and web crawling. Both can be accomplished with off-the-shelf software or in programming environments like Python or R. Crawling and scraping can potentially save huge amounts of time if the alternative is to manually scrape data from webpages. But they require an investment of time to learn how to use them, and this requires some background knowledge about the structure of the World Wide Web.

The web—a common abbreviation for the World Wide Web—consists of billions of interlinked hypertext pages. These pages contain text, images, videos, or sounds and are usually viewed using web browsers such as Firefox or Internet Explorer. Users can navigate the web either by directly typing the address of a webpage (the **URL**) inside a browser or by following the links that connect webpages between them.

The web can be visualized as a typical example of a graph, with webpages corresponding to vertices in the graph and links between pages corresponding to directed edges. For instance, if the page https://umich.edu includes a link to the page www.eecs.umich.edu and one to the page http://med.umich.edu and the later page, in turn, links to the page of the National Institutes of Health (https://www.nih.gov) and back to the https://umich.edu page, it means that these four pages form a subgraph of four vertices with four edges, as is illustrated in Figure 6.1.

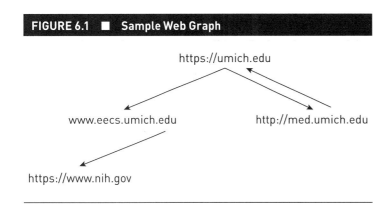

**FIGURE 6.1 ■ Sample Web Graph**

In addition to "traditional" webpages, which account for a large fraction of the data that we currently find online, today's web also includes a number of other data sources, such as sites with user-contributed content (e.g., Wikipedia, *HuffPost*), social media sites (e.g., Twitter, Facebook, Blogger), deep web data (e.g., data stored in online databases such as https://www.data.gov), or e-mail (e.g., Gmail, Hotmail). While some of these sources may not be publicly available (for instance, e-mail is by definition private, and so are a number of Facebook profiles), they still represent data in digital format that account for online traffic.

There are many challenges that come with the use of web data, many of which are highlighted throughout this book. In addition, there are also challenges that are associated with crawling such data, which we address in this chapter.

## WEB STATISTICS

While the size of the web is generally considered to be unknown, there are various estimates concerning the size of the indexed web—that is, the subset of the web that is covered by search engines. Web statistics compiled in 2014 by www.geekwire.com suggested 5 million terabytes of data online, out of which approximately 20% is textual data.

The web is estimated to include more than 600 million web servers and 2.4 billion web users, with about 1 billion Facebook users and 200 million Twitter users (http://royal.pingdom.com/2013/01/16/internet-2012-in-numbers). Estimates of the number of e-mails come from www.radicati.com, which suggests that 154 billion e-mails are sent daily, of which more than 60% are spam.

An interesting statistic refers to the proportion of languages used on the web. Information collected by www.internetworldstats.com in 2015 showed the distribution of language use as illustrated in Figure 6.2.

**FIGURE 6.2 ■ Top Ten Languages on the Web in 2015**

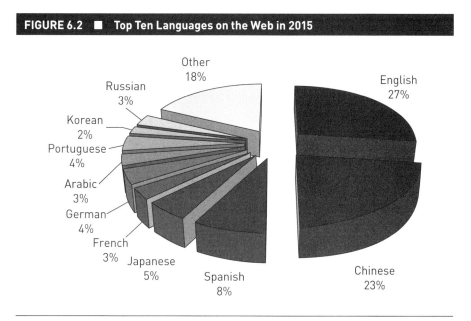

*Source:* Internet World Stats, http://www.internetworldstats.com/stats7.htm

# WEB CRAWLING

Web crawling is the process of building a collection of webpages by starting with an initial set of URLs (or links) and recursively traversing the corresponding pages to find additional links. A collection built this way can be used, for instance, to perform text mining (see Chapter 15), opinion analysis (see Chapter 14), text classification (see Chapter 13), or any other process that requires textual data.

## Processing Steps in Web Crawling

A crawler typically performs the following steps:

1. The crawler creates and maintains a list of URLs to be processed. This list is initially seeded with some manually selected URLs, and it is then iteratively grown into a large set of URLs.

2. The crawler selects a URL from the list (see below for selection strategies), marks it as "crawled," and it fetches the webpage from that URL. The page is processed, and links and content are extracted. This processing can be as simple as just extracting links using a regular expression (regex) that matches all the occurrences of tags such as <a href="http://. . . .">, followed by removal of all the HTML tags to obtain the content of the page. At times, a more sophisticated processing may be required—for instance, when the links also include relative links or links to fragments or when the content of a page includes entire sections devoted to advertisements or other content that needs to be removed.

3. If the content has already been seen, it is discarded. If not, it is added to the collection of webpages to be further processed (e.g., indexed, classified).

4. For each URL in the new set of URLs identified on the page, a verification is made to ensure that the URL has not been seen before, that the page exists, and can be crawled. If all these filters are passed, the URL is added to the list of URLs at Step 1, and the crawler goes back to Step 2.

## Traversal Strategies

An important aspect of any crawler is its web **traversal strategies**. As mentioned before, the web is a graph and therefore different graph traversal algorithms can be applied. One way of traversing the web is called breadth-first, where, given one webpage, we first collect and process all the pages that can be reached from URLs on that page before we move on to other pages. The second way of traversing the web is called depth-first, where, given one webpage, we extract one URL from that page, collect and process the page that can be reached from that one URL, extract again one URL on the page we just processed, and so on until we reach a dead end. Only then do we backtrack and process additional URLs on the pages we have just visited. For instance, Figure 6.3 shows a simple web graph, along with the order of page traversal, starting with Page A, for each of these two strategies.

**FIGURE 6.3  ■  Web Traversal Strategies**

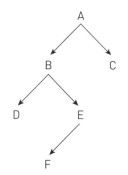

Breadth-first traversal order: A, B, C, D, E, F

Depth-first traversal order: A, B, D, E, F, C

## Crawler Politeness

Most websites have a clear crawling policy which states what **crawlers** can or cannot traverse them and which parts of the site can be crawled. There are two main ways of indicating a crawling policy. The most commonly used one is robots.txt, which is a file that is placed at the root of the website (e.g., www.cnn.com/robots.txt). This file can include a list of crawlers (or agents) that are disallowed for specific portions of the site. For instance, the following content of robots.txt indicates that all the crawlers are disallowed from traversing pages found under/tmp or /cgi-bin; the exception is BadBot, which is disallowed from the entire site:

User-agent: *

Disallow: /tmp/

Disallow: /cgi-bin/

User-agent: BadBot

Disallow: /

Another way of providing a crawling policy is through meta tags included in the HTML of individual pages. There is a special meta tag called robots, which can be used with combinations of values for two aspects: index or noindex (allow or disallow this webpage to be crawled) and follow or nofollow (allow or disallow the crawler to follow links on this webpage). For instance, a webpage could have a robots meta tag as follows:

<meta name="robots" content="index,nofollow">

It states that this page can be crawled, but links on the page cannot be followed.

# WEB SCRAPING

There are several available Internet-based methods for collecting ("scraping") document collections for social science research. There are several traditional methods of acquiring text data for research, including transcribing interviews (e.g., Bamberg, 2004) and downloading text files from digital archives, including news archives such as LexisNexis (https://www .lexisnexis.com) and Access World News (www.newsbank.com/libraries/schools/solutions/ us-international/access-world-news) and digital archives of historical documents (Jockers & Mimno, 2013). As there are a number of useful resources available to help with organizing interview transcripts and with finding and working with digital archives, in this chapter we focus only on newer Internet-based methods for creating corpora from scratch. The first of these methods is known as web scraping, which involves using commercial software and, as needed, programming languages such as Python to identify and download text from one or more pages or archives within a single website. Web crawling involves using programming languages to identify and download text from a large number of websites. While both web scraping and web crawling are powerful tools for data acquisition, they should ideally be used only within a project with a logical and practical research design (see Chapter 5).

# SOFTWARE FOR WEB CRAWLING AND SCRAPING

While researchers with programming backgrounds will generally prefer to use Python or another programming language over commercial web scraping software, commercial scraping software is reasonably easy to use for nonprogrammers, and it may at times have technical advantages over Python and other languages used for web scraping.

Web scraping software is designed to recognize different types of content within a website and to acquire and store only the types of content specified by the user. So, for instance, web scraping software allows a user to search a newspaper website and save only the names of article authors or to search a real estate website and save only the prices, addresses, or descriptions of listed properties. The software works by running *scripts* written by the user. The scripts tell the software on which webpage to start, what kind of text to look for (e.g., text with a certain font size or formatting), what to do with the text that is found, where to navigate next once text is saved, and how many times to repeat the script. Saved text data can be downloaded in a convenient file form such as a comma-separated values (CSV) file or a Microsoft Excel spreadsheet. Although web scraping software is very powerful and relatively user friendly, sites with complex structures often lead scraping software to stall or freeze. Luckily there are many videos and online support forums available for software users.

There are several useful freeware and commercial software products available on the market, and instructional videos for most of these are easy to find on YouTube and other Internet video services or in the manual pages available on Linux via the *man* command. In our own research, we have used *Lynx*, which is a very simple Linux-based command-line browser that allows for automatic processing of a page, including link and content extraction, and the Linux command *wget*, which allows for recursive crawling with a prespecified depth of the crawl. We have also used *Helium Scraper* (www.heliumscraper.com).

## SOFTWARE AND DATA SETS FOR WEB SCRAPING AND CRAWLING

Helium Scraper is an affordable and convenient scraping package with good online and YouTube support (www.heliumscraper.com).

Outwit Hub is another scraper similar in concept to Helium (https://www.outwit.com/products/hub).

FMiner is a scraping package that includes some advanced data extraction features (www.fminer.com).

Mozenda is a comprehensive cloud-based package of scraping tools designed for business applications (www.mozenda.com).

RapidMiner is a "data science platform" with web scraping tools (https://rapidminer.com).

Visual Web Ripper is an affordable, dedicated web scraping package (www.visualwebripper.com).

Import.io offers a powerful suite of data extraction tools (https://www.import.io).

Beautiful Soup is a Python library for extracting data out of HTML files (https://pypi.python.org/pypi/beautifulsoup4).

Lynx and wget are online commands available in almost any Unix/Linux environment, which can be used for direct download of webpages.

## Conclusion

Web scraping and crawling allows for direct access to the raw data available on websites. While scraping typically targets the collection of the text from a page or a site, crawling also involves the identification of new pages to scrape, for the purpose of, for example, building a large collection of web data. This chapter briefly overviewed the main approaches for web scraping and crawling and also gave pointers to a number of programming or off-the-shelf tools that can be used to facilitate this process.

## Key Terms

Crawlers   79

Scrapers   82

Traversal strategies   78

URL   76

Web crawling   75

Web scraping   75

## Highlights

- Web crawling is the process of building a collection of webpages by starting with an initial set of URLs or links and recursively traversing the corresponding pages to find additional links.

- Web scraping generally involves using commercial software and, as needed, programming languages such as Python to identify and download text from one or more pages or archives within a single website.

## Discussion Questions

- How do researchers choose whether to use a web crawler or a web scraper?

- What are some challenges in using crawlers and **scrapers** on websites with complex structures, such as many interlinked pages, graphics, and video?

- Considering your plans for your own research project (its topic, research questions, and at least a preliminary research design), what is the ideal tool for acquiring the data you need? More realistically, given real-world time and resource constraints, what is the best available web crawling or web scraping tool?

# Text Mining Fundamentals

# LEXICAL RESOURCES

## INTRODUCTION

Lexical resources contain a wealth of information on language and play an important role in most text mining applications. There are different types of lexical resources, ranging from simple word lists, which are often generated based on large collections of texts; to dictionaries, which also include phonetic transcriptions, definitions, usage examples, and other information on words; **thesauruses** and **semantic networks**, which also define similarity or other **semantic relations** between words; and **concordances**, which include several contexts where the words occur. Lexical resources can be monolingual, bilingual, or multilingual. Their development is usually labor intensive, as it requires a significant amount of time from experts such as lexicographers, linguists, or psychologists. Some resources took many years to complete; for instance, the *Oxford English Dictionary*, credited as the first comprehensive **dictionary** of the English language, was compiled over 27 years. Additionally, many lexical resources went through several editions over time; for example, WordNet, which is by now the most popular electronic English dictionary, had its first version released in 1991, and since then, it evolved to Version 3.1, released in 2012. More recently constructed lexical resources, such as Wikipedia or Wiktionary, benefited from online crowdsourcing, which comes with the advantage of significantly larger number of contributors at the cost of consistency (and sometimes at the cost of quality).

In this chapter, we provide an overview of several lexical resources that have been widely used in text mining applications. We also provide links to downloadable versions of most of these resources and application programming interfaces (APIs) that can facilitate their use in applications.

## WORDNET

WordNet (Fellbaum, 1998; Miller, 1995) is a dictionary or network started in 1985 by a group led by Miller at Princeton University. WordNet covers the majority of nouns, verbs, adjectives, and adverbs in the English language, along with a rich set of semantic relations that connect these concepts. Words in WordNet are organized in synonym sets, also called synsets. WordNet 3.1 is the latest WordNet version (as of December 2016), and it has a large network of 155,000 words grouped into 117,000 synsets.

Many of the synsets in WordNet are connected to several other synsets via semantic relations, such as hypernymy ("is a"), homonymy ("part of"), and so on. Table 7.1 lists the semantic relations available in WordNet, together with examples.

# BASIC CONCEPTS

A *lexical resource* is a database that contains information about the words in language. Lexical resources can be monolingual, bilingual, or multilingual.

A *dictionary* is an alphabetical list of the words in a language, which may include information such as definitions, usage examples, etymologies, translations, and so on.

A *thesaurus* is a database that groups the words in a language according to their similarity.

A *semantic network* is a network that defines the semantic relations between words.

A *concordance* is an alphabetical list of the words used in a text, along with the immediate contexts where each word appears.

| TABLE 7.1 ■ Semantic Relations in WordNet | | |
|---|---|---|
| Relation | Description | Example |
| Hypernym (nouns, verbs) | A is a hypernym of B means B is an A. | *Canine* is a hypernym of *dog*. |
| Hyponyms (nouns, verbs) | A is a hyponym of B means A is a B. | *Dalmatian* is a hyponym of *dog*. |
| Holonyms (nouns) | A is a holonym of B means B is a part of A. | *Forest* is a holonym of *tree*. |
| Meronyms (nouns) | A is a meronym of B means A is a part of B. | *Tree* is a meronym of *forest*. |
| Coordinates (nouns, verbs) | A is a coordinate of B means A and B have a common hypernym. | *Dalmatian* is a coordinate of *poodle* (they both have *dog* as a hypernym). |
| Troponym (verbs) | A is a troponym of B means doing A is a manner of doing B. | *To march* is a troponym of *to walk*. |
| Entailment (verbs) | A entails B means doing A implies also doing B. | To snore entails to sleep. |
| Related nouns (adjectives) | A has related noun B means A was derived from B. | *Studious* has related noun *study*. |
| Antonym (adjectives, adverbs) | A is an antonym of B means A and B have opposite meanings. | *Beautiful* is an antonym of *ugly*. |
| Similar to (adjectives) | A is similar to B means A and B have similar meanings. | Beautiful is similar to lovely. |

Nouns and verbs are organized into hierarchies, based on the hypernymy and hyponymy relation. Figure 7.1 shows a snapshot of a WordNet noun hierarchy.

Adjectives and nouns are organized into clusters of related words, often with cluster heads that are found in an antonymy relation. Figure 7.2 shows a snapshot of an adjective cluster in WordNet.

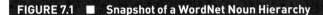

**FIGURE 7.1 ■ Snapshot of a WordNet Noun Hierarchy**

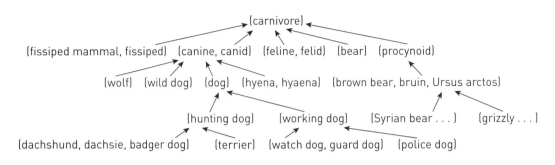

**FIGURE 7.2 ■ Snapshot of a WordNet Adjective Cluster**

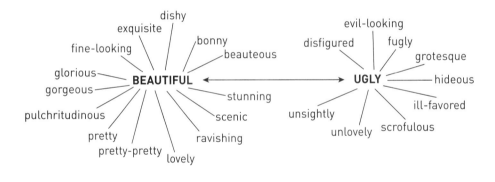

In the following, we take a closer look at two resources that have been built directly on WordNet: WordNet-Affect and WordNet Domains. Chapter 14 also provides a brief overview of SentiWordNet.

## WordNet Domains

WordNet Domains (Magnini & Cavaglia, 2000) is an augmentation of WordNet with domain labels. Every synset in WordNet has been semiautomatically labeled with one or several of 200 domain labels, which reflect the appurtenance of the words in the synset to domains such as *archaelogy, art, sport,* and so forth. In addition to enriching the synsets in WordNet with additional information on their semantic category, the WordNet

**TABLE 7.2 ■ Sample Domains From WordNet Domains**

| Domain | Sample Synsets |
|---|---|
| Sport | (athlete, jock), (game equipment) |
| Building industry | (hospital, infirmary), (railway station, railroad station, train station, railroad terminal, train depot) |
| Literature | (poetry, poesy, verse), (verse, rhyme), (codex, leaf book) |
| Religion | (chapel service, chapel), (monk, monastic), (convent) |

Domains also have the additional benefits of (1) connecting words from different parts of speech, as a domain may encompass verbs, nouns, adjectives, or adverbs, and (2) allowing for principled ways to group similar senses, by merging those synsets in which a word appears and which belong to the same domain. WordNet Domains was used in a large number of applications, including word sense disambiguation, text classification, and joke generation, among others. Table 7.2 shows several domain examples along with synsets in WordNet.

## WordNet-Affect

WordNet-Affect (Strapparava & Valitutti, 2004) is another resource that was created starting with WordNet, by annotating synsets with several emotions. It uses several resources for affective information, including the emotion classification of Ortony, Clore, and Collins (1990). WordNet-Affect was constructed in two stages. First, a core resource was built based on a number of heuristics and semiautomatic processing, followed by a second stage where the core synsets were automatically expanded using the semantic relations available in WordNet.

Table 7.3 shows several sample words for each of the six basic emotions of Ortony and colleagues (1990): anger, disgust, fear, joy, sadness, surprise.

# ROGET'S THESAURUS

*Roget's Thesaurus* (Roget, 1911/1987) is a thesaurus of the English language, with words and phrases grouped into hierarchical classes. A word class usually includes synonyms, as well as other words that are semantically related. Classes are typically divided into sections, subsections, heads, and paragraphs, which are, in turn, divided by part of speech:

**TABLE 7.3  ■  Sample Words From WordNet-Affect**

| Emotion | Sample words |
|---|---|
| Anger | wrath, umbrage, offense, temper, irritation, lividity, irascibility, fury, rage |
| Disgust | horror, foul, disgust, abominably, hideous, sick, tired of, wicked, yucky |
| Fear | terrible, ugly, unsure, unkind, timid, scared, outrageous, panic, hysteria, intimidated |
| Joy | worship, adoration, sympathy, tenderness, regard, respect, pride, preference, love |
| Sadness | aggrieve, misery, oppressive, pathetic, tearful, sorry, gloomy, dismay |
| Surprise | wonder, awe, amazement, astounding, stupefying, dazed, stunned, amazingly |

*Source:* WordNet-Affect. FBK-irst © 2009. All Rights Reserved.

nouns, verbs, adjectives, and adverbs. Finally, each paragraph is grouped into several sets of semantically related words. The most recent version of *Roget's Thesaurus* (Roget, 1911/1987) includes about 250,000 words, grouped into eight broad classes that branch into 39 sections, 79 subsections, 596 head groups, and finally 990 heads.

Table 7.4 shows four sample word sets found under each of the four parts of speech under the head 408 Informality.

**TABLE 7.4  ■  Sample Word Sets in Roget**

| Part of Speech | Sample Set of Semantically Related Words |
|---|---|
| Noun | informality, informalness, lack of formality, lack of ceremony, unceremoniousness, lack of convention, indifference, noncomformity, casualness, offhandedness |
| Verb | be informal, not stand on ceremony, be oneself, be natural, relax, feel at home, make oneself at home, not insist, waive the rules, come as you are, let one's hair down |
| Adjective | familiar, natural, simple, plain, unpretentious, homely, folksy, common, unaffected |
| Adverb | freely, indulgently, tolerantly, unconstrainedly, permissively, loosely, irregularly |

*Source:* Roget's thesaurus, http://www.gutenberg.org/ebooks/22

# LINGUISTIC INQUIRY AND WORD COUNT

Linguistic Inquiry and Word Count (LIWC) was developed as a resource for psycholinguistic analysis by Pennebaker, Francis, and Booth (2001). It has been used in a large number of studies in social, psychological, and linguistic research, addressing tasks such as analysis of psychology traits (Mairesse et al., 2007; Pennebaker & King, 1999), deception (Mihalcea & Strapparava, 2009; Ott, Choi, Cardie, & Hancock, 2011), social analysis of conversations (Stark, Shafran, & Kaye, 2012), prediction of depression (Resnik, Garron, & Resnik, 2013), identification of sarcasm (González-Ibáñez, Muresan, & Wacholder, 2011), and many others.

The 2007 version of LIWC includes more than 2,000 words and word stems grouped into close to 80 word categories. The word categories are grouped into four broad classes: linguistic processes, covering primarily function words and other common words; psychological processes, including social, affective, cognitive, perceptual, biological, and time processes; personal concerns, such as work, money, and religion; and spoken categories, including fillers and other spoken words. The LIWC lexicon has been validated by showing significant correlation between human ratings of a large number of written texts and the rating obtained through LIWC-based analyses of the same texts.

Table 7.5 shows four LIWC categories along with a set of sample words included in these classes.

**TABLE 7.5  ■  Three Sample LIWC Classes With Sample Words**

| Category | Class | Sample Words |
|---|---|---|
| We | Linguistic processes | our, ourselves, we, we'd, we'll, us, let's, we've, we're, let's |
| Optimism | Psychological processes | accept, best, bold, certain, confidence, daring, determined, glorious, hope |
| Achievement | Personal concerns | better, award, ahead, advance, achieve, motivate, lose, honor, climb, first, fail |
| Nonfluencies | Spoken categories | er, umm, uh, um, zz |

*Source:* LIWC (Linguistic Inquiry and Word Count), https://liwc.wpengine.com/.

# GENERAL INQUIRER

The General Inquirer (Stone & Hunt, 1963) is a dictionary program of about 10,000 words grouped into about 100 categories. Two of the most widely used word categories in the General Inquirer are the *positive* and *negative* sentiment categories, which have been overviewed in Chapter 14. In addition to these two word classes, the General Inquirer includes many other word classes that have social and psycholinguistic motivations, and have been widely used for content analysis. Three General Inquirer classes are shown in Table 7.6, together with sample words from these classes.

| TABLE 7.6 ■ Sample Words and Categories in General Inquirer | |
| --- | --- |
| **Category** | **Sample Words** |
| Academ[ic] | academic, astronomy, biology, chemistry, credit, dean, degree, physician, library |
| Ritual | ambush, appointment, affair, bridge, census, commemorate, debut, demonstration |
| Female | aunt, feminine, girl, goddess, her, heroine, grandmother, mother, queen, she |

*Source:* General Inquirer dictionary program, http://www.wjh.harvard.edu/~inquirer/

# WIKIPEDIA

Wikipedia is a free online encyclopedia, representing the outcome of a continuous collaborative effort of a large number of volunteer contributors. Virtually any Internet user can create or edit a Wikipedia webpage, and this "freedom of contribution" has a positive impact on both the quantity (fast-growing number of articles) and the quality (potential mistakes are quickly corrected within the collaborative environment) of this online resource.

The basic entry in Wikipedia is an article (or page), which defines and describes a concept, an entity, or an event, and consists of a hypertext document with hyperlinks to other pages within or outside Wikipedia. The role of the hyperlinks is to guide the reader to pages that provide additional information about the entities or events mentioned in an article. Articles are organized into categories, which, in turn, are organized into category hierarchies. For instance, the article on Alan Turing shown partially in Figure 7.3 is included in the category British cryptographers, which has a parent category named British scientists and so forth.

Each article in Wikipedia is uniquely referenced by an identifier, consisting of one or more words separated by spaces or underscores and occasionally a parenthetical explanation. For example, the article for the entity Turing that refers to the "English computer scientist" has the unique identifier Alan Turing, whereas the article on Turing with the "stream cipher" has the unique identifier Turing (cipher).

**FIGURE 7.3 ■ Snapshot of a Sample Wikipedia Page**

# Alan Turing

From Wikipedia, the free encyclopedia

*"Turing" redirects here. For other uses, see Turing (disambiguation).*

**Alan Mathison Turing** OBE FRS (/ˈtjʊərɪŋ/; 23 June 1912 – 7 June 1954) was an English computer scientist, mathematician, logician, cryptanalyst, philosopher and theoretical biologist.

He was highly influential in the development of theoretical computer science, providing a formalisation of the concepts of algorithm and computation with the Turing machine, which can be considered a model of a general purpose computer.[3][4][5] Turing is widely considered to be the father of theoretical computer science and artificial intelligence.[6]

*Source:* https://en.wikipedia.org/wiki/Alan_Turing. Licensed under the Creative Commons Attribution-Share Alike 3.0 Unported License. https://creativecommons.org/licenses/by-sa/3.0/.

The hyperlinks within Wikipedia are created using these unique identifiers, together with an anchor text that represents the surface form of the hyperlink. For instance, "Alan Mathison Turing OBE FRS, . . . was an English computer scientist" is the wiki source for the first sentence in the example page on Alan Turing in Figure 7.3, containing links to the articles Order of the British Empire, Fellow of the Royal Society, and computer scientist.

One of the implications of the large number of contributors editing the Wikipedia articles is the occasional lack of consistency with respect to the unique identifier used for a certain entity. For instance, Alan Turing is also referred to using the last name Turing, or the full name Alan Mathison Turing. This has led to the so-called redirect pages, which consist of a redirection hyperlink from an alternative name (e.g., Turing) to the article actually containing the description of the entity (e.g., Alan Turing). Another structure that is worth mentioning is the disambiguation page. Disambiguation pages are specifically created for ambiguous entities and consist of links to articles defining the different meanings of the entity. The unique identifier for a disambiguation page typically consists of the parenthetical explanation (disambiguation) attached to the name of the ambiguous entity, as in for example, sense (disambiguation), which is the unique identifier for the disambiguation page of the noun sense.

Wikipedia editions are available for more than 280 languages, with a number of entries varying from a few pages to 4 million articles or more per language. Table 7.7 shows the

10 largest Wikipedias (as of April 2017), along with the number of articles and approximate number of contributors.

Also worth noting are the interlingual links, which explicitly connect articles in different languages. For instance, the English article for the noun sense is connected, among others, to the Spanish article *sentido (percepcion)* and the Latin article *sensus (biologia)*. On average, about half the articles in a Wikipedia version include interlingual links to articles in other languages. The number of interlingual links per article varies from an average of 5 in the English Wikipedia, to 10 in the Spanish Wikipedia, and as many as 23 in the Arabic Wikipedia.

| TABLE 7.7 ■ Number of Articles and Users for the Top Ten Wikipedia Editions | | | |
|---|---|---|---|
| **Language** | **Wiki** | **Articles** | **Users** |
| English | en | 5,391,707 | 30,771,377 |
| Cebuano | ceb | 4,138,135 | 33,996 |
| Swedish | sv | 3,785,049 | 543,852 |
| German | de | 2,048,714 | 2,616,328 |
| Dutch | nl | 1,897,908 | 830,046 |
| French | fr | 1,858,259 | 2,757,540 |
| Russian | ru | 1,384,908 | 2,078,886 |
| Italian | it | 1,346,331 | 1,488,417 |
| Spanish | es | 1,327,066 | 4,564,582 |
| Waray | war | 1,262,379 | 31,594 |

*Source:* http://meta.wikimedia.org/wiki/List_of_Wikipedias. Licensed under the Creative Commons Attribution-ShareAlike 3.0 Unported License. https://creativecommons.org/licenses/by-sa/3.0/.

## Wiktionary

A sister project of Wikipedia, run by the same Wikimedia Foundation, Wiktionary is a volunteer-contributed dictionary, covering a large number of languages. Words in Wiktionary include synonyms and definitions, connections to translations in other languages, and a number of relations such as hyponyms ("is a") and derived terms. A useful piece of information that is available for many words in Wiktionary is the etymology of the words, which connects the current form of a word to earlier versions sometime in other languages.

## BabelNet

BabelNet (Navigli & Ponzetto, 2012) is a very large multilingual resource that has been built by automatically connecting Wikipedias in multiple languages, as well as WordNet dictionaries, Wiktionaries, and more recently other resources such as ImageNet and FrameNet. It currently covers 271 languages, and it includes about 14 million Babel synsets, each such synset containing all the synonyms available for a concept in multiple languages.

---

### Lexical Resources and Application Programming Interfaces

WordNet is one of the largest and most frequently used online dictionaries of the English language. Several APIs are also available (https://wordnet.princeton.edu).

Global WordNet is a website that includes links to WordNet versions in many other languages (many of which are publicly available; http://globalwordnet.org/wordnets-in-the-world).

WordNet Domains and WordNet-Affect include an annotation of WordNet with 200 semantic domains and several affective classes (http://wndomains.fbk.eu).

*Roget's Thesaurus* is one of the oldest thesauruses of the English language. The 1911 version of the *Roget's Thesaurus* is in the public domain, downloadable from this site: www.gutenberg.org/ebooks/22; the newer version of *Roget's Thesaurus* is not publicly available, but it can be accessed online at www.thesaurus.com.

Linguistic Inquiry and Word Count (LIWC) is a lexicon that groups words based on psycholinguistic processes. It can be tested online or used offline by purchasing a license (http://liwc.wpengine.com).

General Inquirer groups words into many categories, and among others, it includes two large sets of positive and negative words (www.wjh.harvard.edu/~inquirer).

Wikipedia and Wiktionary are large crowdsourced resources, available in many languages. The crawling of these resources is discouraged; instead, those who want to use these resources can download entire dumps from this site: https://dumps.wikimedia.org/backup-index.html. Several APIs have been built over time; for instance, this API that can be used to facilitate the access to a Wiktionary dump: https://dkpro.github.io/dkpro-jwktl.

BabelNet includes 14 million synsets in 271 languages. The resource and the API are freely available for research purposes (http://babelnet.org).

## Conclusion

Lexical resources are building blocks for many text mining applications, as they encode words and relations between words in ways that enable a deeper understanding of language. Lexical resources vary from simple, even if often extensive, word lists, to dictionaries, thesauruses, semantic networks, and more recently crowdsourced resources that leverage the knowledge of the "crowds" and often span many languages. This chapter overviewed several of the most frequently used lexical resources in text mining and highlighted the representations used in these resources. While several of these lexical resources took many years to compile, the effort that went into each resource is often paying off by several orders of magnitudes, as they facilitate tens and sometime hundreds of applications.

## Key Terms

| | | |
|---|---|---|
| Concordances    85 | Semantic networks    85 | Thesauruses    85 |
| Dictionary    86 | Semantic relations    85 | |

## Highlights

- Lexical resources are often extensive compilations of information on language and may include lists of words, definitions, translations, relations, and so on.

- WordNet is one of the most frequently used digital dictionary of the English language: It organizes words into synsets (synonym sets) and explicitly encodes a large number of semantic relations between these synsets. Several resources have been built on top of WordNet, including WordNet-Affect, WordNet Domains, SentiWordNet. Versions in other languages also exist.

- Other lexical resources group words based on their polarity, or based on other psychological or linguistic processes. Such resources include *Roget's Thesaurus*, LIWC, or General Inquirer.

- Very large crowdsourced lexical resources also exist, including Wikipedias and Wiktionaries in multiple languages. A resource that has automatically linked many of these resources is BabelNet, which includes 271 languages, and 14 million synsets that cover the representation (synonyms, definitions) of concepts in many languages.

## Discussion Topics

- Discuss the challenges that had to be overcome by the lexicographers who created WordNet. Hint: Think of the variety of dictionaries that existed before WordNet and on which WordNet has built—for example, the *Oxford English Dictionary*, *Roget's Thesaurus*, and *Merriam-Webster Dictionary*. Think also of the challenges associated with the breadth of the coverage of a lexical resource.

- Think of and discuss an application of WordNet that has not been discussed in this chapter.

- Assume you want to create a lexical resource that can support an application of your choice (e.g., politeness recognition, identification of moral values in text). How would you go about creating such a lexical resource?

# 8

# BASIC TEXT PROCESSING

## LEARNING OBJECTIVES

The goals of Chapter 8 are to help you to do the following:

1. Define basic text processing steps, such as **tokenization**, stop word removal, **stemming**, and **lemmatization**.
2. Explain text statistics and laws that govern the distribution of words in text.
3. Explore the basics of **language models**, and evaluate their applications.
4. Discuss the main goals of more advanced text processing steps.

## INTRODUCTION

Text analysis almost invariably requires some form of text processing. Consider the following example of a tweet: Today's the day, ladies and gents. Mr. K will land in U.S. :). If one wants to use information from this piece of text for any form of text mining or other text analysis, it is important to determine what are the tokens in this text—*today, 's, the, day, ladies, and, gents, Mr., K, will, land, in, U.S., :)*—which implies a process that understands that periods in abbreviations (e.g., *Mr.*) and acronyms (e.g., *U.S.*) need to be preserved as such, but there is also punctuation that needs to be separated from the nearby tokens (comma after *day* or period after *gents*). Further, a text preprocessor often normalizes the text (e.g., it may expand *'s* into *is* or the informal *gents* into *gentlemen*), it may try to identify the root or stem of the words (e.g., *lady* for *ladies*, or *be* for *'s*), and it may even attempt to identify and possibly label special symbols such as this emoticon: *:)*.

Text processing can consist of basic steps such as removing the HTML tags from a collection of documents collected from the web, separating the punctuation from the words, removing function words, and applying stemming or lemmatization, or it can take more advanced forms such as annotating text with part-of-speech tags or syntactic dependency trees or other layers of annotations such as mapping words to senses in a dictionary or finding discourse markers. This chapter covers some of the basic text processing steps, addresses the basics of language models, and provides pointers for additional reading for the more advanced text processing.

Basic text processing is usually the first step in any research study that involves linguistic input. Oftentimes, it is sufficient to just remove extraneous tags (e.g., HTML, XML) and tokenize the punctuation, which will result in a set of tokens that can be used to collect statistics or to use as input for other applications such as sentiment analysis or text classification. But there are also times when it is useful to remove the very frequent words (through stop word removal) or obtain the root form of the words (through stemming or lemmatization). The kind of text processing steps that are to be applied is often application dependent: If one wants, for instance, to analyze the language of deception, stop words are useful and should be preserved, but if the goal is to separate computer science texts from biology texts, then stop words can be removed, and one may also benefit from stemming all the input words. There can also be cases when one is interested in identifying all the organizations that appear in a corpus, in which case it is beneficial to have available more advanced annotations such as the ones provided by a **named entity recognition (NER)** tool.

## BASIC CONCEPTS

*Basic text processing* is often the first step in any text mining application and consists of several layers of simple processing such as tokenization, lemmatization, normalization, or more advanced processes such as part-of-speech tagging, syntactic parsing, and others.

*Tokenization* refers to the process of separating the punctuation from the words while maintaining their intended meaning.

*Stop word removal* is the process of eliminating function words such as *the, a, of,* and so on.

*Stemming* is a processing step that uses a set of rules to remove inflections.

*Lemmatization* is the process of identifying the base form (or root form) of a word.

*Language models* are probabilistic representations of language.

The *distribution of words* in language is effectively modeled by two laws: Zipf's law and Heaps' law.

Other, more *advanced text processing* steps that are often used in text mining are part-of-speech tagging, collocation identification, syntactic parsing, named entity recognition (NER), word sense disambiguation, and word similarity.

# BASIC TEXT PROCESSING

## Tokenization

Tokenization is the process of identifying the words in the input sequence of characters, mainly by separating the punctuation marks but also by identifying contractions, abbreviations, and so forth. For instance, given the text "Mr. Smith doesn't like apples," we would like output that has each word as a separate token, as in "Mr. Smith does n't like apples." Tokenization may seem like a trivial process at first, but there are some cases that require special attention. For instance, for a period, we need to distinguish between end of sentence period and markers of acronyms (e.g., U.S.) or abbreviations (e.g., Mr., Dr.). While we do want to separate the end of sentence from the word before, it is preferred to keep the period attached to the acronyms or abbreviations, as they are words that require the period to be well formed. The period also has special meaning and should be kept as is inside numbers (e.g., 12.4) or dates (e.g., 12.05.2015) or IP addresses (100.2.34.58).

- For an apostrophe, we often want to identify the contractions and separate them such that they form meaningful individual words. For instance, the possessive book's should form two words *book* and *'s*. The contractions *aren't* and *he's* should be separated into *are n't*, and *he 's*.

- Quotations should also be separated from the text, as in, for example, "Let it be," which should become " Let it be ".

- For hyphenations, we often leave them in place, to indicate a collocation as in, for example, *state-of-the-art*, although sometimes it may be useful to separate it, to allow for access to individual words, for example, separate *Hewlett-Packard* into *Hewlett-Packard*.

While tokenization is largely language independent, several of the special cases that need to be handled for correct tokenization can be language specific. For instance, abbreviations and contractions are often dependent on language, and thus, one needs to compile a list of such words to make sure that the tokenization of the period is handled correctly. The same applies to apostrophe and hyphenation.

Sometimes the tokenization process also includes other text **normalization** steps, such as lowercasing or the more advanced truecasing (e.g., selecting the correct case for the words *apple* in "There is an apple symbol on my Apple Macbook") or removal of HTML tags, if the text is obtained from a webpage.

Note that the process of tokenization assumes that white spaces and punctuation are used as explicit word boundaries. This is the case with many of the languages that use a Latin alphabet, as well as several other language families, but it is not the case with most

Asian languages. Processing an input source of characters in an Asian language also requires a separate step of word boundary detection, which is often done using supervised learning algorithms. There are also languages that make heavy use of compound words such as German (*Computerlinguistik* means "computational linguistics") or agglutinative languages such as Inuktitut (*Tusaatsiarunnanngittualuujunga* means "I can't hear very well").

## Stop Word Removal

Stop words, also referred to as function words or closed-class words, consist of high-frequency words including pronouns (e.g., *I, we, us*), determiners (e.g., *the, a*), prepositions (e.g., *in, on*), and others. For some tasks, stop words can be useful: For instance, it has been found that they can give significant insights into people's personalities and behaviors (Mihalcea & Strapparava, 2009; Pennebaker & King, 1999). But there are also tasks when it is useful to remove them and focus the attention on content words such as nouns and verbs. Whatever the case, it is important to have the means to identify the stop words in an input text. In general, this is done using a precompiled list of stop words together with an efficient lookup algorithm.

Stop words are clearly language-dependent; thus, an important question is how to create a list of stop words for the language of interest. Well-studied languages, such as English, or Spanish, or Chinese, have several such lists publicly available. If a list of stop words is not available for a given language, relying on the fact that stop words are high-frequency words (see the next section), one can gather word statistics on a very large corpus of texts written in that language and consequently get the top *N*-most frequent words as candidate stop words. Ideally, the corpus should contain a mix of texts from different domains, to avoid high frequency for some words due to their domain specificity (e.g., a collection of texts on computer science will inherently include the word *computer* with high frequency). It is a good practice to also get the feedback of a native speaker on the list of candidate stop words, as sometime it can also include words that are frequent but are not stop words (e.g., *have, get, today*).

## Stemming and Lemmatization

Many words in natural language are related, yet they have different surface forms, which make their recognition nontrivial. While some of these relations are of semantic nature and require dictionary knowledge, as in, for example, *sick* and *ill*, there are also many relations that can be more easily captured through simpler forms of string analysis, as is the case with *construction* and *construct* or *water* and *watered*.

The simplest way to identify the common stem of multiple words is through the process called stemming. Simply put, stemming applies a set of rules to an input word to remove suffixes and prefixes and obtain its stem, which will now be shared with other related words. For instance, *computer, computational*, and *computation* will be all reduced to the same stem: *compute*.

Stemming often produces stems that are not valid words, which is irrelevant if the "consumer" of these stems is a system and not a human. For instance, stemming is used in information retrieval (see Chapter 13), where the stems are fed into the indexing process, and improve the quality of the information retrieval system, without ever being read by the users of that system. Stemming, however, should not be used if the stemmed text is to be read by a human, as oftentimes it is hard to understand. Consider, for example, the text "for example compressed and compression are both accepted as equivalent to compress," which a stemmer will transform into "for exampl compres and compres are both accept as equival to compres."

There are many stemmers out there, the most popular one being the Porter stemmer, which is a simple procedure for removing known affixes in English without using a dictionary. The Porter stemmer consists of a set of transformation rules, such as *sses → ss, ies → i, ational → ate, tional → tion*, which are applied repeatedly on a word until no transformations are obtained. The stemmer was found to work well in evaluations performed in information retrieval systems, where the quality of the retrieval system was improved when applied on stemmed text. It also makes errors, including errors of "comission," such as *organization* and *organ* being both stemmed to *organ* or *police* and *policy* sharing the stem *polic*, or errors of "omission," such as *cylinder* and *cylindrical* or *Europe* and *European* not being stemmed at all. The stemmer is clearly language dependent, but versions of the stemmer for several languages other than English also exist.

The alternative to stemming is lemmatization, which reduces the inflectional forms of a word to its root form. For instance, lemmatization will transform *boys* to *boy, children* to *child*, and *am, are*, or *is* to *be*. Unlike stemming, the output obtained from lemmatization is a valid word form, which is the base form of a word as found in a dictionary. Thus, lemmatization has the benefit that its output is readable by humans; however, this comes at a cost of a more computationally intensive process, as it requires a list of grammatical forms to handle the regular inflections as well as an extensive list of irregular words.

# LANGUAGE MODELS AND TEXT STATISTICS

## Language Models

Language models are probabilistic representations of natural language, which can be used as predictive or explicative models. Very briefly, a language model will capture the probability of seeing certain sequences of words or characters—for instance, given that we have already seen the word *dog*, is it more likely that we will see *barks* or *writes*? Language models can thus be used to propose possible alternatives, given a history of previously occurred words—for example, *dog*. What are possible continuations? Or they can be used to assess likelihood—for example, what is the likelihood of seeing the sequence *dog barks*.

Language models have a very broad range of applications, ranging from spelling corrections (what are the most likely corrections, given an observed incorrect text), to speech recognition (about all possible texts that could be output from an input utterance, which one is more likely), machine translation (which is the most likely translation, given all possible alternatives), handwriting recognition, language recognition, and so forth.

Language models are built on very large corpora (referred to as training corpora), by calculating probabilities of words or sequences of words on the given text collection. Clearly, the larger the collection, the more accurate the language models. Think, for instance, of predicting the likelihood of seeing the sequence *dog eats* by processing the text from this chapter versus processing the text available in some millions of webpages.

The simplest language models are based on unigrams, where we have probabilities associated with individual words. In these models, we mainly count the frequency of individual words, and calculate their probability with respect to the entire set of words in the training corpus. For instance, if we have a collection of 100 words, out of which two are *dog*, the probability of seeing this individual word (or unigram) is $P(dog) = 2/100$.

The next stage is to create bigram language models. We now measure the probability of a word given the word before $P(W_i | W_{i-1})$, which can be calculated as $Count(W_{i-1} W_i)/Count(W_{i-1})$. For instance, we could calculate $P(barks|dog)$ as the number of times we have seen *dog barks* divided by the number of times we have seen *dog*.

Next are trigram models, where we estimate $P(W_i | W_{i-1} W_{i-2})$, then four-grams, where we estimate $P(W_i | W_{i-1} W_{i-2} W_{i-3})$ and so forth. The higher the order of the n-gram models, the better the accuracy of the models, as measured through their predictive or explicative power. The trade-off, however, stands in the amount of data required to train such models, with higher-order n-grams requiring significantly larger training sets to avoid data sparseness. Think, for instance, of calculating individual word probabilities from a corpus of 1 million words versus calculating the probability of sequences of six words at a time (six-grams) from the same corpus. It is likely that we would have seen a lot of the individual words in this corpus, but it is also likely that we have not seen most of the possible sequences of six words in that same corpus. The effect of that is that we will have a lot of zero counts in our six-gram probability estimates, and therefore, the model will end up not being accurate.

Given such language models, we can then combine them to make predictions for entire texts. For instance, if we have the text "I want to eat Chinese food," assuming a bigram model, we can calculate $P(I\ want\ to\ eat\ British\ food) = P(I|start)\ P(want|I)\ P(to|want)$

P(eat|to) P(British|eat) P(food|British). Similarly, with a trigram model, we would calculate P(I | start start) P (want | start I) P(to|I want) P(eat|want to) P(British|to eat) P(food|eat British), and so forth.

## Text Statistics

One of the simplest analyses that one can do on any collection of text is to count words and determine what words occur with higher frequency. Interestingly, despite its complexity, natural language is very predictable: One can, for instance, make a good guess as to what will be the most frequent words in any text collection or make predictions as to what will be the size of the vocabulary (i.e., number of unique words) in a new collection.

For instance, Table 8.1 shows the top 10 most frequent words in one of the benchmark collections from the Text REtrieval Conference (TREC 3). As seen in this table, the most frequent words are generally stop words, as also mentioned in the previous section.

If we plot the frequency of words in a corpus, we generally obtain a curve that looks like the one showed in Figure 8.1.

What this curve shows is that there are a few words that are very common. For instance, words such as *the* or *of* can account for as much as 10% of all the word occurrences in a

| TABLE 8.1 ■ Word Frequencies in TREC 3 (125,720,891 total words, 508,209 unique words) | | |
| --- | --- | --- |
| **Frequent Word** | **Number Occurrences** | **Percentage of Total** |
| the | 7,398,934 | 5.9 |
| of | 3,893,790 | 3.1 |
| to | 3,364,653 | 2.7 |
| and | 3,320,687 | 2.6 |
| in | 2,311,785 | 1.8 |
| is | 1,559,147 | 1.2 |
| for | 1,313,561 | 1.0 |
| The | 1,144,860 | 0.9 |
| that | 1,066,503 | 0.8 |
| said | 1,027,713 | 0.8 |

*Source:* Used with permission of Dr. Bruce Croft.

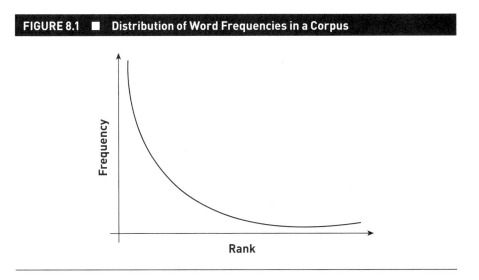

**FIGURE 8.1  ■  Distribution of Word Frequencies in a Corpus**

collection. At the other end of the curve, we have the rare words, which make the "bulk" of the words in a corpus. In fact, it has been shown that half the words in a collection of texts appear only once (these words are called *hapax legomena*, which means "read only once" in Greek).

There are two laws that have been established on word distributions: **Zipf's law** and **Heaps' law**. Zipf's law models the distribution of terms in a corpus and provides a mathematical way to answer this question: How many times does the *r*th most frequent word appear in a corpus of *N* words? Specifically, assuming that *f* is the frequency of a word, and *r* is its rank reflecting the position of the word in a list sorted by decreasing frequency (e.g., in Table 8.1, the word *of* has a frequency of 3,893,790 and has rank 2 in the frequency sorted list), Zipf found the following in 1949, where *k* is a constant that depends on the corpus:

$$f \cdot r = k \text{ (for constant } k\text{)}$$

Zipf's law can be used to make predictions regarding the number of words that have a certain frequency range and generally to show the distribution of words in a corpus.

The second law, called Heaps' law, models the number of words in the vocabulary as a function of the corpus size. The number of unique words (vocabulary) in a collection does not grow linearly with number of words in that collection. This is because words that we have already seen will start repeating as the corpus grows—thus, the shape of vocabulary versus size that generally is as shown in Figure 8.2.

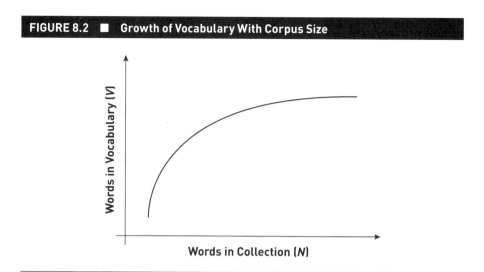

**FIGURE 8.2 ■ Growth of Vocabulary With Corpus Size**

Interestingly, the curve never plateaus either, and this is because there are certain word classes in language, such as numbers and proper names, which are an endless source of new words. So no matter how large a corpus is (and thus its corresponding vocabulary), adding more text to it will likely bring a few more new words.

Heaps' law can be used to answer questions such as these: What is the number of unique words appearing in a corpus of $N$ words? How many words will I have in a collection when I will have a vocabulary of $V$ words? Given a corpus of $N$ words with a vocabulary of $V$ words, Heaps' law states the following, where $K$ and $\beta$ are parameters that can be determined on a given collection of texts:

$$V = KN^{\beta} \text{ with contants } K, 0 < \beta < 1$$

Their typical range is $K \approx 10$–$100$ and $\beta \approx 0.4$–$0.6$. Using this law, one can make predictions as to what will be the vocabulary of a corpus as it grows. For instance, we may know that a collection of legal texts has 1,000,000 words, and a vocabulary of 135,000 words. Heaps' law will help us make a prediction of what will be the size of the vocabulary in a future setting when the corpus will grow to, for example, 5,000,000 words.

# MORE ADVANCED TEXT PROCESSING

As stated at the beginning of this chapter, in addition to basic processing steps, there are other text processing layers that can be applied on any given text. Some of the most commonly used are briefly described next.

## Part-of-Speech Tagging

**Part-of-speech tagging** is the task of assigning each word in an input text with its correct syntactic role, such as noun, verb, and so forth. Most of the algorithms are based on supervised learning and therefore rely on previously annotated data in order to learn how to assign parts of speech to new text. There are also different tag sets that have been proposed, ranging from a handful of tags (e.g., noun, verb) to larger tag sets such as the Penn Treebank (Marcus, Marcinkiewicz, & Santorini, 1993), which contains close to 40 different tags (e.g., NN = common noun singular, NNS = common noun plural, NNP = proper noun, NNPS = proper noun plural).

When annotated data are available, the most basic approach that one could use is to assign each word in a text with its most frequent part-of-speech tag from the annotated data. If, for instance, the word to be annotated is *race* and it was found 118 times with a verb annotation and 206 times with a noun annotation, then this baseline will choose the noun tag merely based on its previous frequency.

More advanced tagging methods, however, go beyond the frequency of the tag and also consider the context. For example, if once again we are to annotate the word *race* and we know that the context is *to race*, intuitively its verb tag will be more likely than in a context such as *the race*, where the noun tag is more probable. To account for context, a part-of-speech tagger will collect sequence probabilities from the annotated data. In their simplest form, these probabilities would consider the likelihood of a tag given the previous tag—for example, p(VB|TO) (probability of the tag verb given that the previous tag is to)—but they can also look further into the history and consider longer sequences of tags. A question that arises is the dependency between tags—in our example that was just given, how would one know that the previous tag is TO, since the tagging of that previous word is itself a probabilistic process. Hidden Markov models (HMMs) can address such situations. For example, the Viterbi algorithm is a recursive algorithm that calculates the probability of the current tag by considering all the various previous tags along with their probabilities. Other flavors of HMMs are the forward and backward algorithms, which are also recursive methods that iteratively compute the likelihood of a sequence of tags.

In addition to HMMs, many other part-of-speech tagging methods have been introduced. For instance, transformation-based tagging such as Brill's (1992) starts by annotating all the words with their most frequent tag, and then it uses annotated data to learn transformation rules such as "if the previous word is *the* change the tag from VB to NN" or "if the next word has the tag NN then change the tag from RB to JJ." Other taggers include maximum entropy tagging (Ratnaparkhi, 1996) or feature-rich graph-based tagging (Toutanova, Klein, Manning, & Singer, 2003); machine-learning methods such as those described in Chapter 9 have also been effectively used for part-of-speech tagging.

## Collocation Identification

The goal of **collocation identification** is to automatically identify sequences of words that have a special meaning when taken as a phrase, such as "mother-in-law" or "kick the bucket." Identifying such collocations can be useful for many purposes: In information retrieval, knowing that the query includes the word *mother-in-law* rather than the individual words *mother, in,* and *law,* it will avoid wrong matches with documents that refer to legal materials; in machine translation, collocations often have a correspondent in the other language that is not a simple composition of the translations of the individual words—keeping with the mother-in-law example, the correct translation in Italian is one word *suocera,* rather than the meaningless sequence "*mama in legge*" obtained from a literal translation.

The methods most frequently used for collocation identification consist of information theoretic measures, which try to identify significant co-occurrences in text. These include pointwise mutual information (PMI), Jaccard coefficient, chi-square, and many others (Church & Hanks, 1990). The gist of these methods is that they calculate a measure of co-occurrence both by assuming that the words in a **collocation** occur together and by assuming independence; these two measures are then combined together in a final metric that reflects the likelihood of the words under consideration to occur together. For example, given the words *wood* and *desk,* in order to determine if the phrase *wood desk* is a collocation or not, one could, for instance, use PMI and calculate the likelihood p(wood) of seeing the word *wood* in a given corpus (the number of times *wood* occurs in the corpus divided by the total number of words in the corpus), the likelihood p(desk) of seeing the word *desk* in the same corpus (using the same count division), and the likelihood p(wood desk) of seeing wood desk in the corpus (the number of times the words *wood* and *desk* occur next to each other in the corpus divided by the total number of words in the corpus). With these inputs, the PMI will be calculated as PMI(wood, desk) = log (P(wood desk)/(P(wood) × P(desk))), and depending on where this value falls with respect to a given threshold, wood desk would be considered a collocation or not (for this particular example, the PMI will likely be very small, which will suggest that wood desk is not a collocation).

## Syntactic Parsing

**Syntactic parsing** often builds upon part-of-speech tagged text and aims to identify syntactic relations between constituents in language. Some parsers will produce constituency syntactic trees (Collins, 2003), often expressed in either tree or parenthetical notation, which can have multiple elements in one syntactic constituent (e.g., identify a noun phrase as being formed by a determiner followed by an adjective followed by a noun). For instance, given the text "I am happy," a constituency parser will produce the following output: (ROOT (S (NP (PRP I)) (VP (VBP am) (ADJP (JJ happy))) (..))), which reflects among others that there is a sentence (S) formed by a noun phrase (NP) and a verb phrase (VP), that the VP is formed by a verb (VBP) and an adjectival phrase (ADJP), and so on.

Other parsers will mainly output dependencies (Klein & Manning, 2004)—that is, binary relations between elements in the text (e.g., an adjective that has a modifier relation to its noun). For example, for the same text considered before, a dependency parser may output the following dependencies nsubj(happy-3, I-1) and cop(happy-3, am-2), which indicates a subject (nsubj) dependency between happy and I, and a copulative (cop) dependency between happy and am.

The most accurate parsers work by training supervised systems on manually parsed data, such as the Penn Treebank (Marcus et al., 1993). Given a large corpus of annotated data, these parsers will learn probabilities for relations between words—for example, the probability for a sentence to be formed by a noun phrase followed by a verb phrase versus a sentence being formed just by a verb phrase. Given all these probabilities learned during the training stage, the parsers will use a dynamic programming algorithm to find the set of rules that apply on a given input.

In addition to supervised parsers, there has also been work on building unsupervised parsers, which are particularly appealing when a parser is needed for a new language.

## Named Entity Recognition

Named entity tagging—sometimes regarded as a specialized case of information extraction (see Chapter 15)—aims to identify named entities from a predefined set, such as person, location, or organization. Named entity tagging is a necessary step for many other applications, such as question answering, conversational technologies; text geolocation, as well as a number of text mining applications where it is important to know the people, locations, or organizations in a text. One could for instance aim to find how peoplecentric a text is, which can be partly addressed by finding all the person mentions in the text, or to find the sentiment toward certain organizations, in which case the identification of the organizations is important.

The most common techniques for named entity tagging combine rules, as available through extensive lexicons that specify the possible values that the entities can take (e.g., Gazetteers) or tokens that may occur before or after an entity (e.g., *Mr.* before a person mention or *Inc.* after an organization mention) with supervised learning, which aims to automatically learn the properties of named entities from previously annotated text. More precisely, using a supervised learning framework as described in Chapter 9, every entity in an annotated (training) text will be transformed into a learning instance, with features (or attributes) that reflect the properties of the entity, including, for example, the value of the words right before and right after the entity, the position in the sentence, the case (uppercase, lowercase), and so on. Given a new text, all the candidate words (e.g., all the nouns) are transformed into a feature vector using a similar set of attributes and consequently labeled as a certain named entity using a machine-learning algorithm (e.g., Person/NotPerson). While many supervised algorithms have been explored for named entity tagging, conditional random fields (CRFs) is among the most successful ones.

The annotated data used to build a named entity tagger can either be obtained automatically by applying a set of rules as described previously (Collins & Singer, 1999), a process often referred to as bootstrapping, described in more detail in Chapter 15, or it can be obtained through manual annotations (Collins, 2002).

## Word Sense Disambiguation

**Word sense disambiguation** maps input words to dictionary senses and is used to identify the meaning of a word as a function of its context. Word meaning annotations can be used for rule-based machine translation, for query expansion in information retrieval, for language learning, and so on. The two most common approaches for word sense disambiguation are supervised approaches based on annotated data and unsupervised approaches that rely on knowledge sources.

When labeled instances for a word are available—for example, a number of manually sense-annotated examples for the noun plant, we can use traditional supervised methods such as those described in Chapter 9 to build a system that can automatically predict the meaning of a word in new text (Yarowsky, 2000).

The alternative is to exclusively use information obtained from lexical resources, such as word meaning definitions, synonyms, hypernyms, and so forth (see Chapter 7). In this case, one could use, for instance, the overlap between the definitions of the meanings of the words in a sentence, to find the set of word senses that maximize this overlap (Lesk, 1986). Note that this method can face a combinatorial explosion, as it aims to simultaneously consider all the meanings of all the words in a text. A simplified and more efficient version of this approach is to disambiguate one word at a time, by measuring the overlap between the meaning definitions of the word and the context where the word occurs, and choose the meaning that has the highest overlap with the context (Banerjee & Pedersen, 2002).

Recent work in word sense disambiguation has also used lexical resources other than dictionaries, such as Wikipedia (Mihalcea, 2007).

## Word Similarity

Measuring **word similarity** or longer sequences such as phrases, sentences, or entire documents is one of the main tasks of the field of natural language processing (NLP) and lies at the core of a large number of applications such as information retrieval, plagiarism detection, short answer grading, textual entailment, and others. A relatively large number of word and text similarity measures have been proposed in the past, ranging from distance-based measures computed on semantic networks or taxonomies, to metrics based on models of distributional similarity learned from large text collections.

Corpus-based measures of word semantic similarity try to identify the degree of similarity between words using information exclusively derived from large corpora. In distributional similarity, words are represented by their distribution in a large corpus (e.g., presence–absence or weight inside the documents in a collection; position inside syntactic dependencies), and consequently, the similarity of two words is measured by the similarity of their vector representations. Latent semantic analysis (LSA; Landauer, Foltz, & Laham, 1998) attempts to bring improvements by reducing these representations to a low-dimensional space, which also captures semantic relations between words. Another related method is the explicit semantic analysis method (Gabrilovich & Markovitch, 2007), which represents each word as a vector that reflects the presence–absence of the word inside Wikipedia articles. Another way to measure the similarity of two words is to calculate their PMI in very large data sets (Turney, 2001) by measuring the likelihood of the words to co-occur together. It is measured as $\log (P(w^1,w^2)/(P(w^1)P(w^2))$, where $P(w^1,w^2)$ is the probability of the two words to appear within a small window, whereas $P(w^1)$ and $P(w^2)$ reflect the probabilities of each of the two words. Words that are similar tend to have higher mutual information, whereas words that are unrelated will have low mutual information. More recently, deep learning approaches have been used to create word embeddings, which are vectorial representations of words, obtained as the output of a neural network trained on very large textual corpora (Mikolov, Sutskever, Chen, Corrado, & Dean, 2013). For instance, Google has released the word2vec tool along with word embeddings pretrained on large news data, where the similarity of two words can be measured by calculating the similarity of their embedding vectors.

# SOFTWARE FOR TEXT PROCESSING

The Natural Language Toolkit, or NLTK, is a collection of Python libraries for text processing, covering tokenization, lemmatization, part-of-speech tagging, and many others. It also includes a variety of document collections and lexical resources (www.nltk.org).

Stanford CoreNLP toolkit is a Java package that includes many language analysis tools, including part-of-speech tagger, syntactic parses, named entity tagger, and others (https://stanfordnlp .github.io/CoreNLP).

LingPipe is a Java toolkit with many text processing tools and a large number of tutorials for core tasks in natural language processing (NLP; http://alias-i.com).

Porter stemmer and other stemmer algorithms have implementations available for several languages (http://snowballstem.org).

WordNet::Similarity is a package for calculating the semantic similarity of words using WordNet (http://wn-similarity.sourceforge.net).

Word2vec includes pretrained word embeddings models as well as code for training word embeddings on new corpora (https://github.com/dav/word2vec).

## Conclusion

Text preprocessing is often applied to text collections before more advanced text mining applications. Depending on the application end goal, lighter **preprocessing** steps (such as tokenization, lemmatization, or normalization) may be sufficient, while in other cases other layers of processing may be required (such as part-of-speech tagging, parsing, and so on). This chapter provided an overview of the main basic text processing tasks and discussed some the main techniques used to address these tasks. For those interested in a more detailed overview of some of these tLingasks, Jurafsky and Martin (2009) provide an excellent introduction to the field of NLP.

## Key Terms

Collocation    109
Collocation
    identification    109

Heaps' law    106
Language models    99
Lemmatization    99

Named entity recognition
    (NER)    100
Normalization    101

*(Continued)*

## Highlights

- Text preprocessing is often used before more advanced text mining algorithms. It facilitates the application of these text mining methods by separating punctuation from the words, normalizing the text, finding the base form of the words, and possibly applying layers of annotations such as part-of-speech or named entity tags, syntactic relations, and so on.

- Basic text processing steps typically consist of tokenization, stop word removal, stemming, or lemmatization.

- More advanced text processing steps may consist of part-of-speech tagging, syntactic parsing, NER, collocation identification, word sense disambiguation, and measures of word similarity.

- Language models are probabilistic representations of language. They can be efficiently built from large textual corpora and often form the foundation of applications such as information retrieval, language identification, various forms of tagging, and so on.

- The distribution of words in language can be described by Zipf's law and Heaps' law. These laws also have practical applications for making estimates of the size of the vocabulary or the size of a corpus for hypothetical situations.

## Discussion Topics

- Assume you want to build a set of basic text processing tools, including a tokenizer, a stop word removal, and a stemmer for a new language, which does not benefit from an existing set of tools as English does. How would you create such tools? Address separately each of the three tools mentioned before.

- How about building more advanced text processing tools for a new language? For instance, how would you build a part-of-speech tagger for Spanish? Hint: Assume you have a parallel corpus, consisting of sentence-aligned English–Spanish text, as well as a part-of-speech tagger for English.

- Pick a text mining application of your choice, and think about the text preprocessing steps that would be required for that application.

# 9

# SUPERVISED LEARNING

## LEARNING OBJECTIVES

The goals of Chapter 9 are to help you to do the following:

1. Recognize the task of **supervised learning** and its large range of applications.
2. Define feature representation and weighting in supervised learning, and classify specific learning algorithms.
3. Evaluate supervised learning methods.
4. Explore available software packages for supervised learning.

## INTRODUCTION

Without us always realizing it, supervised learning has become a technology that is pervasive in our everyday life. Consider, for instance, the problem of predicting tomorrow's weather based on current meteorological information, or consider the problem of predicting whether an incoming e-mail is spam or not, or consider the problem of predicting what movie somebody will like based on their own (and possibly others') history of movies they liked. These, and many others, are all examples where **machine learning** is currently making a difference in our lives by using the knowledge that we have about the past to make predictions about the future.

The field of machine learning is one of the relatively new fields within artificial intelligence, yet it is also one of the most impactful fields, as it has found applications in a very large number of other domains, within and outside computer science. Simply put, the task of supervised learning (also referred to as supervised machine learning or sometimes simply as learning) consists of using an automatic system to learn from a history of occurrences of a certain "event" and consequently make predictions about future occurrences of that event.

As an example, consider one of the tasks mentioned before about weather prediction and specifically the problem of learning whether it will rain or not. We could imagine a set of previous occurrences of the "rain or not" event, along with some representative **features (or attributes)**, as illustrated in Rows 1 through 4 in Table 9.1.

Given these previous occurrences of the rain event, we could imagine a system that could identify an association among sky = overcast, humidity = high, wind = strong and rain and consequently be able to predict that it is likely to rain given the observations from the fifth instance in Table 9.1.

The task of machine learning is therefore to learn how to most effectively make such predictions. An event is characterized by a set of features or attributes and a class. These are very specific to the task being solved: For instance, in our example we use four features—sky, temperature, humidity, and wind—to make predictions about the class rain. These features would be, however, irrelevant for predicting, for example, part of speech of a word, in which case we would use other features such as the word *before*, the word *after*, and so on. Event occurrences are typically represented as vectors of feature values, which represent an observation of a certain instance of that event. In the earlier example, one of the occurrences (Instance 1) has a value of "sunny" for the sky feature, a value of "high" for the humidity feature, and so forth. The event we are trying to predict is typically referred to as the "class." In our example, the class is rain, and it has two possible values: yes or no. Class values are known for the instances we are learning from (generally referred to as training instances) but are unknown for the instances we are trying to make predictions for (often referred to as test instances).

Given the **feature vector** representation of an event, along with specific instances of that event represented as vectors of feature and class values, there are many supervised learning algorithms that can be used. These algorithms are broadly classified into two

| Instance | Sky | Temperature | Humidity | Wind | Rain? |
|----------|-----|-------------|----------|------|-------|
| 1 | Sunny | Warm | High | None | No |
| 2 | Overcast | Warm | High | Strong | Yes |
| 3 | Overcast | Cold | No | None | No |
| 4 | Overcast | Warm | High | Strong | Yes |
| 5 | Overcast | Cold | High | Strong | ? |

TABLE 9.1 ■ Examples of Occurrences for the Event "Rain"

categories: (1) Eager algorithms learn when presented with the training instances and build a model that can then be quickly apply to make predictions for test instances. Most supervised learning algorithms fall under this category. Examples of such algorithms are **decision trees**, neural networks, **support vector machines (SVMs)**, Naive Bayes, and so forth. (2) Lazy algorithms do not do any intensive work at training time and instead reserve most of the learning process for the time when the test instances become available. Nearest neighbor is an example of a lazy algorithm.

There are literally hundreds of applications of machine learning, which cannot possibly be listed all in one place. They range from weather prediction, as in the earlier example, to predictions of language phenomena (e.g., text classification, part-of-speech labeling, word sense predictions), to applications in psychology (e.g., prediction of psychological traits), sociology (e.g., prediction of communication patterns), astronomy (e.g., prediction of star presence or star moves), and so forth. As long as an application requires a prediction being made and as long as there is some history of previously occurring examples where that prediction is known, machine learning can be applied to address the problem. While the amount of training data is an important aspect of any learning task, to some extent even more important is how the data are being represented, in other words, what features are being selected to describe the training and test instances. The following sections address feature representation and weighting and describe three supervised learning algorithms.

# BASIC CONCEPTS

*Machine learning* is a field in artificial intelligence that deals with the development of programs that gives computers the ability to learn from past experiences.

*Supervised learning* is the task of learning from a set of labeled instances (also referred to as training data) and using the learned models to make inferences on new unseen data.

**Unsupervised learning** is the task of drawing inferences without explicit labeled data. One of the most common types of unsupervised learning is clustering.

*Features (or attributes)* are measurable properties of an event being observed.

*Feature vectors* are collections of such properties, used to represent an instance of an event. The same type of feature vectors are used to represent the previous instances (the history of the event) as well as the future instances (for which predictions are to be made).

*Training data* are the collection of instances of an event used to train a machine-learning algorithm. The instances are also associated with a classification, which is often manually assigned.

*Test data* are the collection of instances of an event used to test a machine-learning algorithm. The algorithm will automatically make a prediction of the instances in the test data.

# FEATURE REPRESENTATION AND WEIGHTING

The features used to represent the instances of a learning problem can fall under two different types. They could be discrete features, taking values out of a finite set. For example, the value of the sky feature in the example shown in Figure 9.1 can be either sunny or overcast. The values for a discrete feature do not have to be set a priori. Rather, it is typical to infer the set of values based on the training and test instances being observed. Features can also be continuous—that is, they take numerical values, which can be either integer or real values, positive or negative. It is also possible that the value of a feature is not observable for a certain instance, in which case it is typical to use a question mark to reflect the lack of information for that attribute for that instance.

Not all the features selected to describe a learning problem are equally useful. It is therefore important to have ways to measure the weight of each feature. This is generally done automatically by the learning algorithms themselves, which sift through the training instances and calculate how discriminatory each feature is (in other words, how much that feature helps in finding the right class for an instance).

Importantly, the weights associated with features are also a way to analyze and interpret a classification data set. Consider, for example, the problem of classifying the gender of the author of a text. It is, of course, useful to be able to say that a supervised learning algorithm—for example, a decision tree—can separate the two classes with an accuracy of 75%. But it is even more useful to be able to say that certain features—for example, the frequency of certain pronouns or other patterns in the data—are the ones that contribute most toward this classification, which can lead to insights into the differences between the two genders.

## Feature Weighting

There are different weighting metrics that can be used to weight features. One of the most commonly used measures is information gain. Although the calculation of information gain is an integral part of most learning algorithms, we briefly describe it here, as it is simple to understand and can be used as a tool for data analysis.

Given a collection $S$ of positive and negative instance, let $p$ be the probability of an instance to be positive, and $q$ the probability of an instance to be negative. We define its entropy as Entropy($S$) = $-p \log p - q \log q$. The entropy is at its maximum when $p = q = 1/2$ and at its minimum when $p = 1$ and $q = 0$ (we use the assumption that $\log 0 = 0$). For instance, if $S$ contains 14 examples: 9 positive and 5 negative, Entropy($S$) = $-$ (9/14) log (9/14) $-$ (5/14) log (5/14) = 0.94.

We can now define information gain as the expected reduction in entropy when we split a data set $S$ based on a certain feature $A$.

$$Gain(S,A) = Entropy(S) - \sum_{v \in Values(A)} \frac{|S_v|}{|S|} Entropy(S_v)$$

Figure 9.1 shows an example of how information gain is calculated for two binary features. In this example, we have the problem of classifying a text, represented as a set of words, as either computer science (labeled as C) or biology (labeled as B). We assume a set of 14 training instances, consisting of 9 instances that belong to the Class C, and 5 that belong to the Class B. We have two features under consideration: one feature, named computer, with values yes or no (depending on whether the word *computer* is present in an instance) and a second feature named cell—again, with values yes or no. We can then calculate the entropy of this data set before we split the data based on either of these two features; as before: Entropy($S$) = − (9/14) log (9/14) − (5/14) log (5/14) = 0.94. We can also calculate the entropy of the data after following each of the branches for a certain feature. For example, if we follow the branch yes for the feature computer, meaning that we only look at those instances where this feature has a value of yes, we will find three instances in Class C and 4 in Class B, which corresponds to an entropy of Entropy($S_{Computer=yes}$) = −(3/7) log (3/7) − (4/7) log (4/7) = 0.985. Similarly, if we follow the branch no for the same feature, the entropy of the resulting set will be Entropy($S_{Computer=no}$) = 0.592. We can now combine all these entropy values to calculate the information gain, by weighting each of the entropies corresponding to branches of the feature computer. There are seven instances

---

**FIGURE 9.1  ■  Sample Calculation of Information Gain for Two Features**

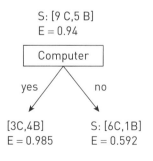

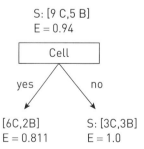

that fall under the branch yes for the feature computer, and thus Entropy($S_{Computer=yes}$) will be weighted as 7/14. Just as a coincidence in this example, the entropy corresponding to the other branch will also have a weight of 7/14. After all the calculations are complete, we will conclude that among the two features considered, computer has a higher discriminatory power for this specific classification problem (with an information gain of 0.151, as compared to the information gain of cell, which is 0.048).

# SUPERVISED LEARNING ALGORITHMS

There is a very large number of supervised learning algorithms that have been proposed to date, many of which have one or more publicly available implementations, as stand-alone code or part of machine-learning packages. Some of the most popular supervised learning algorithms are Naive Bayes (covered in detail in Chapter 13), regressions, decision trees, **instance-based learning**, SVMs, **deep learning** with neural networks (these five algorithms are covered next), perceptrons, and random forests.

## Regression

Regression is the simplest machine-learning algorithm and has been originally introduced in the field of statistics as a way of associating input values (e.g., size of a house) with an output dependent variable (e.g., sale price). There are many types of regression algorithms, including linear regression, which assumes that all the inputs and the output are scalar values, and logistic regression, where the output variable is categorical.

Similar to the functionality of a neuron, described later in this section, a linear regression is typically a linear combination of the input features, and the main goal is to learn the value of the weights that will best approximate the output. For instance, assuming three input values $a_1$, $a_2$, $a_3$, the linear regression function will have the form $x = a_1w_1 + a_2w_2 + a_3w_3 + b$, where $w_1$, $w_2$, $w_3$ are weights to be learned, $b$ is a bias parameter that often is also learned, and $x$ is the dependent variable to be predicted by the model. To transform the linear regression into a logistic regression, the output can be passed through the logistic function $1/(1 + e^x)$.

As with other learning algorithms, training a regression function assumes the availability of a training data set, for which we know the value of the input features along with the output variable. The goal of the training stage is to learn the parameters of the model; thus, in the example given previously, learn the parameters $w_1$, $w_2$, $w_3$, and $b$. To do this, we first assign the parameters with random values and then iterate through the training examples and apply corrections to these values, such that the computed $x$ variable for each training instance is adjusted to match the actual $x$ output for that instance. For instance, assuming the problem of predicting the sale price of a house (output variable) based on its size (input feature), if the predicted price for a training instance using the existing model is $50,000, but the actual price is $75,000, the error will be used to correct the model parameters.

## Decision Trees

Decision tree learning (Quinlan, 1993) is one of many algorithms for eager learning, where a decision tree is built during the training stage and later used for making classification decisions on test instances. A decision tree is a structure that looks like a flowchart, where each internal node represents a test on one of the features, and the nodes represent classification decisions. For instance, Figure 9.2 shows one possible decision tree for the weather problem with the features shown in Table 9.1.

As any eager learner, in a decision tree learning process most of the time is spent in training, when the decision tree is built. There are a very large number of different decision trees that can be put together for one data set. In Figure 9.2, we show one possible decision tree for the features in Table 9.1; one could also imagine a tree that has *sky* at the root, or *humidity*, and then branches that use the other available features. As it turns out, the selection of features for inclusion in the decision tree can have an impact both in terms of effectiveness (how correct the classifications made with a decision tree are) as well as in terms of efficiency (how fast such classifications can be made at test time).

The typical process for building a decision tree is to iteratively select features based on their weight. Using information gain as a **feature weighting** measure (other weighting

**FIGURE 9.2   ■   Sample Decision Tree Using Features Shown in Table 9.1**

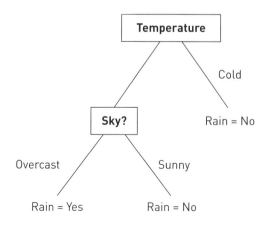

metrics can also be used), the most informative feature is selected from among all the features available and added as the root of the decision tree. Next, for each of the possible values of the feature selected as root, we determine the set of instances that have that feature value and once again determine the most informative feature from among the remaining features, with the information gain being measured on that set of instances. A branch is stopped when we reach a decision leaf, which is the case when we have one or multiple instances under a branch that have the same classification decision.

For example, if we choose temperature as the most informative feature for the instances in Table 9.1 and include it as the root of the tree, we will first consider its warm value and determine the most informative feature on the set of Instances 1, 2, and 4 from among the features sky, humidity, and wind. We then repeat the same process for its cold value, and in this case, we will have reached a decision node, as we have a consensus over the classification for all the instances in this set (there is only one instance with a temperature value of cold, and we can thus make a decision when we notice this value). Assume we find sky to be the next most informative feature; we then apply the same process for each of its values and so on.

Sometimes decision trees can grow overly large, in which case the process of "pruning" can be applied, with the goal of reducing the complexity of the tree while keeping the accuracy of the classifier. There are different pruning techniques, one of the simplest being to replace each node with its most popular (frequent) class and keep the replacement if it does not affect the prediction accuracy.

## Instance-Based Learning

Instance-based learning is a form of lazy learning and includes algorithms such as k-nearest neighbors (or KNN, for short) and kernel machines. The main idea underlying instance-based learning, in general, and KNN, in particular, is that a test instance can be classified by finding the most similar training instances and using their class as a label. Consider, for instance, the example shown in Figure 9.3, in which we want to classify the point labeled with a question mark as either a rectangle or a circle. A KNN algorithm will try to find the KNN and find the majority class among those instances. In this example, if we select the three-nearest neighbors, as shown inside the circle, the label will be dictated by the rectangle training instances, which are a majority.

Depending on the number of neighbors being considered, a different class may be assigned. For instance, in Figure 9.3, we could also apply seven-nearest neighbors, in which case the label will be a circle.

A central issue for these algorithms is the measure of distance being used to decide which are the closest training instances for a given test instance. It is common to use a Euclidian distance, but other distance metrics can also be used. Considering the vector

**FIGURE 9.3 ■ Illustration of *k*-Nearest Neighbors**

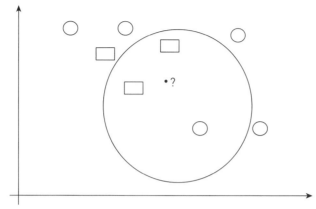

representations discussed previously, and assuming a training vector X and a test vector Y, the Euclidian distance will be given by $\sqrt{\sum (x_i - y_i)^2}$. In recent years, various kernel measures have been often used, where a kernel is simply a similarity measure defined over a certain set of inputs (e.g., there are string kernels, which define the similarity of two strings; tree kernels, which measure the similarity of tree structures)

## Support Vector Machines

The underlying idea behind SVM algorithms (Vapnik, 1995) is to identify a hyperplane (or set of hyperplanes) that can provide the best separation between the training data instances. Among all possible separation hyperplanes, SVM algorithms try to identify the one that has the largest distance to the nearest training instance of any class, as that will be reflected into a lower generalization error of the classifier.

Consider, for instance, the task of separating the rectangle and circle instances shown in Figure 9.4. Multiple hyperplanes can be drawn, including $H_1$, which does not separate well the two classes; $H_2$, which separates the rectangles and circles, but with a small margin, as it is very close to a rectangle instance; and $H_3$, which again separates the instances in the two classes, with a larger margin. We will eventually choose this separation hyperplane and consequently determine the class of a new unknown item depending on where it falls with respect to this hyperplane. For example, the instance marked with a question mark in Figure 9.4 will be labeled as a rectangle, as it falls on the side of the selected hyperplane $H_3$ that belongs to the rectangle instances.

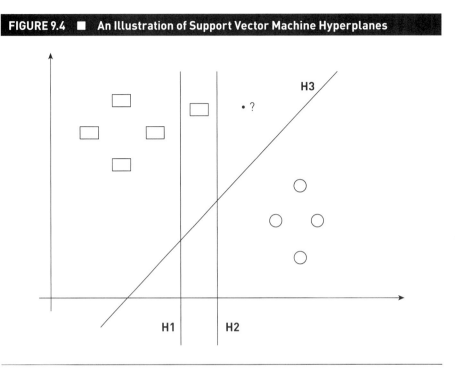

**FIGURE 9.4 ■ An Illustration of Support Vector Machine Hyperplanes**

Given the feature vector representations discussed previously, in the feature space $X$, any hyperplane can be written as $w.X + b = y$. We then want to find the vector of weights $w$ and parameter $b$ so that the hyperplane separates all the instances in the training data with the largest margin. This is a quadratic optimization problem, which can be solved by using Lagrangian multiplier methods.

Note that SVM algorithms were devised to solve binary classification problems—that is, separate between instances belonging to two classes. However, any multiclass classification can be translated into a set of binary classifications, by performing multiple classifications of one versus all. Assume, for instance, we have three classes: A, B, and C. We can, thus, perform three binary classifications: A versus (B or C), B versus (A or C), and C versus (A or B).

## Deep Learning With Neural Networks

Deep learning (Goodfellow, Bengio, & Courville, 2016) is one of the newest branches of machine learning and consists of algorithms that aim to learn high-level representations of the data that can be used for effective learning. In a way, deep learning can be thought of as a process in which the features themselves are being learned. Rather than doing careful feature engineering, which is required by most of the other learning algorithms, the premise of deep learning is that with enough data, features can be automatically learned.

Various deep learning architectures have been proposed, including deep neural networks, recursive neural networks, and convolutional neural networks, with a broad number of applications in computer vision, bioinformatics, and natural language processing (NLP). In this chapter, we briefly overview deep neural networks, which found many applications in language processing and text mining.

The core unit of a neural network is the neuron. Simply put, a neuron acts like a function that takes several inputs and produces an output, as illustrated in Figure 9.5. In this figure, the inputs are $a_1$, $a_2$, and $a_3$, and the output is $o_1$. The edges that go into the neuron are weighted, and these weights are generally learned when the network is trained. In addition to the input variables, the neuron often also takes an additional input in the form of a bias $b$, whose value is also learned during training. The neuron will then take all these inputs, combine them linearly, and apply a nonlinear function on top of this computation. For the example in Figure 9.5, the linear combination of the inputs will produce $x = a_1w_1 + a_2w_2 + a_3w_3 + b$, which is then passed through a nonlinear function such as the logistic function $1/(1 + e^{-x})$, and the result of this computation will be the output $o_1$.

Now consider several such neurons, organized in layers, as in the example shown in Figure 9.6. Each element in this network has the functionality of the neuron we just described, with the outputs of a layer feeding as inputs to the next layer. The first set of inputs would be obtained directly from the input data, while the last set of outputs will represent the classifications to be made.

**FIGURE 9.5**

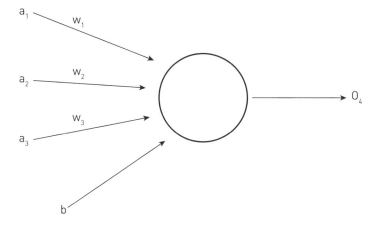

**FIGURE 9.6**

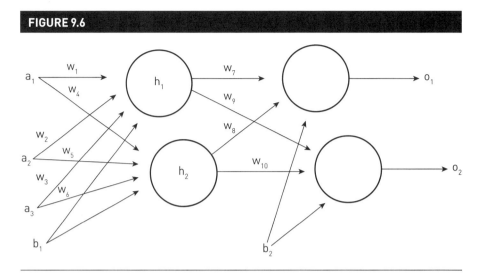

The key aspect of a successful such deep neural network is its training, during which we learn the weights for the edges, the bias terms, and sometimes even the representations to be used for the inputs. The way this process works is as follows. First, we initialize the network to a random set of small weights and biases. We then pass through the entire network, complete all the computations as described previously (i.e., the neuron computation), and produce a set of outputs. This set of outputs can either be used as is, be passed through a so-called softmax layer that normalizes these outputs to produce a distribution of probabilities, or be passed through a regression layer that generates a final output. We then compare this set of outputs against the correct outputs in the training data and, depending on the errors observed, correct the weights and biases through a mechanism known as backpropagation. Very briefly, backpropagation determines at each neuron the effect that a weight (or bias) had on the output error of that neuron and applies a correction in order to minimize the amount of error. This entire process is repeated several times, until the output error is reduced to a very small number, in which case the network is considered to be "trained," and it can take new inputs to predict an output. Inside these networks, while the inputs are obtained directly from the data, the intermediate (hidden) layers are analogous to the features used by other learning methods, except that now these features have been automatically learned.

Deep neural networks can be used to make predictions based on input data, similar to the previously described machine-learning algorithms. Interestingly, deep neural networks have also been successfully used to learn word representations, in which a very large number of training instances are created automatically from raw text. For instance, considering the example "the dog chases the cat," a training instance can be created in which the context words *the, dog, the, cat* are used as input to predict the central word *chases* (Mikolov, Sutskever, Chen, Corrado, & Dean, 2013; note that the reverse can also be done, i.e., use *chases* as input and *the, dog, the, cat* as outputs). Millions of such naturally occurring textual examples can create millions of "free" training examples, which can be used to train a deep neural network that has the effect of constructing word representations that account for the context where these words occur. Using word2vec, which is one popular implementation of these deep neural networks to construct word representations, it was found that simple and intuitive vector operations can be applied on these representations. For instance, word2vec(king) − word2vec(man) + word2vec(woman) results in a vector that is very close to word2vec(queen).

# EVALUATION OF SUPERVISED LEARNING

As with any automatic systems, it is important to have ways to evaluate supervised learning systems. Usually this is done on test data that are independent from the training data, using metrics such as accuracy, precision, or recall. Accuracy is defined as the total number of test instances that are correctly classified, out of the total number of test instances. Precision and recall are defined with respect to one given class $C_i$, the precision being the total number of instances correctly labeled as $C_i$ by the system out of the total number of instances labeled as $C_i$ by the system, and recall being the total number of instances correctly labeled as $C_i$ by the system out of the total number of instances labeled as $C_i$ in the entire test data.

For more robust results, experiments are generally run over multiple training or test data splits, and the results obtained for different splits are averaged. That is, given a set of labeled instances, say 1,000, we could take 90% of this set and use it for training, and the remaining 10% for test, then divide the 1,000 instances in another 90%–10% split and repeat the evaluation, and so on. This also leads to **N-fold cross-validation** evaluations, when the set of labeled instances is split into $N$ subsets, then one subset is used for test and the remaining $N-1$ subsets are used for training, then another subset is used for test and the remaining $N-1$ subsets for training, and so on $N$ times, followed by an average over the set of $N$ results. An alternative to that is leave-one-out cross-validation, where the test set consists of one single instance, and the training set consists of the remaining instances; this process again is repeated several times, for each instance in the data set.

Also important during the evaluation is to gain insights into the effectiveness of the various features used. One way to do that is to simply look at the feature weights learned by the algorithm. For instance, if we consider information gain as the weight metric, those features that have a higher information gain are presumably more important (or useful) than those with lower information gain. Another way to gain such insights is to perform **feature ablation**. Specifically, this means that the supervised learning algorithm is run on the data set using one feature at a time (forward feature ablation) or by removing one feature at a time from the entire set of features (backward feature ablation). The intuition behind this process is that either by considering only one feature in the learning process or by considering the entire set of features except for one feature, we can determine how useful that feature is for the overall system.

Finally, extremely relevant for the evaluation of any classification system is its **learning curve**: How is the performance of the classifier affected by the size of the training data? To generate this curve, one can run the classification system on fractions of the training data and determine its accuracy on the same test set. Figure 9.7 shows two sample learning curves, with accuracies measured for two classifiers on fractions of training data ranging from 10% to 100%. Learning curves can be very insightful, as they can determine the course of future experiments: Should one focus on gathering more data (see the learning curve in Figure 9.7[a], where the curve has an ascending trend), or are the data sufficient and one should focus on engineering more sophisticated features (see the learning curve in Figure 9.7[b], where the curve has plateaued after a certain number of training instances)?

FIGURE 9.7 ■ Learning Curves for Two Classifiers/Data Sets

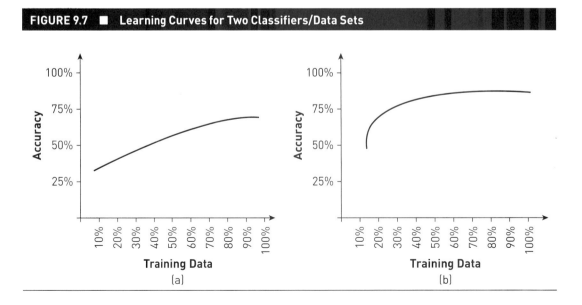

# SOFTWARE FOR SUPERVISED LEARNING

Weka is an extensive collection of Java tools for machine learning, covering a very large number of learning algorithms, including the ones described in this chapter, along with several others (www.cs.waikato.ac.nz/ml/weka).

Scikit is a Python package with many machine-learning algorithms (http://scikit-learn.org).

Caret is a collection of machine-learning tools implemented in R (http://cran.r-project.org/web/packages/caret).

Theano is a Python library that can be used to power deep learning implementations (alongside with other advanced mathematical computations; http://deeplearning.net/software/theano).

SVM-Light is a C implementation of support vector machines (SVMs), optimized for speed (http://svmlight.joachims.org).

Decision trees implementations are available in many programming languages, including as a suite of Perl tools (http://search.cpan.org/~avikak/Algorithm-DecisionTree-1.41).

## Conclusion

Machine learning is a field in artificial intelligence that has had a very significant impact on a large number of problems in a diverse set of domains, ranging from information management, to linguistics, to astrophysics, and many others. Given the history associated with a certain event (e.g., weather), machine learning will first represent the instances in this history as feature (or attribute) vectors and then use these representations along with the class (or category) associated with them to make predictions about the classification of future instances. This chapter covered aspects relevant to feature representation and weighting, as well as several learning algorithms including decision trees, instance-based learning, SVMs, and deep learning. The chapter also addressed the problem of machine-learning evaluation and ways to gain insight into the performance of the algorithm and the various features through learning curves and feature ablation.

## Key Terms

Decision trees   117

Deep learning   120

Feature ablation   128

Feature vector   116

Feature weighting   121

Features (or attributes)   116

Learning curve   128

Instance-based
   learning   120

Machine learning   115

*N*-fold cross-validation   127

Supervised learning   115

Support vector machines
   (SVMs)   117

Unsupervised learning   117

## Highlights

- Given the history of an event, machine-learning algorithms aim to make predictions about that event in the future. Specifically, instances from the history and the future of the event are represented as feature vectors that include observable attributes, with the instances from the past also being associated with classes (or categories), so that learning algorithms can then be used to make predictions of these classes for the instances from the future.

- Instances of an event are typically represented as feature vectors. A feature is an observable attribute of that event (e.g., temperature), which can take discrete or continuous values.

- Not all the features selected to describe a learning problem are equally useful. It is therefore important to have ways to measure the weight of each feature. This is generally done automatically by the learning algorithms themselves, but it can also be done as a separate process.

- There are many learning algorithms, broadly grouped into two classes: (1) eager algorithms (e.g., decision trees, SVMs), which attempt to learn generalizations from the training data and then apply these generalizations to make predictions on the test data, and (2) lazy algorithms (e.g., instance-based learning), which perform most of the calculations at test time by identifying training instances that are most similar to a given test instance and making a prediction based on that.

- Machine-learning algorithms are evaluated through measures such as accuracy, precision, and recall, which determine the number of correct predictions (with respect to a gold standard) made on a test data set.

## Discussion Topics

- Discuss the advantages and disadvantages of eager learners versus lazy learners.

- As discussed in this chapter, there are two broad types of features: (1) continuous and (2) discrete. Assume you have a learning algorithm that can only learn with discrete features. How could you transform your continuous features into discrete features?

- Consider a social science research project of your choice, and think of how you could address it as a machine-learning problem. Think about what features you would use to represent the data instances in your project, what algorithm you would use for learning, how would you evaluate its performance, and so on.

# Text Analysis Methods From the Humanities and Social Sciences

# ANALYZING NARRATIVES

## INTRODUCTION

Humans are a storytelling species; we are "*Homo fictus* (fiction man), the great ape with the storytelling mind" (Gottschall, 2012, p. xiv). We tell stories to others, and to ourselves, every day, and those stories motivate us to action and elicit the whole range of our emotions, from love and wonder to anger and shame. Storytelling appears to be fundamental to human communication, but what are stories, exactly? How do they differ from other forms of communication? And how can the stories we tell each other be analyzed scientifically?

In the social sciences and humanities, researchers who are interested in storytelling work in the field known as narrative analysis (or narratology). Narrative analysis refers to a family of approaches to analyzing texts that take a narrative (story) form. Narrative analysis is performed within anthropology, sociology, literary studies, and other academic fields to analyze how people interpret their social worlds and the events and people in them and how they develop social identities through the stories they tell about themselves and others. Narrative analysts study all sorts of texts, including interview transcripts, newspaper articles, speeches, plays, and works of literature.

Narrative analysis focuses on the ways people make and use stories to interpret the world. Narrative analysis does not treat narratives as stories that transmit a set of facts about the world and so is generally not primarily interested in whether stories are objectively true or not. Narrative researchers view narratives as social products that are produced by people in specific social, historical, and cultural contexts. Narratives are understood to be interpretive devices that people use to represent themselves and their worlds to other people (and to themselves). Narratologists argue that people's representations of themselves often take the form of stories and that **public stories** circulating in popular culture provide resources people use both to construct their personal narratives and identities (Ricoeur, 1991) and to link the present to the past. Such stories are often found in interview accounts (Gee, 1991).

Theories of narrative suggest that the main elements that give texts narrative form are *sequences* and *consequences* of events by which narratives organize, connect, and evaluate events as meaningful for particular audiences. With these elements, storytellers interpret the social world for their audiences. Narratologists characterize stories in terms of **transformation** (change over time) of **characters** and actions that are brought together in a **plotline**. Stories bring together many plot elements, including digressions and subplots, in what is known as a process of **emplotment** (White, 1978). Narratives must have a point, and their point often takes the form of a moral message.

## BASIC CONCEPTS

*Narratives* are stories that people tell each other and themselves to interpret and motivate social behavior.

*Public stories* are narratives that circulate in popular culture.

*Emplotment* refers to the process of bringing together characters and actions into a plot that involves change over time.

A *story grammar* is a basic narrative structure that is repeated across many diverse narrative genres.

# APPROACHES TO NARRATIVE ANALYSIS

There are several major approaches to narrative analysis, three of the most influential being *structural*, *functional*, and **sociological approaches**.

**Structural approaches** to narrative analysis operate mainly at a *textual* level of analysis, which is to say they focus on texts themselves rather than the social and historical contexts in which stories emerge, circulate, and change. The focus of structural narrative analysis is what is known as a **story grammar**. An early theorist of story grammars, Propp (1968) argued that the fairy tale has a narrative form that is central to all storytelling. The fairy tale is structured not by the nature of the characters in it but by the function they play in the plot, and the number of possible functions is fairly small. In his influential structural approach to narrative, Labov (1972) defined *narrative* as "one method of recapitulating past experience by matching a verbal sequence of clauses to the sequence of events which (it is inferred) actually occurred" (Labov 1972, pp. 359–360; see also Labov & Waletzky, 1967, p. 20). For Labov (1972), a **minimal narrative** is "a sequence of two clauses which are temporally ordered." The skeleton of a narrative thus consists of a series of temporally ordered clauses called **narrative clauses** (Labov, 1972, pp. 360–361). While narratives require narrative clauses, not all clauses found in narrative are narrative clauses. Labov provided the following example:

a.  I know a boy named Harry.

b.  Another boy threw a bottle at him right in the head.

c.  He got seven stitches.

In this narrative passage, only Clauses B and C are narrative clauses. Clause A is a **free clause** in Labov's terminology because it does not have a temporal component. It can be moved freely within the text without altering the text's meaning. This is not so with narrative clauses, where a rearrangement of the clauses typically results in a change in meaning (Labov, 1972, p. 360). Labov also proposed that there are six distinct functional parts in a fully formed narrative: the (1) abstract, (2) orientation, (3) complicating action, (4) evaluation, (5) result or resolution, and (6) coda. Of these six parts, only the complicating action, which constitutes the main body of clauses and "usually comprises a series of events" (Labov & Waletzky, 1967, p. 32), is "essential if we are to recognize a narrative" (Labov, 1972, p. 370). See Table 10.1.

The functionalist approach to narrative analysis was pioneered by the psychologist Bruner (1990). Bruner argued that humans' ordering of experience occurs in two basic modes. The first is the **paradigmatic mode**, or **logico–scientific mode**. This mode

**TABLE 10.1 ■ Examples of Narrative Analysis Studies**

|  | Qualitative Studies | Mixed Methods Studies |
|---|---|---|
| Structural narrative analysis | Laird, McCance, McCormack, and Gribben, 2015 | Franzosi, De Fazio, and Vicari, 2012 |
| Functional narrative analysis | Stroet, Opdenakker, and Minnaert, 2015 | |
| Sociological narrative analysis | Andersen, 2015 | Mische, 2014 |

attempts to fulfill the ideal of a formal, mathematical system of description and explanation and is typical of argumentation in philosophy and the natural sciences. In contrast, in the **narrative mode** of organizing experience in which events' particularity and specificity as well as people's involvement, accountability, and responsibility in bringing about specific events are more centrally important than are logical considerations.

Functionalist analysis of narrative differs from structuralist analysis in that rather than focusing on the structural elements of texts themselves it focuses on what particular stories *do* in the contexts of people's everyday lives. For Bruner, some of the functions of narrative include *solving problems*, *reducing tension*, and *resolving dilemmas*. Narratives allow people to deal with and explain mismatches between the exceptional and the ordinary. Narratives are not required when events occur that are perceived as ordinary but are needed to allow people to recast unfamiliar or chaotic experiences into causal stories in order to make sense of such experiences and to render them familiar and safe. Closely related to Bruner's approach are Vygotsky's functionalist *social development theory* (Wertsch 1985), and Halliday's (1985) *systemic functional grammar*, as well as the psychologist Michael Bamberg's research that uses functionalist narrative methods. Bamberg investigates adolescent and postadolescent identity formation and the emergence of professional identities (Bamberg, 2004; see Chapter 1).

Functionalist approaches to narrative have influenced what is known as the "life story tradition" in the fields of narratology, psychology, and management research. Psychologists have used autobiographical narratives both for research and in their therapeutic practice. Their interest is not mainly in the content of life stories per se but in how individuals recount their histories: what they emphasize and omit, their stance as protagonists or victims, and the relationships their stories establish between teller and audience (see Rosenwald & Ochberg, 1992). For life story researchers, personal stories are not only ways of sharing with someone else, or oneself, information about one's life but are also means by which personal identities are fashioned.

## CONCEPT CHECK

Structural narrative analysis focuses on texts themselves rather than the social contexts in which they are produced and received. A concept to this approach is the "story grammar," which is a narrative form that is central to all storytelling, such as, for example, the fairy tale story. Structural analysts analyze stories in terms of sequence of clauses and events, often using quantitative and mixed methods in addition to qualitative methods.

Functionalist narrative analysis examines what particular stories *do* in the context of everyday life, such as solving problems, reducing tension, and resolving dilemmas. Functionalist narratives analysis often focuses less on *what* people say than on *how* they tell stories about themselves and others: what they emphasize and omit, how they portray themselves and others as protagonists or victims, and how they fashion their personal identities through their stories. Functionalist analysis is performed mainly with qualitative methods.

Sociological narrative analysis analyzes texts as reflections of cultural, historical, and political contexts in which particular stories are told by particular narrators to particular audiences. Sociological analysis makes use of qualitative research methods including especially comparative historical methods.

A third approach to narrative analysis is a sociological approach that focuses on the cultural, historical, and political contexts in which particular stories are told by particular narrators to particular audiences. The British sociologist Plummer's *Telling Sexual Stories* (1995) is one such sociological narrative analysis of "coming out stories." Plummer (1995) argued that such stories are "rites of a sexual story-telling culture" (p. i). This culture, which emerged in the late 20th century, involved the transformation of experiences that were once seen as personal, private, and pathological into public and political stories. Plummer's study of the proliferation of these types of stories is based on transcribed interviews with people narrating their own biographical stories involving recovering from rape or coming out as gay or lesbian and of fashioning personal identities based on participation in communities based on common sexual identity or political goals related to intimate experience.

## PLANNING A NARRATIVE ANALYSIS RESEARCH PROJECT

There is no agreed-upon procedure for planning a narrative analysis research project. As is the case for many qualitative research methods (Creswell, 2014, p. 46), research design in narrative analysis is often *emergent*. The initial plan for a narrative analysis project cannot be tightly prescribed, but instead the plan is likely to shift and change during data collection and preliminary analysis. Your research questions may change as patterns emerge in your data, and as a consequence, you may choose to alter your data collection strategy and tactics. Still, narrative analysis will ideally follow the concept of *methodological congruence* advanced by Richards and Morse (2013; see Creswell, 2014, p. 50). Methodological congruence refers to the purposes, questions, and methods of a research project being interconnected and interrelated so that the study appears as a cohesive whole rather than a collection of independent parts.

## SPOTLIGHT ON THE RESEARCH
### Analyzing Relationship Breakups

Sahpazia, P., & Balamoutsoua, S. (2015). Therapists' accounts of relationship breakup experiences: A narrative analysis. *European Journal of Psychotherapy & Counselling*, *17*(3), 258–276.

The psychologists Sahpazia and Balamoutsoua used narrative analysis to present therapists' accounts of terminations of their own romantic relationships and to explore ways these have affected their life and identity. Sahpazia and Balamoutsoua's sample includes four counselors who have experienced a breakup from a significant relationship. The data were gathered through semistructured interviews consisting of seven questions. Participants shared that their breakup experience led them to personal growth experiences that helped them become more empathic, congruent, and helpful therapists.

Although there is no agreed-upon recipe for performing narrative analysis, narrative researchers are expected to design their study with a general understanding of the intent and rationale for conducting qualitative research. Narrative analysis research designs generally follow the traditional approach of presenting a problem, asking a question, collecting data to answer the question, and analyzing the data in order to answer the question. Creswell's (2014, pp. 53–55) criteria for good qualitative research apply to narrative analysis, including the need to employ rigorous data collection procedures, beginning with a single focus or concept to be explored, having a detailed methods section, and adhering to the highest possible ethical standards (see Table 10.2; see Chapter 3).

| TABLE 10.2 ■ Narrative Analysis Research Design Principles |
| --- |
| Make sure that **data collection** procedures are as rigorous as possible. |
| Use a **recognized approach** to narrative analysis. |
| Analyze your data at **multiple levels of abstraction** and from unusual angles. |
| Adhere to the highest possible **ethical standards**. |

*Source:* Adapted from Creswell (2014, pp. 53–55).

## QUALITATIVE NARRATIVE ANALYSIS

Approaches to narrative analysis that are basically qualitative in nature and reliant on human interpretation of texts are used widely in the social sciences and humanities. In the social sciences, qualitative approaches are especially popular in applied research fields such as education, health, management, and tourism research. In these fields, most published research takes either a structural, functional, or sociological approach to the texts being analyzed, although some studies combine elements of several of these approaches.

An example of a qualitative study that takes a **functional approach** to narrative analysis is a 2015 paper by the education researchers Stroet, Opdenakker, and Minnaert (2015), who conducted a narrative analysis of teacher–student interactions in two differently organized classrooms. Their goal was to better understand manifestations of both positive and negative dimensions of need supportive teaching by relating these dimensions to the educational approaches of schools. For the two schools, Stroet and colleagues analyzed seventh-grade math and language lessons and found both striking differences and similarities between the classes in manifestations of need supportive teaching.

Health and human performance researchers Busanich, McGannon, and Schinke (2014) took a different approach from the study by Stroet and colleagues; Busanich and colleagues used structural narrative analysis and social constructionism (see Chapter 4) to compare an elite male and female distance runner's disordered eating experiences. Their data were transcripts of four in-depth interviews, with both runners participating in two separate interviews. The runners' experiences were framed by cultural narratives around food, body, and exercise. Busanich and colleagues found that both runners drew upon a performance narrative to construct running experiences and self-identities as elite athletes and that when elite athletic identity became threatened by moments of perceived failure, disordered eating thoughts and behaviors emerged for both runners.

The sociologist Andersen (2015) conducted a functional and sociological narrative analysis to investigate how addiction "recovery narratives" develop in real time during drug treatment. Building on the sociology of storytelling and ethnographic fieldwork conducted at two drug treatment institutions for young people in Denmark, Andersen argued for studying stories in the context of their telling. Through a narrative analysis of both story content and story process she discovered that (1) stories of change function locally as an institutional requirement; (2) professional drug treatment providers edit young people's storytelling through different techniques; (3) the narrative environment of the drug treatment institution shapes how stories make sense of the past, present, and future; and (4) storytelling in drug treatment is an interactive achievement. Andersen used NVivo (see Appendix D) to code her field notes, interviews, and transcriptions of treatment sessions.

Nursing researchers Fors, Dudas, and Ekman (2014) investigated acute coronary syndrome patients' perceptions of their illness during their hospital stay using structural narrative analysis. Fors and colleagues conducted an interview study in two coronary care units at a hospital in Sweden. The 12 participants included five women and seven men. Patient narratives were recorded, transcribed, and analyzed using a "phenomenological hermeneutic" approach to narrative analysis. A main theme that emerged was "awareness that life is lived forwards and understood backwards." Two minor themes included a sense of "struggling to manage the acute overwhelming phase." The phenomenological hermeneutic approach used, inspired by Ricoeur's interpretation theory (Lindseth & Norberg, 2004), involved interpreting the meaning of a text in a "structural and comprehensive way" (Fors et al., 2014, p. 432).

Health researchers Laird, McCance, McCormack, and Gribben (2015) conducted a structural narrative analysis to illuminate the experiences of patients who received care in hospital wards during the intervention phase of a program to develop person-centered practice. Twenty-six patients were recruited from four different hospital sites in one health care organization, focusing on patients who were admitted to the nine wards or units where the nursing teams were participating in a practice development program that promoted person-centeredness. The interviews were audio recorded at 4-month intervals and transcribed. Structural narrative analysis of the transcripts revealed one main theme of vulnerability at the junctures of systems, care processes, and nurses' responses. There were also subthemes of confronting vulnerability; experiencing exemplary care; experiencing misalignments in systems, care processes, and nurses' responses; and sharing in a sense of belonging with ward nurses.

# MIXED METHODS AND QUANTITATIVE NARRATIVE ANALYSIS STUDIES

Since the 1980s, social scientists have developed methods of narrative analysis that integrate qualitative methods within mixed method research designs (see Chapter 5; Teddlie & Tashakkori, 2008; Tashakkori & Teddlie, 2010). These research designs involve analyzing patterns of words in narratives using software and statistical tools.

In sociology, one of the most prominent mixed method approaches to narrative analysis is the analysis of "narrative grammars" developed by Franzosi and his colleagues, who refer to their approach as quantitative narrative analysis (QNA). Franzosi and his collaborators quantify a basic structural element of what the psychologist Bruner termed the "narrative mode" of ordering experience. That element is a social cognitive process whereby people interpret situations of all kinds in terms of basic social relations of actors, actions, and objects of action. Franzosi's (1987) term for these sequential structures is the "**semantic triplet**" or "S-A-O triplet" (for *subject*, *action*, and *object*). His method of analyzing texts' semantic sequences involves teams of manual coders coding collections of historical texts, such as newspaper archives line by line for S-A-O triplets. Franzosi and his collaborators have applied this method in studies of newspaper accounts of lynchings (Franzosi et al., 2012) and of the rise of fascism (Franzosi, 2010). Recently Sudhahar, Franzosi, and Cristianini (2011) have developed a working system for large-scale QNA of news corpora. Their system identifies the key actors in a body of news and the actions they perform by analyzing their position in the overall network of actors and actions, analyzing the time series associated with some of the actors' properties, generating scatter plots describing the subject/object bias of each actor, and investigating the types of actions associated with each actor. Applying their automated system to 100,000 *New York Times* articles about crime published between 1987 and 2007, they found that men were most commonly responsible for crimes against the person, while women and children were most often crime victims. The sociologist Cerulo (1998) has used narrative analysis in her studies of "victim" and "perpetrator" sequences in newspaper headlines, and Ignatow (2004) analyzed narrative grammars in a multimethod sociological study of transcripts of shipyard union leaders' meetings (see Chapter 12).

The sociologist Roberts and his colleagues have developed another mixed method of narrative analysis that they term **modality analysis**. Similar in some ways to Franzosi's narrative grammars, the modality analysis is intended for cross-cultural and cross-linguistic comparative research (Roberts, 2008). Modality analysis evaluates languages by analyzing modal clauses in multiple large collections of text in multiple languages in order to identify what activities the users of each language treat as possible, impossible, inevitable, or contingent. Roberts and his colleagues have used their method to analyze the characteristics of many different cultures based on studies of Arab and Hindi newspapers (Roberts, Zuell, Landmann, & Wang, 2010) and Hungarian newspapers (Roberts, Popping, & Pan, 2009).

More recently, Mische (2014) analyzed online documents from the United Nations Conference on Sustainable Development and the accompanying People's Summit held in Rio de Janeiro in 2012. While reading the documents, Mische and her team of graduate students noticed that the different groups who participated in online deliberations used different grammatical and narrative elements. Her team subsequently developed a coding scheme to analyze predictive, imperative, and subjunctive verb forms in these documents, which they hand coded using NVivo (see Appendix D).

The management researchers Gorbatai and Nelson (2015) used the Linguistic Inquiry and Word Count (LIWC) dictionary (Tausczik & Pennebaker, 2010; see Appendix C) and topic models (see Chapter 16) to examine the role of language in the success of online fund-raising, which is a new form of entrepreneurial project financing. Gorbatai and Nelson evaluated the influence of linguistic content on fund-raising outcomes based on data from the website Indiegogo. They hypothesized that gender inequality in favor of women versus men in online fund-raising is explained in part by linguistic differences between men and women in terms of language they use. They analyzed four different dimensions of language content in campaign descriptions, including positive language, vividness, inclusive language, and business language. The results of their analysis showed a link between linguistic choices and fund-raising outcomes.

# SOFTWARE FOR MIXED METHODS AND QUANTITATIVE NARRATIVE ANALYSIS

SAS is an analytics platform that is widely used in industry as well as academia (https://www.sas.com/en_us/home.html).

Program for Computer-Assisted Coding of Events (PC-ACE) is a data entry program for historical events based on research by Franzosi, De Fazio, and Vicar (2012) and his colleagues on semantic grammar. It was used with UCINET and NVivo (https://launchpad.net/pcace/+download).

UCINET is a free program for visualizing data from social networks and forms of networks.

It is included as a component of NetDraw (https://sites.google.com/site/ucinetsoftware/home).

NetDraw is a free Windows program for visualizing social network data (https://sites.google.com/site/netdrawsoftware/home).

NVivo is qualitative data analysis software (QDAS) that features relatively elaborate organizing functions that allow users to link together text data in a variety of ways. It is widely used in the social sciences and is particularly suited for discourse analysis (e.g., Mische, 2014).

## Conclusion

Stories are fundamental to how humans order experience. Because of the ubiquity and power of narrative in social life, it is not surprising that narrative analysis is one of the most important and influential approaches to text analysis in the social sciences and humanities. The studies reviewed in this chapter can each be used as a template for your own narrative analysis research project, whether it is a qualitative or mixed method study. Be sure to refer to Appendices A through I, and especially B and D, as you make decisions about research design (see Table 10.2), collect your data, and choose software.

## Key Terms

Characters    134

Emplotment    134

Free clause    135

Functional approach    139

Logico–scientific mode    135

Minimal narrative    135

Modality analysis    141

Narrative analysis    133

Narrative clauses    135

Narrative mode    136

Paradigmatic mode    135

Plotline    134

Public stories    134

Semantic triplet    141

Sociological approaches    135

Story grammar    135

Structural approaches    135

Transformation    134

## Highlights

- Narrative analysis refers to a family of approaches to analyzing texts that take the form of stories.

- Narrative analysis can focus exclusively on texts themselves or on the social contexts in which texts emerge, circulate, and change.

- While narrative analysis methods are primarily qualitative and interpretive, social scientists are developing mixed methods of narrative analysis and combining narrative analysis with other text mining and text analysis methods.

## Review Questions

- What are some of the ethical concerns raised by narrative analysis research?

- What is the key value of conducting research using narrative analysis methods?

- How can researchers using narrative analysis techniques avoid bias?

## Developing a Research Proposal

In the data that you are collecting, or have collected, for your own project, what narrative elements have you noticed? What kinds of stories, including public stories, do people tell each other? Are there repeated categories of protagonists, antagonists, or sequences of actions? Can you speculate as to the social functions these stories serve or to the connections between these stories and the social and historical circumstances in which they emerged?

Next, having identified narrative elements in your data, review the studies surveyed in this chapter and choose one that is most similar to the research project you are developing. Using research databases such as Google Scholar, Web of Science, or JSTOR, access the study you have chosen and several recent studies that cite it. Read all of the studies you download carefully, focusing on their research designs. Write down some ways your own study can build from the studies you have read, either by applying their methods to new data, making changes to their methods, or doing both.

## Further Reading

Franzosi, R. (2010). *Quantitative narrative analysis*. Thousand Oaks, CA: Sage.

Sahpazia, P., & Balamoutsoua, S. (2015). Therapists' accounts of relationship breakup experiences: A narrative analysis. *European Journal of Psychotherapy & Counselling, 17*(3), 258–276.

Smith, S., & Watson, J. (2010). *Reading autobiography: A guide for interpreting life narratives*. Minneapolis: University of Minnesota Press.

# ANALYZING THEMES

The goals of Chapter 11 are to help you to do the following:

1. Explain how human communication is structured by themes.
2. Describe **thematic analysis** techniques from the social sciences and humanities.
3. Evaluate various approaches to thematic analysis.
4. Choose an approach and the appropriate software tools to conduct a thematic analysis.

## INTRODUCTION

Just as works of literature have themes, so, too, do people's conversations about their daily lives, their family and friends, politics, technology, fashion, and countless other topics. For example, in a seminal paper that used thematic analysis techniques, the anthropologist Strauss (1992) analyzed interviews with a retired blue-collar worker and found that, when asked to discuss his life experiences, he repeatedly referred to ideas associated with money, businessmen, greed, siblings, and "being different." Strauss concluded that these ideas represented important themes in his life. But while we may think we have the ability to recognize themes in ordinary language without the help of specialized training or software, how are we able to do this, and how can we know if the themes we identify in texts are in fact the most prominent or important themes?

Social scientists have developed methods to perform thematic analysis with greater rigor and objectivity than is possible from reading texts and hoping that themes will simply reveal themselves as if by magic. These thematic analysis methods provide core skills that can be used for many different types of text mining and text analysis.

The organizational theorist and thematic analysis pioneer Boyatzis (1998) characterized thematic analysis not as a specific method but as a tool to use across different methods and theoretical approaches. Similarly, Bernard, Wutich, and Ryan (2016) considered **thematic coding** to be a process that is compatible with several analytic approaches rather than a specific methodological approach in its own right (Braun & Clarke, 2006; Ryan & Bernard, 2010). Because thematic analysis techniques are used within many research traditions and toward many different ends, the results of thematic analysis depend critically on researchers' theoretical and metatheoretical positions (see Chapter 4).

# BASIC CONCEPTS

*Codes* are labels that are applied by the researcher to words or passages in texts that share common characteristics.

*Repeated reading* occurs in the early stages of thematic analysis. It involves immersion in a collection of texts and searching for themes while reading the texts carefully and taking extensive notes.

At a minimum, thematic analysis involves organizing and describing texts in detail. But thematic analysis can go further than organization and description of texts by allowing for interpretation of various aspects of the research topic (Boyatzis, 1998). While thematic analysis is widely used in the social sciences, there is little clear agreement about how best to go about doing it. Braun and Clarke (2006) suggested that it is a poorly "branded" method that is not widely viewed as a "named" analysis in contrast to more widely recognized approaches such as narrative analysis (see Chapter 10).

## HOW TO ANALYZE THEMES

In thematic analysis, writing is an integral part of every phase of a research project (see Chapter 17). Writing generally begins in a project's initial stages with the writing out of ideas and potential coding schemes and then continues through coding and analysis phases.

Thematic analysis starts when the researcher notices patterns of meaning in a collection of texts—either during the process of acquiring the texts or soon after. The endpoint of thematic analysis is the reporting of the content and meaning of the patterns of themes in the texts. While thematic analysis allows researchers to interpret overarching themes and subthemes in texts, it does not allow them to make claims about language use or the "fine-grained functionality of talk" (Braun & Clarke, 2006). Still, themes are understood to capture something important about textual data in relation to a research question or questions.

In thematic analysis, themes can be identified either inductively or deductively (see Chapters 4 and 5). A bottom-up, inductive approach means that the themes identified are directly linked to the texts being analyzed (Patton, 1990). In this approach, if the corpus has been constructed specifically for the research project—for instance, by transcribing interviews or focus group interactions—the themes identified may bear little relationship to the specific questions that were asked of the participants (see Toerien & Wilkinson, 2004). In contrast, top-down, deductive thematic analysis is driven by researchers' theoretical and substantive questions (see Chapters 4 and 5).

## RESEARCH IN THE SPOTLIGHT
### Coulson's Studies of Online Support Groups

Coulson, N. S. (2005). Receiving social support online: An analysis of a computer-mediated support group for individuals living with irritable bowel syndrome. *CyberPsychology & Behavior, 8*(6), 580–584.

The psychologist Coulson examined the nature of socially supportive communication that within a computer-mediated support network for individuals affected by irritable bowel syndrome. Using a deductive (see Chapter 4) form of thematic analysis, Coulson examined 572 posted messages in terms of five main categories of social support, including emotional, esteem, information, network, and tangible assistance. He found that the primary function of this group was the communication of informational support within the areas of symptom interpretation, illness management, and interaction with health care professionals.

Coulson, N. S., Buchanan, H., & Aubeeluck, A. (2007). Social support in cyberspace: A content analysis of communication within a Huntington's disease online support group. *Patient Education and Counseling, 68*(2), 173–178.

In this study from 2007, the psychologists Coulson, Buchanan, and Aubeeluck investigated online support groups for Huntington's disease, which is an inherited disorder characterized by a progressive degeneration of the brain. Due to the nature of the symptoms, the genetic element of the disease, and the fact that there is no cure, patients with Huntington's disease and those in their support network often experience considerable stress and anxiety. The researchers' content analyzed 1,313 messages using a modified version of the social support behavior code developed by other researchers. Their findings were that group members most frequently offered informational and emotional support followed by network support. Esteem support and tangible assistance were shared least frequently.

Thematic analysis is not a linear method but rather a recursive one where the analyst moves back and forth as needed throughout the many phases of a project. The first steps in a thematic analysis are for the researcher to acquire a collection of texts and to immerse herself in the texts via **repeated reading** (Braun & Clarke, 2006). Such immersion and repeated reading involves searching for themes while reading the texts carefully and taking extensive notes.

Formal coding is the next step. Formal coding starts with the researcher generating initial codes based on the notes taken while actively and repeatedly reading the texts. An important question to address in terms of coding is what counts as a theme. This is a question of the frequency of the occurrence of a theme within each text as well as across the entire collection of texts being analyzed. While ideally there will be a number of instances of the theme within the collection of texts, more instances do not necessarily mean the theme is more crucial. There are no agreed-upon answers to the question of what proportion of a collection of texts or documents needs to display evidence of a theme for it to be considered a main or overarching theme. The relative importance of a theme is not necessarily based on quantifiable measures but rather on whether it captures something important in relation to the overall research question (Braun & Clarke, 2006).

Codes identify a feature of the corpus that is interesting to the researcher and refer to "the most basic segment, or element, of the raw data or information that can be assessed in a meaningful way regarding the phenomenon" (Boyatzis, 1998, p. 63). Coding can be done either manually or with specialized software (see Appendix D). If coding manually, you can write notes on the texts themselves by using highlighters, colored pens, or sticky notes to indicate potential patterns. Qualitative data analysis software (QDAS;

## RESEARCH IN THE SPOTLIGHT
### Analyzing Climate Change Doubt

Boussalisa, C., & Coan, T. G. (2016). Text-mining the signals of climate change doubt." *Global Environmental Change, 36*, 89–100.

Environmental researchers Boussalisa and Coan analyzed longitudinal data on texts produced by think tanks that are skeptical of global climate change. These think tanks generate climate change skepticism despite a broad scientific consensus that the Earth is getting warmer and that the rise in average global temperature is predominantly due to human activity. Boussalisa and Coan provided a systematic overview of conservative think-tank skeptical discourse based on a collection of over 16,000 documents from 19 organizations produced between 1998 and 2013. They analyzed key themes in the corpus in order to examine the relative prevalence of science- and policy-related discussion, finding that discussion of climate science has generally increased over the period examined.

see Appendix D) allows you to perform these functions digitally. However, this coded data differ from the units of analysis, which are the themes developed in the next phase of thematic analysis.

After initial manual or software-assisted coding, the next phase of thematic analysis begins when all the texts have been initially coded and you have a list of different codes identified in the data. At this point, you will refocus on themes rather than codes. The various different codes are sorted into potential themes, and coded data extracts are collated within the identified themes. In this phase, you may use visual representations such as matrices or mind maps (see Appendix G) to help sort codes into themes. You may also begin to consider the relationships between different levels of themes, such as between overarching themes and subthemes. You can review, revise, and organize themes and possibly recode your data based on the revised set of themes. Your goal is for words and ideas associated with themes to link in a meaningful way while the themes are all distinctly different from one another (Patton, 2014; see Table 11.1).

There are several observational techniques available to sort coded text into themes. One technique is to identify themes by recognizing repetitions in coded text. This was the technique used by Strauss (1992) in her thematic analysis of interviews with a retired blue-collar worker discussed at the beginning of this chapter. Another technique is to identify local terms that are used in unfamiliar ways. Such **indigenous categories** (Patton, 1990) can provide insights into the typologies and classification schemes of the community being investigated. Well-known examples of studies of indigenous classifications are anthropologist Spradley's (1972) analysis of tramps' typology of different types of "flops" (places to sleep), and sociologist Becker's (1993) analysis of medical students' indigenous category of "crock." As is discussed further in Chapter 12, another way you can identify themes in texts is to focus on metaphorical language. It is also possible to analyze transitions, or naturally occurring shifts in content (Bernard et al., 2016), that may take the form of pauses or specific phrases (see Silverman, 1993, pp. 114–143).

| TABLE 11.1 ■ Phases of Thematic Analysis Research |
| --- |
| Start with a research question (deductive) or with data (inductive) |
| Acquiring data |
| Repeated reading |
| Coding |
| Sorting into themes |
| Consider revising coding scheme |

# CONCEPT CHECK

*Themes* are main ideas or underlying meanings in a text or collection of texts. In thematic analysis, themes are understood to capture something important about the data in relation to the research question or questions.

*Subthemes* are subunits of major themes in a text. They appear less frequently and/or are less central to the meaning of the text than its major themes.

*Indigenous categories* are local terms that are used in unfamiliar ways. Such terms can provide insights into themes and subthemes of the community being investigated.

## EXAMPLES OF THEMATIC ANALYSIS

Thematic analysis techniques are used by researchers in business, counseling, education, psychology, and many other fields. While many researchers using these techniques rely on repeated reading and hand coding of texts, others use QDAS tools such as NVivo and Dedoose (see Appendix D) or general purpose text mining software such as SAS Text Miner.

For example, the management researchers Jones, Coviello, and Tang's (2011) study of academic research on international entrepreneurship is an example of an inductive (see Chapters 4 and 5) thematic analysis. Jones and colleagues (2011) constructed a corpus from 323 journal articles on international entrepreneurship published between 1989 and 2009. Using ABI/INFORM and EBSCO search engines, they inductively analyzed themes and subthemes in their data. This involved examining the subject matter of international entrepreneurship research and synthesizing and categorizing it into major themes and then subthemes. Based on their synthesis and organization of the international entrepreneurship research literature, they discussed issues, inconsistencies, and interim debates in the field. They concluded that international entrepreneurship research has several coherent thematic areas.

In another inductive study, the psychologists Halberstadt and her colleagues (2016) used thematic analysis to explore how children experience gratitude. The researchers asked 20 parents in six focus groups to talk about their views of gratitude in young children. They used Dedoose (see Appendix D) to analyze themes in the transcripts, finding that the parents described children as grateful for both tangible and intangible gifts. Parents identified multiple cognitive, emotional, and behavioral aspects of gratitude in their children as well as four cognitive and emotional barriers to experiencing gratitude.

Gerontology researchers Strachan, Yellowlees, and Quigley (2015) performed a thematic analysis on transcripts of group interviews conducted with nine general practitioners that is similar to the study conducted by Halberstadt and her colleagues (2016). The general practitioners were asked about their assessment and treatment of older patients and their expectations and experience of referral to secondary care. Strachan and colleagues (2015) discussed how their findings highlight discrepancies between assumptions about general practitioners' attitudes and actions toward older patients with mental disorders and the practitioners' own accounts.

Mental health researchers Shepherd, Sanders, Doyle, and Shaw (2015) assessed how Twitter is used by people who have experienced mental health problems. Shepherd and colleagues (2015) followed the #dearmentalhealthprofessionals on Twitter and conducted a thematic analysis to identify common themes of discussion. They found 515 unique communications that were related to the specified conversation. The majority of the material related to four overarching themes: (1) the impact of diagnosis on personal identity and as a facilitator for accessing care, (2) balance of power between professional and service user, (3) therapeutic relationship and developing professional communication, and (4) support provision through medication, crisis planning, service provision and the wider society.

The clinical psychologists Attard and Coulson (2012) conducted an inductive (see Chapters 4 and 5) thematic analysis of messages exchanged within online support groups for patients living with Parkinson's disease. Attard and Coulson collected data from four forums and found that participation in the forums allowed patients to share experiences and knowledge, form friendships, and help them cope with the challenges of living with Parkinson's disease. Conversely, a lack of replies, the experience of Parkinson's disease symptoms, a lack of personal information, fragility of online relationships, and misunderstandings and disagreements all appeared to compromise the online experience.

The nursing researchers Fereday and Muir-Cochrane (2006) used a hybrid process of inductive and deductive thematic analysis to interpret raw data in a doctoral study on the role of performance feedback in the self-assessment of nursing practice. Using NVivo (see Appendix D), the authors demonstrated how analysis of the raw data from interview transcripts and organizational documents progressed toward the identification of overarching themes that captured the phenomenon of performance feedback as described by participants in the study.

The psychologists Frith and Gleeson's 2004 study of male body image is a theoretically driven thematic analysis. In order to better understand how men's feelings about their bodies influence their clothing practices, Frith and Gleeson used a snowball sampling strategy (see Chapter 5) to recruit undergraduate psychology students who answered four written questions about clothing practices and body image. Thematic analysis of the students' answers revealed four main themes relevant to the research question: (1) practicality of clothing choices, (2) lack of concern about appearance, (3) use of clothing to conceal or reveal the body, and (4) use of clothing to fit cultural ideals. Frith and Gleeson concluded that their study demonstrates the pervasive and mundane role of clothing in men's self-surveillance and self-presentation and the range and complexity of the processes involved in clothing the body.

The communications researcher Lazard, Scheinfeld, Bernhardt, Wilcox, and Suran (2015) used SAS Text Miner to perform a thematic analysis of tweets generated by users who participated in a Centers for Disease Control and Prevention live Twitter chat. Users' tweets were collected, sorted, and analyzed to reveal major themes of public concern with the symptoms and life span of the virus, disease transfer and contraction, safe travel, and protection of one's body.

# SOFTWARE FOR THEMATIC ANALYSIS

Thematic analysis is traditionally performed with very little software, although many thematic analysts are choosing to work with qualitative data analysis software (QDAS) packages (see Appendix D) such as the following:

Dedoose is a relatively new cloud-based application for qualitative and mixed methods analysis.

It is particularly suited for collaborative research and can be used on any device (e.g., Halberstadt et al., 2016; www.dedoose.com).

NVivo is widely used in the social sciences and features organizing functions that allow users to link together text data in a variety of ways (e.g., Fereday & Muir-Cochrane, 2006; www .qsrinternational.com).

## Conclusion

The thematic analysis studies reviewed in this chapter can each be used as a template for your own thematic analysis research project, or you can choose to use thematic analysis procedures within research projects that use other methodologies. In any case, be sure to refer to the appendices as you make decisions about research design, data, and software.

## Key Terms

Indigenous categories    149
Repeated reading    148
Thematic analysis    145
Thematic coding    146

## Highlights

- Thematic analysis involves, at a minimum, organizing and describing texts in detail. But it can go further than that by allowing for interpretation of various aspects of the research topic.

- Thematic analysis is not a specific method but rather a tool that can be used across different methods and theoretical approaches.

- Thematic coding is compatible with several analytic approaches.

- The results of a thematic analysis depend critically on the researchers' theoretical and metatheoretical positions (see Chapter 4).

## Review Questions

- What are themes, and how do social scientists analyze them?

- In what ways can thematic analysis stimulate social problem solving by researchers?

- How has thematic analysis come to be at odds with more computationally intensive forms of text analysis such as sentiment analysis and topic modeling?

## Developing a Research Proposal

Consider how thematic analysis techniques of coding and sorting coded text into themes and subthemes can be used in your own research project. What words or phrases can you code as representative of a theme or subtheme.

If you choose to analyze metaphors (see Chapter 12) or topics (see Chapter 16), consider how techniques for thematic analysis can help you increase the rigor and precision of your analysis. Are metaphors used haphazardly, or does repeated reading reveal thematic patterns? In topic modeling, can topics modeled in texts be grouped in terms of themes?

## Further Reading

Attard, A., & Coulson, N. (2012). A thematic analysis of patient communication in Parkinson's disease online support group discussion forums. *Computers in Human Behavior, 28*(2), 500–506.

Boyatzis, R. E. (1998). *Transforming qualitative information: Thematic analysis and code development*. Thousand Oaks, CA: Sage.

# ANALYZING METAPHORS

The goals of Chapter 12 are to help you to do the following:

1. Learn the basic concepts of **cognitive metaphor theory (CMT)**.
2. Theorize why social scientists analyze metaphorical language and summarize different approaches.
3. Recognize the benefits and drawbacks of different strategies for analyzing metaphor.
4. Explore available software tools for metaphor analysis.

## INTRODUCTION

Like narratives (see Chapter 10) and themes (see Chapter 11), **metaphors** are common in everyday language and are arguably a basic element of human communication. The computer scientist and cognitive neuroscientist Feldman (2006) gave the example of the metaphor of "spinning your wheels," which is able to communicate an amazing amount of information with just a few words:

> Imagine yourself trying to teach the meaning and usage of a phrase like "spinning your wheels" to a friend who knows English but comes from a culture where the phrase isn't used. Let's begin with the simplest, literal meaning of this idiomatic

expression. If your friend's culture did not have cars, the task would be enormous. You would first have to explain what an automobile is, how it works, and how a car's wheels might spin in mud, in sand, or on ice without the car moving. One would also have to explain the typical effect of this on the driver, namely, frustration at not being able to get the car to move. (p. 10)

For Feldman and other researchers, working in cognitive neuroscience and related fields, metaphors like spinning your wheels are interesting because they communicate information quickly and efficiently by activating preexisting complex knowledge structures. For social scientists, however, the spinning your wheels metaphor is not particularly interesting in and of itself. But what is interesting is that different groups of people may use this metaphor in different situations or perhaps at higher or lower rates. For instance, if within a large corporation workers in one unit described their work using metaphors related to spinning your wheels, while in another unit workers talked about being "pushed too hard" or being "under pressure" to perform, these forms of metaphorical language could teach a social scientist a great deal about the cultures operating within the organization.

Metaphorical language takes a number of grammatical forms, including **analogy**, **simile**, and **synecdoche**. But in all cases, metaphorical language involves figures of speech that make implicit comparisons in which a word or phrase ordinarily used in one domain is applied in another. While metaphor has long been a topic of literary scholarship, it was only in 1980 with the publication of Lakoff and Johnson's *Metaphors We Live By* that metaphor came to be an object of social science research. Lakoff and Johnson's approach to metaphor has come to be known as CMT and has provided the conceptual foundation for the field of **cognitive linguistics** (Gibbs, 1994; Kovecses, 2002; Lakoff & Johnson, 1999; Sweetser, 1990).

Today, CMT and a variety of metaphor analysis techniques are used to gain insights into how individuals and social groups interpret social reality. While originally a form of literary interpretation, metaphor analysis is now used widely in the humanities as well as in social science fields such as anthropology, communications, and sociology. As we will see, it is also used by researchers in the fields of counseling, education, health, and management.

We begin this chapter with a brief overview of CMT before discussing some of the different approaches that have been developed for conducting metaphor analysis. Along the way, we review exemplary published studies from several social science disciplines, including anthropology, communications research, counseling, educational research, management, psychology, political science, and sociology, focusing on these studies' research methods and research designs.

# COGNITIVE METAPHOR THEORY

The basic claim of CMT is that language is structured by metaphor at a neural level and that metaphors used in natural language reveal cognitive models (or "schemas") shared by members of social groups. Thus, metaphor is a central and indispensable structure of thought and language, and all natural language is characterized by the presence of conventional metaphorical expressions organized around prototypical metaphors, which Lakoff and Johnson have referred to as **conceptual metaphors**. These are linguistic expressions of the conventional pattern of thought of a group or society (Kovecses, 2002). For instance, Lakoff and Johnson argued that in many cultures people conceptualize *argument* in terms of a *battle*. This prototypical conceptual metaphor influences the way people talk about the act of arguing, for instance when they use phrases such as "attack a position," "indefensible," "strategy," "new line of attack," "win," and "gain ground" (Lakoff & Johnson, 1980, p. 7).

According to CMT, metaphors originate in a process of "phenomenological embodiment" (Lakoff & Johnson, 1999, p. 46). They are formed when perceptual and sensory experiences form an embodied **source domain**, such as pushing, pulling, supporting, balance, straight–curved, near–far, front–back, and high–low, are used to represent abstract entities in a **target domain** (Boroditsky, 2000; Lakoff, 1987; Richardson, Spivey, Barsalou, & McRae, 2003).

## BASIC CONCEPTS

*Metaphor* is a figure of speech in which a word or phrase is applied to something to which it is not literally applicable.

*Cognitive metaphor theory (CMT)* is the theory developed by cognitive linguists that posits that metaphors structure language at a neural level and that metaphors used in natural language reveal cognitive models shared by members of social groups.

*Conceptual metaphors* are prototypical metaphors that are linguistic expressions of the conventional pattern of thought of a group or society.

The *source domain* of a metaphor is the set of perceptual and sensory experiences (e.g., the sensory experience a wheel spinning in mud) are used to represent abstract entities.

The *target domain* of a metaphor is the set of abstract entities (e.g., the idea of making inadequate progress) that is represented metaphorically by rich perceptual and sensory experiences from a source domain.

CMT is capable of explaining universal aspects of language and culture as well as cultural variation (Kovecses, 2002). While languages' phenomenological foundations are universal, societies and social groups differ in terms of the associations they make between conceptual metaphors and abstract target domains. In other words, different societies and groups use different sets of metaphors to construct and interpret social reality in different ways. An implication of CMT for social research is that studying the distribution of metaphor in natural language can reveal how commonsense ideas are constructed and negotiated within groups.

## APPROACHES TO METAPHOR ANALYSIS

Influenced by CMT, researchers have developed a number of strategies for metaphor analysis. While the three strategies discussed next do not exhaust the possibilities for analyzing metaphor in social science research, these approaches can help you to get started developing a manageable research project (see Table 12.1).

| TABLE 12.1 ■ Metaphor Analysis Research Design Strategies | |
| --- | --- |
| | **Examples** |
| Start with an anomaly | Ignatow, 2003; Ignatow and Williams, 2011 |
| Compare two groups | Rees, Knight, and Wilkinson, 2007 |
| Analyze a subculture | Schmitt, 2000, 2005 |

A first research strategy for metaphor analysis is to begin your analysis with an anomalous or unexpected example of metaphorical language. This is basically an inductive method (see Chapters 4 and 5). For instance, the sociologist Ignatow and communications researcher Williams noticed that around 2010 that the metaphor "anchor baby" had entered popular culture (the phrase refers to children born in the United States to undocumented migrant parents who are thought to have been conceived in order to improve their parents' chances of attaining citizenship). This seemed anomalous because the phrase was widely seen as racist and dehumanizing and prior to about 2007 had been used almost exclusively on anti-immigrant websites with small audiences. Ignatow and Williams (2011) analyzed the rates of use of the phrase over time and across media platforms using Google Advanced Search and other software tools.

A second productive research strategy is to start your project by choosing two or more groups to compare to attempt to answer a research question. This strategy is basically deductive (see Chapter 4) in that it requires you to systematically select groups to compare (see Chapter 5 on case selection) so that your data can be used to test hypotheses derived from your research question. An example of this strategy is a 2007 study by the education researchers Rees, Knight, and Wilkinson, who used ATLAS.ti (see Appendix D) to analyze metaphors in strategically collected transcripts of discussions of doctor–patient interactions by patients, medical students, and doctors. Their analysis revealed six prototypical metaphors associated with the target domain of student/doctor–patient relationships: the relationship as war, hierarchy, doctor-centeredness, market, machine, and theater. All of these metaphors except the theater metaphor emphasized the oppositional quality of student/doctor–patient relationships. In their paper, Rees and colleagues (2007) distinguished between the unconscious use of metaphorical linguistic expressions by their participants and use of metaphorical expressions that serves a rhetorical function. They argued that although analyzing metaphorical language is not without its difficulties, the construction of metaphoric models can help researchers to better understand how people conceptualize and construct student/doctor–patient relationships.

A third metaphor analysis strategy, closely related to the second, deductive strategy used by Rees and colleagues (2007) is the psychologist Rudolf Schmitt's subcultural strategy. Schmitt (2000, 2005) developed a qualitative method of text analysis centered on metaphor, a "rule-based and step-by-step approach" that is based on an inductive inferential logic (p. 2). Schmitt's strategy operates at a sociological level of analysis (see Chapter 5) that involves making inferences about the community that generates the text being analyzed. The goal is to "discover sub-cultural thinking patterns" (Schmitt, 2005, p. 365). The first step is for the researcher to choose a topic of analysis. Schmitt gave the example of abstinence taken from his own empirical work on metaphors for abstinence and alcoholism. The next step is to assemble a "broad-based collection of background metaphors" (Schmitt, 2005, p. 370) for the topic. These metaphors can be collected from sources such as encyclopedias, journals, and specialist and generalist books. In Schmitt's own work, **background metaphors** include metaphors for the effects of drinking alcohol such as being more "open" versus "fencing off" from others. The third step is to analyze the metaphors used in the natural language of the subgroup. This involves creating the second document collection, identifying metaphors in that collection, and then reconstructing metaphorical concepts from those metaphors. The fourth and final step is to compare the metaphorical concepts from the two document collections in order to learn about the culture and psychology of the subgroup in comparison to the culture and psychology of the general population.

# QUALITATIVE, QUANTITATIVE, AND MIXED METHODS

Once you have gotten started with a metaphor analysis project by noticing an anomalous use of metaphor, selecting groups or organizations to compare, or identifying a subculture of interest using Schmitt's strategy, the next step is to choose a method of metaphor analysis. Available methods can be roughly categorized into qualitative methods, mixed methods (qualitative and quantitative), and quantitative methods. Metaphor analysis studies using the strategies reviewed previously have been conducted in many social science fields as well as in applied research fields such as education and management. In this section, we review exemplary recently published studies from these diverse areas, focusing on their research methods and research designs.

## Qualitative Methods Studies

Cognitive linguists themselves have performed qualitative studies of metaphors used in natural language and in formal documents. For instance, both Lakoff (1996) and Chilton (1996) studied metaphors related to security used in political discourse. Charteris-Black (2009, 2012, 2013) has developed a rhetorically based approach to metaphor known as **critical metaphor analysis** that draws on methodologies and perspectives developed in cognitive linguistics, corpus linguistics, and critical linguistics. He has used the approach to examine metaphors from the domains of political rhetoric, press reporting, religion, and the communications of a wide range of political leaders. He has also worked jointly with sociologists on the relationship among gender, language, and illness narratives. And Goatly (2007) investigated how conceptual metaphor shapes thought and behavior in fields including architecture, engineering, education, genetics, ecology, economics, politics, industrial time management, medicine, immigration, race, and sex. He has argued that the ideologies of early capitalism used metaphor themes historically traceable through Hobbes, Hume, Smith, Malthus, and Darwin and that these metaphorical concepts support neo-Darwinian and neoconservative ideologies up to the present day. Hart (2010) has advocated for a cognitive linguistic approach to critical discourse analysis (CDA; see Chapter 1). Hart's approach involves a semantic analysis of particular lexical, grammatical, and pragmatic features found in political and media discourse. More narrowly, it investigates the conceptual structures that are associated with different language usages and the ideological functions that such structures may serve. He has applied this framework primarily in the context of anti-immigration discourse (Hart, 2010).

Qualitative metaphor analysis has been performed in many social science fields. For example, anthropologists began analyzing metaphorical language in the 1970s (Sapir &

## SPOTLIGHT ON THE RESEARCH
Metaphors in Leadership Communication

Charteris-Black, J. (2012). Comparative keyword analysis and leadership communication: Tony Blair—A study of rhetorical style." In L. Helms (Ed.), *Comparative political leadership* (pp. 142–164). Basingstoke, England: Palgrave Macmillan

In this study of the rhetorical style of former British prime minister Tony Blair, Charteris-Black has drawn on methodologies and perspectives developed in cognitive linguistics, corpus linguistics, and critical linguistics. He analyzed Blair's political rhetoric using the corpus linguistics software package WordSmith (see Appendix F) and used the results of his analysis to adjudicate between major theories of leadership.

Specialized software used:

WordSmith

www.lexically.net/wordsmith

Crocker, 1977). Fernandez's 1991 edited collection *Beyond Metaphor* provides a good overview of early ethnographic work on metaphor. For an overview of more recent linguistic anthropological research, see Danesi's (2012) *Linguistic Anthropology: A Brief Introduction*.

In management research, the linguists Sun and Jiang (2014) used the corpus tool Wmatrix (see Appendix F) to study metaphors used in Chinese and American corporate mission statements. They found differences in the use of source domains for three conventional conceptual metaphors: (1) brands are people, (2) business is cooperation, and (3) business is competition. They also found that different corporate identities and ideologies were associated with different patterns of metaphor use, with Chinese corporate identity being more competition-oriented while American corporate identity was more oriented toward cooperation.

O'Mara-Shimek, Guillén-Parra, and Ortega-Larrea (2015) introduced the concept of crisis solution marketing (CSM) to explore how metaphor can be used to present information to propose "solutions" to "problems" that are discursively constructed in the media. O'Mara-Shimek and colleagues (2015) explored the relationship between editorial positioning and ideology in financial news and by examining metaphors used to describe the nature of the stock market in online reporting on the stock market crash of 2008. In the *New York Times* and the *Wall Street Journal*, animate–biological metaphors depict the stock market "in terms of a living being that must be 'nurtured' through intervention as opposed to being 'left alone,' which is more consistent with laissez-faire approaches to economic crisis scenarios" (O'Mara-Shimek et al., 2015, p. 103).

In education research, Cameron (2003) and others have used CMT to analyze figurative language used by students and teachers in classroom settings. And Olthouse (2014) analyzed how 124 undergraduate education majors conceptualize giftedness. The education majors completed the phrase "a gifted student is _____" by using a metaphor and then explained their choice of metaphor. Qualitative metaphor analysis revealed that preservice teachers conceive of giftedness as "rapid memorization of content knowledge and showy demonstrations of achievement" (p. 122). They believe that giftedness is rare and that intelligence is generalizable.

Gatti and Catalano (2015) analyzed the learning to teach process of one novice teacher, Rachael, enrolled in an urban teacher residency in the United States. Critical metaphor analysis (see Charteris-Black, 2009, 2012, 2013) reveals conflicting frames of learning to teach, including frames of *teaching is a journey* and *teaching is a business*.

The environmental studies researcher Asplund (2011) examined communicative aspects of climate change, identifying and analyzing metaphors used in specialized media reports on climate change and discussing the aspects of climate change these metaphors emphasize and neglect. Through a CDA of the two largest Swedish farm magazines over the 2000–2009 period, Asplund found that *greenhouse*, *war*, and *game* metaphors were the most frequently used. The analysis indicates that greenhouse metaphors are used to ascribe certain natural science characteristics to climate change, game metaphors to address positive impacts of climate change, and war metaphors to highlight negative impacts of climate change. The paper concluded by discussing the contrasting and complementary metaphorical representations farm magazines use to conventionalize climate change.

The environmental researchers Shaw and Nerlich (2015) explored the emergence of a global climate change mitigation regime through an analysis of the language employed in international science policy reports. Assuming that a global climate regime can only operate effectively on the basis of a shared understanding of climate change, they performed a thematic (see Chapter 11) and metaphor analysis of 63 policy documents published between 1992 and 2012. They found that global climate science policy discourses universalize the myriad impacts of a changing climate into a single dichotomous impacted versus not impacted scenario and aim to govern climate change according to economic principles of cost–benefit analysis. These discourses "use metaphors that draw on narrative structures prevalent in the wider culture to produce and legitimate a reductionist representation of climate change" (p. 34) that undermines public understanding of and engagement with climate change by marginalizing policy framings which do not align with the prevailing dichotomous framing.

Information science researchers Puschmann and Burgess (2014) used CMT to assess values and assumptions encoded in the framing of the term *big data*. Their metaphor analysis of online news items about big data reveals that it is framed as either a natural force to be controlled or a resource to be consumed.

In media studies, Bickes, Otten, and Weymann (2014) have analyzed the German media presentation of the so-called Greek financial crisis, which caused an unexpected uproar in Germany. Bickes and colleagues (2014) examined the role of the media in shaping negative public opinion in Germany toward Greece. Analyzing metaphor use in 122 online articles, the researchers found remarkable differences in the evaluation and presentation of the crisis in the news outlets *Spiegel* (Germany), the *Economist* (United Kingdom) and *Time* magazine (United States).

The sociologist Santa Ana (2002) combined CDA (see Chapter 1) and metaphor analysis. Santa Ana's data are newspapers that he used to study mass media representations of Latino/as in the United States.

Political scientists have analyzed metaphorical language in policy documents, speeches, and other political texts to explore the ways metaphors mediate relations between countries and other political actors. For example, a 2004 edited collection by Beer and De Landtsheer (2004) includes chapters on the metaphors that have guided and shaped American foreign policy in the public arena since the start of the Cold War. The studies in this collection cover metaphors for democracy, war and peace, and globalization. The chapters' authors analyze sports metaphors in Desert Storm discourse, disease metaphors used during the Cold War for the threat of communism, and path metaphors used in deliberations over United States foreign policy toward Cambodia, among other conceptual metaphors (see also Carver & Pikalo, 2008).

## Mixed Methods Studies

Social scientists have developed a number of mixed methods strategies for metaphor analysis. Generally, these involve human coding of metaphors in combination with statistical tests for both interrater reliability and differences in rates of metaphor use across multiple document collections. The document collections are typically produced by social groups with different social or cultural backgrounds. Where qualitative metaphor analysis is mostly inductive, mixed methods research is mostly deductive, although it often involves abductive inference as well (see Chapter 5).

The social psychologist Moser (2000) has developed a metaphor-based method of text analysis that she has applied in her research on the psychology of work and organizations. Moser's mixed methods approach involves categorizing metaphors for the self during transitions from school to work. The self-concept is highly complex and abstract and is thus often represented with metaphors. The subjects Moser studied were Swiss German students who participated in a questionnaire study about their anticipated transition from university to work. A subsample of 12 students was included in the study and interviewed about their experiences with success and relationship quality and their expectations and wishes for the future. The transcribed interviews were analyzed thematically and for self-related metaphors and other aspects of the students' self-concepts. Moser's quantitative analysis of these data revealed statistically significant relationships between themes and metaphors and between metaphors and self-concepts. There was a general preference for scientific and technological metaphors, followed by container, path, visual, balance, war, and economic metaphors. Metaphor use is also significantly influenced by variables such as students' general orientation toward the future, field of study, and gender.

Clinical psychologists have analyzed metaphors used by subjects in psychoanalytic therapy (Buchholz & von Kleist, 1995; Roderburg, 1998), and cognitive and experimental psychologists have studied metaphors as examples of mental models (Johnson-Laird, 1983). But within psychology, only Schmitt (2000, 2005) has developed a qualitative method of text analysis centered on metaphor. Schmitt's (2000) "rule-based and step-by-step approach" is idiographic and qualitative and is based on inductive inferential logic (p. 2). It operates at a sociological level of analysis that involves making inferences about the community that generates the text being analyzed and involves a multiple-document-collection data selection strategy (see Chapter 2). The goal of Schmitt's (2005) method of systematic metaphor analysis is to "discover sub-cultural thinking patterns," and his method accomplishes this in several steps (p. 365). The first step is for the researcher to choose a topic of analysis. Schmitt gives the example of abstinence from his own empirical work on metaphors for abstinence and alcoholism. The next step is to assemble a "broad-based collection of background metaphors" for the topic (Schmitt, 2005, p. 370). These metaphors can be collected from sources such as encyclopedias, journals, and specialist and generalist books. In Schmitt's own work, background metaphors include metaphors for the effects of drinking alcohol such as being more open versus fencing off from others. The third step is to analyze the metaphors used in the natural language of the subgroup. This involves creating the second document collection, identifying metaphors in that collection, and then reconstructing metaphorical concepts from those metaphors. The fourth and final step is to compare the metaphorical concepts from the two document collections in order to learn about the culture and psychology of the subgroup in comparison to the culture and psychology of the general population.

The sociologists Schuster, Beune, and Stronks (2011) have used mixed methods to study metaphorical constructions of hypertension among ethnic groups in the Netherlands. Rather than using secondary data, as is the case for most of the studies reviewed previously, Schuster and colleagues (2011) collected their own data by transcribing interviews they performed with members of three ethnic groups in the Netherlands.

Management researchers Gibson and Zellmer-Bruhn (2001) used mixed methods of metaphor analysis to study concepts of teamwork across national organizational cultures. Their theoretically driven research used a deductive inferential logic and featured a research design with multiple document collections. It operated at a sociological level of analysis (see Chapter 5) that allowed the researchers to analyze texts in order to learn about the organizations and society that produced them. This project's goal was to test a well-known theory of the influence of national culture on employees' attitudes (Hofstede, 1980) with a research design that included strategic selection first of four nations (France, the Philippines, Puerto Rico, and the United States) and then of four organizations (p. 281). The researchers conducted interviews that they transcribed to form their corpora, which they analyzed using QSR NUD*IST (see Appendix D on NVivo) and TACT (Bradley, 1989; Popping, 1997). These software packages were used to organize the qualitative coding of five frequently used teamwork metaphors, which were then used to create dependent variables for hypothesis testing using multinomial logit and logistic regression.

## Quantitative Methods Studies

Both qualitative and mixed methods metaphor analysis are ultimately reliant on human interpretation and coding of metaphors in texts. Such coding is subject to coder fatigue, coder bias, and problems of coder interrater reliability. It is also time-intensive, and the time required for training and coding has thus far limited researchers' ability to scale up metaphor analysis for use with big data. But today the situation is changing rapidly, as several research teams in computer science and related fields are developing computer-assisted methods for automatically detecting metaphors in texts.

Early attempts by Fass (1991) and more recent work by Mason (2004) relied on predefined semantic and domain knowledge to attempt to identify metaphor in texts. Birke and Sarkar (2007) approached the problem by considering literal and nonliteral usages to be different sense of a single word. Hardie, Koller, Rayson, and Semino (2007) repurposed semantic annotation tools in order to extract possibly metaphoric phrases from texts. Turney, Neuman, Assaf, and Cohen (2011) identified metaphorical phrases by assuming that these phrases consist of both a more concrete and a more abstract term. They derived an algorithm to define the abstractness of a term and then used this algorithm to contrast the abstractness of adjective–noun phrases. Phrases were labeled as metaphorical when the difference between the abstractness of the noun and the abstractness of the adjective passed a predetermined threshold.

Recently Gandy, Neuman, and their colleagues (Gandy et al., 2013; Neuman et al., 2013) have developed a number of interrelated algorithms that have been able to identify metaphorical language in texts with a high level of accuracy. Their work is based on Turney and colleagues (2011) key insight that a metaphor usually involves a mapping from a concrete domain to a more abstract domain. The algorithms are thus based on a target noun's abstractness and its accompanying adjective's number of dictionary definitions (if there is only one, the adjective cannot be part of a metaphor). If none of the most common concrete nouns that are commonly associated with the adjective are present, the target noun is coded as metaphorical.

Even if they are not ready to be used for social science research quite yet, the recent successes by computational linguists in automating metaphor extraction suggest that there is great potential for automated methods of metaphor analysis to be used in social science text mining applications in the near future.

# SOFTWARE FOR METAPHOR ANALYSIS

Software packages and programming tools used for metaphor analysis include qualitative data analysis software (QDAS) packages such as the following:

ATLAS.ti (e.g., Rees, Knight, & Wilkinson, 2007)

MAXQDA (e.g., Schuster, Beune, & Stronks, 2011)

NVivo (e.g., Gibson & Zellmer-Bruhn, 2001; see Appendix D)

Occasionally, researchers use more specialized software packages such as the following

TACT (e.g., Gibson & Zellmer-Bruhn, 2001)

TextAnalyst (e.g., Ignatow, 2009; see Appendix C)

Wmatrix (e.g., Sun & Jiang, 2014; see Appendix F)

WordSmith (e.g., Charteris-Black, 2012; see Appendix F)

## Conclusion

Metaphor analysis is widely used in the social sciences and humanities. Researchers analyze metaphorical language to gain insights into groups' cultures and beliefs using a variety of qualitative and mixed methods research designs. Often, researchers use comparative research designs that analyze a group's metaphor use in comparison with another group or with a larger population. Other studies begin with an anomalous, or surprising, pattern of metaphorical language observed in the media or on social media platforms and seek to establish and explain the pattern.

## Key Terms

Analogy   156

Background metaphors   159

Cognitive linguistics   156

Cognitive metaphor theory
 (CMT)   155

Conceptual metaphors   157

Critical metaphor
 analysis   160

Metaphor   155

Simile   156

Source domain   157

Synecdoche   156

Target domain   157

## Highlights

- Metaphor analysis is used widely in the humanities and in social science fields such as anthropology, communications, and sociology.

- Metaphor analysis is generally based on CMT, which posits that language is structured by metaphor at a neural level and that analyzing metaphors can reveal the interpretive schemas shared by members of a group or community.

- Strategies for metaphor analysis research include beginning with an anomalous or unexpected example of metaphorical language, comparing metaphors used by two or more groups in order to answer a research questions, and comparing metaphors used by members of a subculture to metaphors used in mainstream society.

- Although current metaphor analysis research methods rely on human interpretation, computational linguists and other computer scientists are developing new tools for automated metaphor analysis.

## Review Questions

- How do researchers choose between qualitative, mixed methods, and quantitative metaphor analysis techniques?

- What are some challenges in analyzing metaphors in different cultures and subcultures?

## Developing a Research Proposal

If you have already acquired texts to be used as data for your project, carefully read a sample of your data, focusing on metaphorical language. Are there metaphors that are repeated in the text? Is their use widespread? In what situations, and for what purposes, do they seem to be used? Are they unusual metaphors or "dead metaphors" that are commonly used in ordinary language?

Next, choose a metaphor analysis study reviewed in this chapter that is similar to your own research project. Use research databases to access the study and a few studies that cite it. Read all the studies you download carefully, taking notes on their research design and methods. Based on the patterns of metaphorical language you observed in your data, can you design a study that can build from the studies you have read—either by applying their metaphor analysis methods to your data or by adjusting their methods, or combining several of the methods reviewed in this chapter?

## Further Reading

Boroditsky, L. (2000). Metaphoric structuring: Understanding time through spatial metaphors. *Cognition, 75*(1), 1–28.

Carver, T., & Pikalo, J. (2008). *Political language and metaphor: Interpreting and changing the world.* New York, NY: Routledge.

Lakoff, G., & Johnson, M. (1980). *Metaphors we live by.* Chicago, IL: University of Chicago Press.

# Text Mining Methods From Computer Science

## PART V

# 13

# TEXT CLASSIFICATION

## LEARNING OBJECTIVES

The goals of Chapter 13 are to help you to do the following:

1. Describe the task of **text classification**, its history, and applications.
2. Follow the main steps involved in a text classification approach: feature representation and weighting as well as text classification algorithms.
3. Analyze the inner workings of two classification algorithms: **Naive Bayes** and **Rocchio classifier**.
4. Explore available data sets and software packages for text classification.

## INTRODUCTION

Whether you know it or not, you are likely reaping the benefits of text classification several times a day. Consider, for instance, the communication that you do by e-mail: More than half of the e-mails being sent at any given time are spam, yet your inbox probably does not see much spam. The reason for that gap is a spam text classifier that every mail server runs behind the scenes and separates legitimate e-mail from spam. Another example of a text classifier that you likely use daily is that of language recognition: Search engines like Google or Bing use classification techniques to detect the language of your query so that they can direct your query to collections of online documents written in the same language. And the list of examples of text classification in action can continue: text geolocation, opinion classification, document topic detection, and so forth.

How can we automatically build such text classifiers? Of course, reading every incoming document is out of question, and even if that were a possibility, the process of manual labeling would be unscalable and inconsistent. Instead, researchers have developed automatic techniques that are able to learn from history (e.g., a collection of e-mails labeled as spam or nonspam) and therefore predict if a new text should be directed to one's inbox or in the spam folder. This chapter provides an overview of text classification, starting with its early stages of manual labeling and rule-based systems and continuing to the large number of automatic classification methods that we have today.

## WHAT IS TEXT CLASSIFICATION?

Text classification (sometimes also referred to as text categorization) is the task of assigning texts to one or more predefined categories. Formally, given a representation R of a text T and given a fixed set of categories $C = \{C_1, C_2, \ldots, C_n\}$, the task of text classification is to determine a mapping from R to a category in C. This is typically done by learning how to make such mappings from a set of texts that have been already mapped to categories in C. This is referred to as training data and is used to learn associations between their representations and the $C_i$ categories. In the e-mail spam example just given in the previous section, assuming that the representation R used for the texts consists of the words in those texts, a possible association that a classifier would learn could be for instance that *mortgage* and *interest* are more often associated with spam e-mail than legitimate e-mail, whereas *dinner* and *baby* would occur more frequently in nonspam e-mails.

Categories can often be hierarchical, as, for instance, in the case of the categories in Figure 13.1, which represent a possible classification of a number of areas in artificial intelligence.

It is important to differentiate between text classification and **text clustering**. The former refers to the task of grouping texts into categories; however, in text clustering the categories are not known a priori. Given a set of texts, a clustering system will identify that certain texts are more similar to one another than others and should be assigned to the same cluster, but it will not give a name to this cluster. Moreover, the number of clusters that a collection of texts will be split into is often not known. Thus, text classification is often thought of as a supervised task, whereas text clustering is often unsupervised (as with anything, there are exceptions, as there are text classification methods that are unsupervised and text clustering methods that are supervised).

**FIGURE 13.1 ■ Example of Hierarchical Categories**

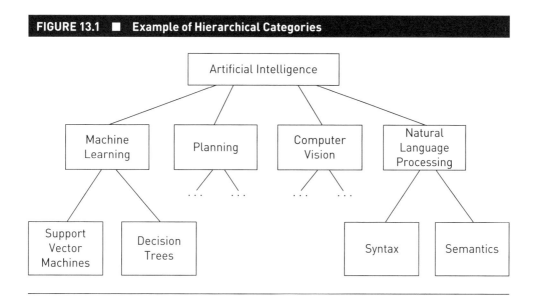

## A Brief History of Text Classification

In the early days, the classification of texts was done manually by "domain experts" who were familiar with the topics of the texts being classified. This was, for instance, the approach taken by Yahoo when creating their "browsing" capability: Each new webpage was manually assigned with one or more categories. As expected, this classification approach was highly accurate, in particular when the data set was relatively small and the team of experts categorizing documents was also small (so as to avoid inconsistency among annotators). But the approach quickly became intractable, as the number of documents that needed to be classified grew to a very large number (webpages in Yahoo's case).

The next step in the history of text classification was rule-based systems, which used queries consisting of combinations of words to determine the category of a text. For instance, if a text included the words *bank* and *money* and *interest*, there could be a rule that would say that this text was part of the financial domain. LexisNexis, for instance, used such rule-based systems, using complex query languages. The accuracy of these systems was generally very high, but they once again suffered from a scalability issue because building and maintaining these rules was an expensive process.

After this, machine learning came into the picture, and supervised or semisupervised learning became the de facto approach for text classification. There are currently numerous algorithms that are available for automatic classification, ranging from nearest neighbor and Naive Bayes to decision trees and support vector machines (SVMs). These systems come at the cost of annotated data, which is required to train the supervised algorithms, but they have the benefit of scalability, as once trained they can be used to classify essentially any amount of unlabeled data.

## BASIC CONCEPTS

*Text classification* is the process of assigning texts to one or more predefined categories.

The set of predefined categories can be organized into hierarchies, in which case we talk about *hierarchical text classification*.

*Text clustering* is the process of grouping texts into clusters of texts based on their similarity. These clusters are often unnamed.

Text classification is typically *supervised*—that is, it assumes a collection of previously labeled texts that can be used for training. Text clustering is typically *unsupervised*, as clusters of similar texts can be identified without input from previously annotated texts.

## APPLICATIONS OF TEXT CLASSIFICATION

Text classification is one of the most widely used applications of text mining or artificial intelligence. The following are just a handful of examples of text classification applied to real-life problems.

### Topic Classification

Topic classification is used to categorize documents by their topic, be it computer science, music, or biology (McCallum & Nigam, 1998). This task is often used to organize web texts (see, for instance, the Open Directory Project [http://dmoztools.net.] where millions of webpages are organized into a hierarchy of categories such as fitness, software, and real estate). Table 13.1 shows one example of a text from the topic of computer science (left) and another from the topic of music (right).

### E-Mail Spam Detection

This is perhaps the most ubiquitous application of text classification, being in use every day by practically all the users of an e-mail service. Spam detectors usually run "behind the scenes" in any e-mail server and run on top of the stream of incoming e-mails to determine

| TABLE 13.1 ■ Examples of Texts Classified by Topic | |
| --- | --- |
| As a discipline, computer science spans a range of topics from theoretical studies of algorithms and the limits of computation to the practical issues of implementing computing systems in hardware and software. The Association for Computing Machinery (ACM), and the IEEE Computer Society (IEEE-CS) identify four areas: (1) theory of computation, (2) algorithms and data structures, (3) programming methodology and languages, and (4) computer elements and architecture. | The notes of the 12-tone scale can be written by their letter names A to G, possibly with a trailing sharp or flat symbol, such as A♯ or B♭. This is the most common way of specifying a note in English speech or written text. In northern and central Europe, the letter system used is slightly different for historical reasons. In these countries' languages, the note called simply B in English (i.e., B♮) is called H, and the note B♭ is named B. |
| Computer Science | Music |

Source: Wikipedia, "Computer Science", https://en.wikipedia.org/wiki/Computer_science and Wikipedia, "Musical Notation", https://en.wikipedia.org/wiki/Musical_notation.

whether an e-mail should be sent to the user's inbox or to the spam folder. This is an application where it is very important to keep the rate of false positives very low even if it comes at the cost of some false negatives. In other words, one would ideally want to avoid losing any legitimate e-mail to the spam folder, even if some spam e-mail makes it to the user's inbox. This constraint also dictates some of the parameter settings used for text classification for spam detection, with only high-confidence spam being filtered out. Table 13.2 shows an example of a legitimate e-mail and a spam e-mail.

| TABLE 13.2 ■ Legitimate E-Mail and Spam E-Mail | |
| --- | --- |
| Hi John, | Dear John Doe, |
| I hope you are doing well. Have you found a job after your graduation? I was wondering if you could tell me where is the web camera that you used for the emotion detection experiments? Is it still in Dr. Yong's lab? I had borrowed it from Prof. Doe in the CSE department, and I should eventually return it to him at some point. | ICISA (International Conference on Information Science and Applications) has been scheduled on May 6–9, 2014, in Seoul, South Korea. The final paper submission date is **February 28th, 2014**. Please make sure to submit your paper before this date! ICISA will be holding its 5th annual conference. ICISA 2014 paper submission system is now open and ready for you to upload your paper. |
| Legitimate E-Mail | Spam E-Mail |

Source: Author's personal collection.

## Sentiment Analysis/Opinion Mining

An application that has received an increasing amount of attention during recent years is that of sentiment analysis (also referred to as opinion mining; Mihalcea, Banea, & Wiebe, 2007; Pang & Lee, 2008; Wiebe, Wilson, & Cardie, 2005). The classification is performed between positive and negative sentiment and is used to detect consumer sentiment for given products (e.g., a positive or a negative review of an iPhone) to monitor a company's brand, to detect product or service issues for targeted customer service, and so on. Table 13.3 shows examples of a positive and a negative review of the movie *Big Hero 6*.

| TABLE 13.3 ■ Positive and Negative Reviews of the Movie *Big Hero 6* | |
| --- | --- |
| I actually wasn't planning to watch this particular movie, until my friends told me it was a good movie and that I should watch it. I decided to try it and see how it goes. I instantly fell in love with Baymax. He's huggable and simply adorable. Along with that, he's a HEALTHCARE companion! It was certainly a HILARIOUS movie, and I enjoyed every last bit of it. . . .All I have to say is that this movie is definitely one worth watching, especially if you like humorous animated film. | I hate this movie for having one of the most cookie-cutter plots imaginable and for trying to build tension where there is none. I am tired of kids' movies trying to be something they're not. You can only have so much drama, because only so many things can possibly happen in a kids' movie. This isn't *Breaking Bad* or *Django*; Baymax isn't going to snap and kill anyone. It just won't happen ever. So why would the movie pretend it could happen. All this fake drama that leads to nothing makes for a very boring and hollow movie. |
| Positive Review | Negative Review |

*Source:* IMDB.com. Zeta-One, http://www.imdb.com/title/tt2245084/reviews and Alexpskywalker, http://www.imdb.com/title/tt2245084/reviews-57.

## Gender Classification

Text classification is also used for tasks aimed at "author profiling"—that is, determining the age, gender, or political orientation of the author of a text (Koppel, Argamon, & Shimoni, 2002; Liu & Mihalcea, 2007). While text classification has also been applied to more traditional texts such as books or other works of fiction, the interest in author profiling has grown with the explosion of social media. It is an interesting task not only for what it achieves but also because it is one of the few examples in artificial intelligence where a computer performs better than a human. Consider, for instance, the example of texts written by a man or a woman illustrated in Table 13.4. As it turns out, people generally have a hard time figuring out if a text was written by a man or a woman, mainly because some of the most useful clues to gender detection consist of function words (such as *we* or *of* ), which we do not naturally pay attention to. Computers instead do better at this task, as they are not used, as we are, to focus their "attention" on content words only and instead can quickly count the function words that are useful for this classification task.

| TABLE 13.4 ■ Texts Written by a Woman and a Man | |
| --- | --- |
| I can go get this stuff. But I try to keep myself on a weekly budget with buying frivolous things. Plus, I unfortunately got a traffic ticket I have to pay off, along with a trip to the doctor this week. That stuff is just being put on hold.<br><br>http://compulsivesammi.blogspot.com | One of the top picks to be McCain's running mate is Louisiana Gov. Bobby Jindal. He's a fascinating guy. Young, Indian-American, conservative, Christian, policy wonk on education and healthcare, part of a new breed of technocratic Reform Republicans like Rudy Guiliani who care more about getting things done than anything else. He may be a little too nerdy for McCain, but I like him.<br><br>http://fearandbloggingcincinnati.blogspot.com |
| Female-Authored Text | Male-Authored Text |

*Sources:* "A Setback," *Compulsively Yours,* May 8, 2015, compulsivesammi.blogspot.com, accessed May 5, 2017; "This Day in History," *Fear and Blogging in Cincinnati,* November 4, 2008, http://fearandbloggingcincinnati.blogspot.com/, accessed May 15, 2017.

## Deception Detection

Yet another difficult task is that of identifying deceits in text (Mihalcea & Strapparava, 2009; Newman, Pennebaker, Berry, & Richards, 2003; Ott, Choi, Cardie, & Hancock, 2011). This has found applications not only in the legal domain but also in the detection of false reviews and deceptive posts on social media. As with author profiling, the linguistic clues that are most useful for the detection of deceit consist of function words (e.g., deceivers use self-referring expressions such as *I* or *we* less often); thus, humans have often very low performance at this task. Table 13.5 shows examples of deceptive and nondeceptive texts.

## Other Applications

Apart from the examples illustrated previously, there are many other applications of text classification. Some additional examples include the classification of texts by their language (e.g., English vs. Chinese vs. Romanian), the classification of the genre of a

| TABLE 13.5 ■ Examples of Truthful and Deceptive Texts | |
|---|---|
| My best friend never gives me a hard time about anything. If we don't see each other or talk to each other for a while, it's not like anyone's mad. We could not see each other for years, and if we met up it would be like nothing happened. A lot of people in life can make you feel like your being judged, and most of the time make you feel that what your doing isn't good enough. My best friend is one of the few people I don't feel that way around. | My best friend is very funny. He's always making jokes and making people laugh. We're such good friends because he can also be very serious when it comes to emotions and relationships. It keeps me from getting too relaxed and making a mistake like taking advantage of our friendship or not making an effort to keep it going. He's a pretty fragile person, and although it can be hard to keep him happy sometimes, it's all the more rewarding. |
| Truthful Text | Deceptive Text |

*Source:* Data collected via Amazon Mechanical Turk, 2008–2009.

text (e.g., editorials versus movie reviews versus news), emotional content detection (e.g., happy versus sad versus angry), classification with respect to a specific dimension of the reader (e.g., interesting to me versus not interesting to me), and many others.

# APPROACHES TO TEXT CLASSIFICATION

The most successful methods for text classification are data-driven, meaning that they rely on collections of manually (or semimanually) annotated texts to automatically learn patterns of associations between words (or other textual clues) and the text classes (or categories). A first required step to enable such automatic classifiers is the representation of texts, addressing questions such as these: What are the clues (or features, or attributes) that are helpful for the task? and What should be the weight assigned to such clues? The second step consists of the actual learning mechanism, with a broad choice of machine-learning algorithms. Finally, when we talk about text classification, we also have to talk about evaluation: How do we know that a certain classification method works better than another? This section provides answers to all these questions.

## Representing Texts for Supervised Text Classification

Most text classification systems use a very high-dimensional feature space consisting of the words in the texts. That is, given a collection of texts, we can extract the *vocabulary* of that collection by identifying all the unique words. The words in the vocabulary will then constitute the feature space; therefore, each text in the collection will be represented as a vector in this space, using weights that represent the importance of a word in a given text.

Consider, for instance, a simple example with just two texts: "today is a beautiful day" and "today is the day." The vocabulary consists of six words (*a, beautiful, day, is, the, today*); thus, the vectors used to represent these texts will all have a length of six. Assuming a very simple weight scheme, which just looks for the presence of a word in a text, the feature vector for the first text will be (1, 1, 1, 1, 0, 1) and for the second text will be (0, 0, 1, 1, 1, 1).

While individual words (also referred to as unigrams) are the most frequently used features for text classification, other features can also be used. For instance, one can also use sequences of two words at a time—bigrams, trigrams, and so on. In the previously given example, the vocabulary of bigrams would be (today_is, is_a, a_beautiful, beautiful_day, is_the, the_day), and the feature vectors for the two texts would be (1, 1, 1, 1, 0, 0) and (1, 0, 0, 0, 0, 1, 1). Of course, the higher the order of the n-grams used to generate the features, the sparser the representations will be.

In addition to word-based features, one can also use word classes to create features for text classification. There are many lexical resources that can be used as a source of word classes, such as WordNet, *Roget's Thesaurus*, or Linguistic Inquiry and Word Count (LIWC; see Chapter 7). In this representation, rather than using individual words, we use classes of words to create each feature. For instance, assuming the class of words WE, including words such as *we, us, ourselves, our*, and so on, and assuming a simple weighting scheme that uses the frequency of words, the value of this feature will be the total number of occurrences of WE words inside the text. Using this technique of creating a cumulative weight for each word class, we can generate feature vectors that include one feature for each class—for example, 80 features if we use LIWC, 700 to 1,000 features if we use *Roget's*, and so on.

### Feature Weighting and Selection

Given the high-dimensional feature space typically used in text classification, **feature weighting** and feature selection play an important role. The question is this: How can we weight features so that we give higher weight to features that are more important for a given text than for others? Intuitively, we would like to give a low weight to words such as *is, a, have,* and *give* instead of high weight to words such as *mining, classroom,* or *history*. Even among these last three words, if we think, for instance, about the topics being discussed in this book, history and classroom should have lower weights than mining.

There are several ways to create feature weights. The simplest method is to use binary weights, which are either 0 or 1 depending on whether a word (or other n-gram) appears in a text or not. Another method is to use the term *frequency*, which counts the number of occurrences of a word in a text. Yet another method is the term frequency inverse document frequency (tf idf), which determines the term frequency of a word, as before, and then it divides it by the total number of texts where that word appears. Finally, a somewhat more advanced weighting method is information gain, which was presented in more detail in Chapter 9.

## Text Classification Algorithms

Once texts are represented as feature vectors, they can be run through any supervised classification algorithm to automatically classify new incoming texts as belonging to one or more categories. Some of these algorithms will also produce a confidence measure associated with the classification, which will indicate the extent to which a certain test item can be accurately classified by the automatic categorizer.

The task of supervised learning was presented in Chapter 9, and many of the algorithms described in that chapter can be directly applied to the classification of texts. For instance, one can use SVMs or instance-based learning (see Chapter 9) to create learning models from the training instances, which can then be applied on the test instances. In this chapter, we present two classifiers that have been more widely used in conjunction with text classification.

### Naive Bayes

Although Naive Bayes is one of the earliest algorithms for text classification, it is still one of the most widely used classification methods. Naive Bayes is based on the Bayes theorem from probability theory, which states the conditional probability of an Event $C$ given an Event $T$.

$$P(C \mid T) = \frac{P(T \mid C)P(C)}{P(T)}$$

The Bayes theorem can be very easily inferred from the probability of joint events. The probability of $C$ and $T$ happening together can be written as $P(C,T) = P(C \mid T)P(T)$ or as $P(C,T) = P(T \mid C)P(C)$. The Bayes theorem follows directly from equating these two different ways of writing $P(C,T)$.

Assuming the feature vector representation of a Text T that we discussed before, let us say $\langle t_1, t_2, \ldots, t_n \rangle$; in text classification, we want to find the Category $C_i$ in $C$ such that it has the maximum probability given text $T$. In other words, we want to find the category that satisfies $C = \underset{C_i \in C}{\operatorname{argmax}} P(C_i \mid t_1, t_2, \ldots, t_n)$. Using the Bayes theorem, it follows that we want to find $C = \underset{C_i \in C}{\mathrm{argmax}} \dfrac{P(t_1, t_2, \ldots, t_n \mid C_i) P(C_i)}{P(t_1, t_2, \ldots, t_n)}$. Given that the nominator is the same, regardless of the Category $C_i$ under consideration, we can rewrite this as $C = \underset{C_i \in C}{\mathrm{argmax}} \, P(t_1, t_2, \ldots, t_n) \mid C_i) P(c_i)$. An important assumption made in the Naive Bayes algorithm (and the reason for the "naive" in its name) is the conditional independence of the features in a text representation. We assume that the features $t_i$ inside a text are independent of each other, which allows us to rewrite the last equation as $C = \underset{C_i \in C}{\mathrm{argmax}} \, P(C_i) \prod_{t_k \in T} P(t_k \mid C_i)$. This final rewrite makes the algorithm tractable and easily computable. We can compute $P(C_i)$ by counting the number of texts in the training data that are labeled with Category $C_i$ and dividing that by the total number of texts in the training data. We can compute $P(t_k \mid C_i)$ by counting the number of texts in the training data that are labeled with Category $C_i$ and include feature $t_k$, out of all the texts in the training data that are labeled with Category $C_i$: $P(C_i) = \dfrac{N(C = C_i)}{N}$ and

$$P(t_k \mid C_i) = \frac{N(T_k = t_k, C = C_i)}{N(C = C_i)}.$$

One final step that is often required is smoothing, which refers to the process of handling cases where there are no observations for a certain event (i.e., zero counts). To address this, the last probability is often rewritten as $P(t_k \mid C_i) = \dfrac{N(T_k = t_k, C = C_i) + 1}{N(C = C_i) + k}$ where $k$ is the size of the vocabulary (unique words) in the training data.

### Rocchio Classifier

The Rocchio classifier builds upon the ideas of the vector-space model used in information retrieval (Salton, 1989), as it uses a measure of similarity between the representation of a test item and the representation of the training items.

In the training stage, the Rocchio classifier builds a prototype vector for each category in C: For each category, it identifies all the texts that are labeled with that category and adds up their feature vectors, thereby creating one feature vector also called the prototype vector for that category.

In the test stage, we calculate the similarity between the feature vector of the test text and each of the prototype vectors for the categories in C. As with the vector-space model in information retrieval, multiple similarity measures can be used, with cosine similarity being the most widespread one. These similarity scores are then used to rank the categories with respect to their relevance to the test text.

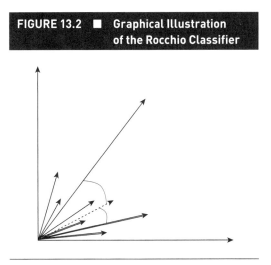

**FIGURE 13.2 ■ Graphical Illustration of the Rocchio Classifier**

Figure 13.2 shows a graphical illustration of the Rocchio classifier: The single-line arrows are the vector representations for the training documents in Category C1, and the double-line arrows are the vector representations for the training documents in Category C2. From these vectors, the prototype vectors are built (the long single- or double-line arrows). The cosine similarity measures between the vector of the test text (the dashed arrow), which results in the selection of the category represented with a double line.

### Bootstrapping in Text Classification

Another aspect of interest in automatic text classification is how to make effective use of raw textual data, which often comes at no cost. Assume, for instance, that we have 100 texts labeled for their topic, and we have 1,000,000 texts that are unlabeled. The question is this: How do we make use of the unlabeled examples to improve the accuracy of a text classifier? There are several answers to this question, but the one that is often used in text classification is **bootstrapping**. This is a method where we train one or more classifiers on the existing training data and automatically label the raw texts. We then select the instances that are labeled with high confidence; move them to the training data set, thus increasing its size; and then repeat the process of training and annotation. The training data set will therefore grow over time and with it the accuracy of the system.

There are different ways of providing a confidence score for the classification. Among them, there is self-training, where a single classifier is used and the confidence score from the learning algorithm itself is used for the bootstrapping process. Another way is cotraining, where two classifiers are used in combination, and the agreement between the classifier is used as an indication of confidence. In this method, only instances where the two classifiers agree are selected for addition into the growing training set.

There are several issues that need to be addressed to apply bootstrapping in process. For instance, an important question is how many items to allow for addition into the training set in each iteration. Another question concerns the number of iterations that the classifier should run, as the general trend in bootstrapping is that the accuracy of the classifier(s) generally goes up for a few iterations, followed by a decrease due to the growing number of errors in the training data set.

Figure 13.3 illustrates the general bootstrapping process. Starting with a seed training data set, one or more classifiers are trained and used to identify items that can be confidently labeled inside a large raw data set. Those items are added to the training data set, and the process is repeated for several iterations.

**FIGURE 13.3 ■ Bootstrapping Text Classification**

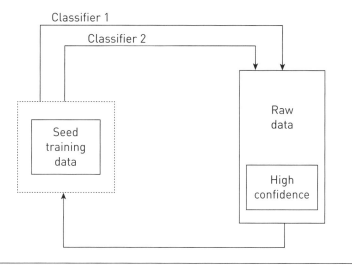

## Evaluation of Text Classification

The methodology to evaluate text classification systems is the same as the evaluation used for general supervised learning methods. The reader is pointed to Chapter 9 to read about evaluation techniques and metrics and about learning curves.

# SOFTWARE FOR TEXT CLASSIFICATION

MALLET (Machine Learning for Language Toolkit) is a collection of Java tools for statistical language processing, which also includes text classification and topic modeling (http://mallet .cs.umass.edu).

AI::Categorizer is an easy-to-use Perl package for text classification, which implements several classification algorithms (http://search .cpan.org/~kwilliams/AI-Categorizer-0.09/lib/ AI/Categorizer.pm).

Natural Language Toolkit (NLTK) is a comprehensive toolkit for natural language processing (NLP), which also includes software for text classification (www.nltk.org).

Weka is a machine-learning toolkit written in Java that can be used for text classification once the input texts have been converted into feature vectors (http://www.cs.waikato.ac.nz/ml/weka).

*(Continued)*

(Continued)

Scikit is a machine-learning toolkit written in Python that can also be used for text classification (http://scikit-learn.org).

Examples of Data Sets for Text Classification

There are several publicly available data sets that can be used to test text classification methods, including the following:

Reuters is a news data set classified into topics (https://kdd.ics.uci.edu/databases/reuters 21578/reuters21578.html).

Deception data sets include several collections of texts explicitly labeled for their truthfulness (http://web.eecs.umich.edu/~mihalcea/downloads .html).

Language identification data sets consist of texts labeled for their language (http://people.eng .unimelb.edu.au/tbaldwin/#resources).

Other data sets, such as the ones described in Chapter 14, can also be used as input to text classifiers.

## Conclusion

Text classification is one of the most widely used computational linguistic methods, with a broad spectrum of applications covering spam detection, language recognition, opinion mining, and deception detection, to name just a few. The key to a successful text classifier is not only the classification algorithm—as most machine-learning algorithms can also be applied to text classification—but also the features used to represent the text and the amount of labeled data available. For those who do not want to invest research or development efforts into the problem of text classification, setting in place a text classifier for a new task can be as simple as gathering a data set representing the task and using one of the off-the-shelves tools for text classification.

## Key Terms

Bootstrapping    182

Feature weighting    179

Naive Bayes    171

Rocchio classifier    171

Text classification    171

Text clustering    172

## Highlights

- Text classification, also referred to as text categorization, is the task of assigning texts to one or more predefined categories.

- Text clustering is a closely related task in which the classification categories are not known a priori. Instead, given a set of texts, a clustering system will group into a cluster those texts that are similar to one another, without naming the resulting clusters.

- Text classification has many real-life applications, including spam detection, age and gender detection, language recognition, topic classification, deception detection, and others.

- Text classification is usually approached in two stages: (1) feature representation and weighting, in which raw words or linguistic resources are used to generate features and (2) supervised learning, in which a machine-learning algorithm such as Naive Bayes, Rocchio classifier (covered in this chapter), SVM, decision trees (covered in Chapter 9) is used to build a predictor for new previously unseen text.

- Bootstrapping is a powerful technique that can build large training data sets for text classification starting with a handful of labeled instances (seeds).

## Discussion Topics

- Think of and discuss an application of text classification that has not been addressed in this chapter. Where could you get the data to power this classification application?

- As the number of iterations in a bootstrapping process increases, the amount of annotated data grows, but at the same time the quality of the annotations decreases. Discuss possible ways to determine the optimal number of bootstrapping iterations.

- Some text classification applications are language specific. For instance, most of the work to date on deception detection has assumed English data. How could we leverage a text classification application built for one language to create a similar application for another language—for example, how could we leverage the existing deception detection classifiers built for English to create a deception classifier for Chinese or Spanish?

# OPINION MINING

## INTRODUCTION

The recent growth of social media has led to an unprecedented amount of opinions being shared on the most diverse topics: People post their reviews of products on websites such as Amazon, share hotel reviews on Expedia or Hotels.com, give travel advice on TripAdvisor, share opinions about parenting on websites such as BabyCenter, discuss political views on news media websites such as CNN or *HuffPost*, and so on and so forth. Not only has it become impossible to track all these opinions being shared online, but making decisions based on such opinions also requires an understanding of their content and the sentiment they express.

A large number of applications can build upon automatic techniques for opinion analysis. For instance, one could imagine a more expressive text-to-speech synthesis that accounts for the sentiment being expressed in the text to be spoken (Alm, Roth, & Sproat, 2005), thus making for more natural human computer interactions. Another application is that of creating timelines of sentiment changes in online forums or news, allowing one to monitor peaks of positive or negative sentiment in public opinion (Balog, Mishne, & de Rijke, 2005; Lloyd, Kechagias, & Skiena, 2005). Customer relationship management (Kim & Hovy, 2006) has also received a significant amount of attention from many companies, where customer forums are being monitored for expressions of negative sentiment about a product or brand, thus allowing the customer service department to intervene in a timely manner. Opinions are also mined from product reviews (Hu & Liu, 2004), which can inform an individual about the pros and cons of a product she is considering purchasing or can inform the companies themselves about the strong and weak points of their products. Other applications that found benefits in the use of opinion mining are question answering (Yu & Hatzivassiloglou, 2003), conversation summarization (Carenini et al., 2008), and text semantic analysis (Esuli & Sebastiani, 2006a; Wiebe & Mihalcea, 2006).

## WHAT IS OPINION MINING?

An important kind of information that is conveyed in many types of written and spoken discourse is the mental or emotional state of the writer or speaker or some other entity referenced in the discourse. News articles, for example, often report emotional responses to a story in addition to the facts. Editorials, reviews, weblogs, and political speeches convey the opinions, beliefs, or intentions of the writer or speaker. A student engaged in a tutoring session may express his or her understanding or uncertainty.

Opinions are expressions of private states, such as emotions, sentiments, evaluations, beliefs, and speculations in natural language. Opinions have attributes, including who is expressing the opinion, the type(s) of attitude being expressed, about whom or what the opinion is being expressed, the sentiment (or polarity) of the opinion (i.e., whether it is positive or negative), and so on.

Opinion mining is defined as the task of identifying such private states in language. Opinion mining is usually divided into two main subtasks: (1) **subjectivity analysis**, which identifies if a text contains an opinion, and correspondingly labels the text as either subjective or objective, and (2) **sentiment analysis**, which further classifies an opinion (or subjective text) as either positive, negative, or neutral. For example, consider the following sentence:

*The choice of Miers was praised by the Senate's top Democrat, Harry Reid of Nevada.*

## RESEARCH IN THE SPOTLIGHT
### Studying Mood in the Humanities

Acerbi, A., Lampos, V., Garnett, P., & Bentley, A. (2013, March 20). The expression of emotions in 20th century books." *PLOS ONE.* Retrieved from http://journals.plos.org/plosone/article?id=10.1371/journal.pone.0059030

In this article, a team of anthropologists and computer scientists report trends in the usage of "mood" words in 20th-century English-language books. Alberto Acerbi and his colleagues used a data set provided by Google that includes word frequencies in approximately 4% of all books published up to 2008. The results show distinct historical periods of positive and negative moods, a general decrease in emotion-related words through time and that in books American English has become decidedly more "emotional" than British English in the past half-century.

Specialized resource used:

WordNet-Affect

http://wndomains.fbk.eu/wnaffect.html

---

In this sentence, the phrase "was praised by" indicates that an opinion is being expressed. The opinion, according to the writer of the sentence, is being expressed by Reid, and it is about the choice of Miers, who was nominated to the Supreme Court by President Bush in October 2005. The type of the attitude is a sentiment (an evaluation, emotion, or judgment), and the polarity is positive (Wilson, 2008).

We can judge the subjectivity and sentiment (or polarity) of texts at several different levels. At the document level, we can ask if a text includes an opinion and, if so, whether that opinion is mainly positive or negative. We can perform more fine-grained analysis and ask if a sentence contains any subjectivity. For instance, consider the following examples from Wilson (2008). The first sentence that follows is subjective (and has positive polarity), but the second one is objective, because it does not contain any subjective expressions:

*He spins a riveting plot, which grabs and holds the reader's interest.*

*The notes do not pay interest.*

Even further, individual expressions may be judged—for example, that *spins, riveting,* and *interest* in the first sentence just given are subjective expressions. A more interesting example appears in this sentence: Cheers to Timothy Whitfield for the wonderfully horrid visuals. While the word *horrid* would be listed as having negative polarity in a word-level subjectivity lexicon, in this context, it is being used positively: The words *wonderfully horrid* express a positive sentiment toward the visuals (similarly, *cheers* expresses a positive sentiment toward *Timothy Whitfield*).

We can also classify word *senses* according to their subjectivity and polarity. Consider, for example, the following two senses of *interest* from WordNet (Miller, 1995):

> *"Interest, involvement—(a sense of concern with and curiosity about someone or something; 'an interest in music')"*

> *"Interest—a fixed charge for borrowing money; usually a percentage of the amount borrowed; 'how much interest do you pay on your mortgage?'"*

The first sense is subjective, with positive polarity. But the second sense is not (non-subjective senses are called objective senses)—it does not refer to a private state. Word- and sense-level subjectivity lexicons are important because they are useful resources for *contextual subjectivity analysis* (Wilson, 2008)—recognizing and extracting private state expressions in an actual text or dialogue.

## BASIC CONCEPTS

An *opinion* is the expression of a *private state*, such as an emotion, a sentiment, an evaluation, a belief, or a speculation.

*Opinion mining* is the task of identifying opinions in text. Opinion mining is usually performed in two stages: (1) *subjectivity analysis*, in which opinions are identified, and *sentiment analysis*,

in which an opinion is classified according to its polarity (positive, negative, neutral).

Subjectivity and sentiment analysis can be performed at different *levels of granularity*: documents, sentences, words or phrases, and word senses.

## RESOURCES FOR OPINION MINING

There are two main types of resources used in opinion mining: (1) lexicons, which consist of extensive listings of words and phrases annotated with a subjectivity, sentiment, and/or emotion labels, and (2) corpora, which are collections of sentences or short documents labeled for subjectivity or sentiment. These resources constitute the foundations for automatic supervised or unsupervised methods to identify opinions in text, as described in the following section.

## Lexicons

One of the most frequently used lexicons is perhaps the subjectivity and sentiment lexicon provided with the **OpinionFinder** distribution (Wiebe, Wilson, & Cardie, 2005).

The lexicon was compiled from manually developed resources augmented with entries learned from corpora. It contains 6,856 unique entries, out of which 990 are multiword expressions. The entries in the lexicon have been labeled for part of speech as well as for reliability—those that appear most often in subjective contexts are *strong* clues of subjectivity, while those that appear less often, but still more often than expected by chance, are labeled *weak*. Each entry is also associated with a **polarity label**, indicating whether the corresponding word or phrase is positive, negative, or neutral. To illustrate, consider the following entry from the OpinionFinder lexicon *type=strongsubj word1=agree pos1=verb mpqapolarity=weakpos*, which indicates that the word *agree* when used as a verb is a strong clue of subjectivity and has a polarity that is weakly positive.

Another lexicon that has been often used in polarity analysis is the **General Inquirer project** (Stone, 1968). It is a dictionary of about 10,000 words grouped into about 180 categories, which have been widely used for content analysis. It includes semantic classes (e.g., animate, human), verb classes (e.g., negatives, becoming verbs), cognitive orientation classes (e.g., causal, knowing, perception), and others. Two of the largest categories in the General Inquirer are the valence classes, which form a lexicon of 1,915 positive words and 2,291 negative words.

**SentiWordNet** (Esuli & Sebastiani, 2006b) is a resource for opinion mining built on top of WordNet, which assigns each synset in WordNet with a score triplet (positive, negative, and objective), indicating the strength of each of these three properties for the words in the synset. The SentiWordNet annotations were automatically generated, starting with a set of manually labeled synsets. Currently, SentiWordNet includes an automatic annotation for all the synsets in WordNet, totaling more than 100,000 words.

## Corpora

Subjectivity and sentiment annotated corpora are useful not only as a means to train automatic classifiers but also as resources to extract opinion mining lexicons. For instance, a large number of the entries in the OpinionFinder lexicon mentioned in the previous section were derived based on a large opinion-annotated corpus.

The MPQA corpus (Wiebe et al., 2005) was collected and annotated as part of a 2002 workshop on multiperspective question answering (thus, the MPQA abbreviation). It is a collection of 535 English-language news articles from a variety of news sources manually annotated for opinions and other private states (i.e., beliefs, emotions, sentiments, speculations). The corpus was originally annotated at clause and phrase level, but sentence-level annotations associated with the data set can also be derived via simple heuristics (Wiebe et al., 2005).

Another manually annotated corpus is the collection of newspaper headlines created and used during the recent SemEval task on "Affective Text'" (Strapparava & Mihalcea, 2007). The data set consists of 1,000 test headlines and 200 development headlines, each of them annotated with the six Ekman emotions (anger, disgust, fear, joy, sadness, surprise) and their polarity orientation (positive, negative).

Two other data sets, both of them covering the domain of movie reviews, are a polarity data set consisting of 1,000 positive and 1,000 negative reviews as well as a subjectivity data set consisting of 5,000 subjective and 5,000 objective sentences. Both data sets were introduced in Pang and Lee (2004) and have been used to train opinion mining classifiers. Given the domain specificity of these collections, they were found to lead to accurate classifiers for data belonging to the same or similar domains. More recently, a much larger movie review data set has been introduced (Maas et al., 2011), consisting of 50,000 full-length reviews collected from the IMDB website.

Research in sentiment analysis has also benefited from the growing number of product reviews available online, on websites such as Amazon, which can be used to build very large sentiment annotated data sets (Hu & Liu, 2004). Such reviews are usually available in many languages, thus enabling the construction of sentiment analysis tools in languages other than English (Nakagawa, Inui, & Kurohashi, 2010).

## RESEARCH IN THE SPOTLIGHT
### Eshbaugh-Soha's Study of Presidential News Coverage

Eshbaugh-Soha, M. (2010). The tone of local presidential news coverage. *Political Communication*, 27(2), 121–140.

In this study from 2010, the political scientist Eshbaugh-Soha analyzed the emotional tone of local news coverage of the presidency. Eshbaugh-Soha used theories of media politics, based primarily on the profit-seeker model of news coverage, to explore the impact of newspaper characteristics, audience preferences, and story characteristics on local newspaper coverage of the presidency. Based on a sample of 288 stories taken from the Bill Clinton and George W. Bush administrations, he demonstrated that everyday local newspaper coverage of the presidency is slightly more negative than positive and that audience support for the president, newspaper resources, and corporate ownership affect the tone of local newspaper coverage of the presidency.

# APPROACHES TO OPINION MINING

There are a large number of approaches that have been developed to date for sentiment and subjectivity analysis in English. The methods can be roughly classified into two categories: (1) rule-based systems, relying on manually or semiautomatically constructed lexicons, and (2) machine-learning classifiers, trained on opinion-annotated corpora.

Among the rule-based systems, one of the most frequently used is OpinionFinder (Wiebe et al., 2005), which automatically annotates the subjectivity of new text based on the presence (or absence) of words or phrases in a large lexicon.

## RESEARCH IN THE SPOTLIGHT
### Hand Coding Sentiment in Media

Bail, C. (2012). The fringe effect: Civil society organizations and the evolution of media discourse about Islam since the September 11th attacks. *American Sociological Review*, 77(6), 855–879.

The sociologist Bail analyzed sentiment in newspaper data using hand coding and plagiarism detection software (see also Corley, Collins, & Calvin, 2011). Their goal was to study how civil society organizations deploy messages that resonate with social discourses and also create cultural change. Bail developed an evolutionary theory of how discursive fields settle after major historical events and used plagiarism detection software to compare 1,084 press releases about Muslims produced by 120 U.S. civil society organizations to 50,407 newspaper articles and television transcripts produced between 2001 and 2008. Although most organizations deployed pro-Muslim discourses after the September 11th attacks, Bail showed how anti-Muslim fringe organizations came to influence the mass media through displays of anger and fear.

Specialized software used:

WCopyfind plagiarism detection software

http://plagiarism.bloomfieldmedia.com/word press/2014/06/26/new-release-wcopyfind-4-1-3

Gephi network visualization software

https://gephi.org

Briefly, the OpinionFinder high-precision classifier relies on three main heuristics to label subjective and objective sentences: (1) If two or more strong subjective expressions occur in the same sentence, the sentence is labeled *subjective*; (2) if no strong subjective expressions occur in a sentence, and at most two weak subjective expressions occur in the previous, current, and next sentence combined, then the sentence is labeled *objective*; (3) otherwise, if none of the previous rules apply, the sentence is labeled *unknown*. The classifier uses the clues from a subjectivity lexicon and the rules mentioned previously to harvest subjective and objective sentences from a large amount of unannotated text; the data are then used to automatically identify a set of extraction patterns, which are then used iteratively to identify a larger set of subjective and objective sentences. In addition to the high-precision classifier, OpinionFinder also includes a high-coverage classifier. This high-precision classifier is used to automatically produce an English labeled data set, which can then be used to train a high-coverage subjectivity classifier. When evaluated on the MPQA corpus, the high-precision classifier was found to lead to a precision of 86.7% and a recall of 32.6%, whereas the high-coverage classifier has a precision of 79.4% and a recall of 70.6%.

Another unsupervised system worth mentioning, this time based on automatically labeled words or phrases, is the one proposed in Turney (2002), which builds upon earlier work by Hatzivassiloglou and McKeown (1997). Starting with two reference words—*excellent* and *poor*—Turney classified the polarity of a word or phrase by measuring the fraction between its **pointwise mutual information (PMI)** with the positive reference (excellent) and the PMI with the negative reference (poor). The PMI of two words $w_1$ and $w_2$ is defined as the probability of seeing the two words together divided by the probability of seeing each individual word: $PMI(w_1,w_2) = p(w_1,w_2)/p(w_1)p(w_2)$. The polarity scores assigned in this way are used to automatically annotate the polarity of product, company, or movie reviews. Note that this system is completely unsupervised and thus particularly appealing for application to other languages.

When annotated corpora is available, machine-learning methods are a natural choice for building subjectivity and sentiment classifiers. For example, Wiebe, Bruce, & O'Hara (1999) used a data set manually annotated for subjectivity to train a machine-learning classifier, which led to significant improvements over the baseline. Similarly, starting with semiautomatically constructed data sets, Pang and Lee (2004) built classifiers for subjectivity annotation at sentence level, as well as a classifier for sentiment annotation at document level. To the extent that annotated data are available, such machine-learning classifiers can be used equally well in other languages.

Recently, a sentiment analysis tool based on deep learning techniques has been introduced in conjunction with a Sentiment Treebank (Socher et al., 2013), where fine-grained sentiment labels at word and phrase level are used together with a parse tree to compose the sentiment of a text. Unlike most of the earlier methods that assumed a text to have a consistent sentiment, this compositional method allows for changes of sentiment inside a text, as in "I generally like the phone, but I am not very fond of the tiny keyboard," where a positive and a negative sentiment are mixed in the same sentence.

While much of the research work to date on opinion mining has been applied to English, work on other languages is growing, including Japanese (Takamura, Inui, & Okumura, 2006), Chinese (Zagibalov & Carroll, 2008), German (Kim & Hovy, 2006), and Romanian (Mihalcea, Banea, & Wiebe, 2007).

# SOFTWARE AND RESOURCES FOR OPINION MINING

Many of the resources and tools described in this chapter are publicly available, even if in some cases their availability is restricted to research use only. Lexicons that are publicly available include the following:

OpinionFinder includes words and phrases that are indicators of subjectivity, along with a polarity markup (http://mpqa.cs.pitt.edu/opinionfinder).

General Inquirer includes lists of words grouped into categories reflective of psycholinguistic processes, human behaviors, named entities, and others. It includes two extensive lists of positive and negative words (www.wjh.harvard.edu/~inquirer).

SentiWordNet is a resource built on top of WordNet, with automatic and semiautomatic sentiment annotations for a large number of word senses (http://sentiwordnet.isti.cnr.it).

WordNet-Affect is another extension of Word-Net, which includes affective labels assigned to word senses. Of specific interest are the six emotion categories: (1) anger, (2) disgust, (3) fear, (4) joy, (5) sadness, and (6) surprise (http://wndomains.fbk.eu/wnaffect.html).

Corpora publicly available, among others, are as follows:

Movie review data set (www.cs.cornell.edu/people/pabo/movie-review-data)

Movie review data set (large; http://ai.stanford.edu/~amaas/data/sentiment)

Product review data sets (https://www.cs.uic.edu/~liub/FBS/sentiment-analysis.html#datasets)

MPQA (http://mpqa.cs.pitt.edu/corpora/mpqa_corpus)

Emotion and sentiment labeled data (http://web.eecs.umich.edu/~mihalcea/affectivetext)

Subjectivity and sentiment analysis tools include the following:

OpinionFinder, which in addition to an extensive lexicon, also includes software for subjectivity analysis (http://mpqa.cs.pitt.edu/opinionfinder)

Deep learning for sentiment analysis implementing recursive neural networks for sentiment analysis (https://nlp.stanford.edu/sentiment)

Provided a collection of annotated data, tools for subjectivity or sentiment analysis can be easily built by applying off-the-shelf machine-learning packages such as the following:

Weka (http://www.cs.waikato.ac.nz/ml/weka)

Scikit (http://scikit-learn.org/stable)

## Conclusion

Opinion mining is one of the fastest growing areas within the fields of computational linguistics and social sciences, having received a lot of attention not only from the research communities but also from the commercial enterprises where opinion mining has found many practical applications. Simple techniques can work remarkably well, given the appropriate set of resources; thus, the application of opinion mining to new problems, domains, or languages often starts with the development of resources. For those who do not want to depart from the typical scenarios (e.g., sentence-level sentiment analysis, or product review classification), a large number of resources and tools exist.

## Key Terms

General Inquirer project   191
OpinionFinder   191
Opinion mining   187

Pointwise mutual information (PMI)   194
Polarity label   191
Sentiment analysis   188

SentiWordNet   191
Subjectivity analysis   188
WordNet-Affect   196

## Highlights

- Opinions are expressions of private states, such as emotions, sentiments, evaluations, beliefs, and speculations in natural language. Opinions have attributes, including who is expressing the opinion, the type(s) of attitude being expressed, about whom or what the opinion is being expressed, the sentiment (or polarity) of the opinion.

- Opinion mining has a wide number of applications, including mining of product review, name branding, customer relationship management, political polls based on social media, text-to-speech synthesis, mood and personality analysis, and others.

- Opinion mining is usually divided into two main subtasks: (1) subjectivity analysis, which identifies if a text contains an opinion, and (2) sentiment analysis, which classifies an opinion as either positive, negative, or neutral.

- The main resources used for opinion mining are lexicons (e.g., OpinionFinder, General Inquirer, SentiWordNet, **WordNet-Affect**) and subjectivity and sentiment annotated corpora (e.g., movie reviews, product reviews, MPQA).

- The main approaches to opinion mining are rule-based (using lexicons) and data-driven (using annotated data and lexicons).

## Discussion Topics

- What are the trade-offs between rule-based sentiment classifiers that rely on lexicons and data-driven approaches based on annotated corpora?

- Think of and discuss a new application of opinion mining that was not addressed in this chapter.

- Try to identify connections between opinion mining and political science. What are interesting areas of investigation that make use of opinion mining and are relevant to topics of interest to political scientists?

# 15

# INFORMATION EXTRACTION

## LEARNING OBJECTIVES

The goals of Chapter 15 are to help you to do the following:

1. Define the task of **information extraction (IE)** and its applications.
2. Explain entity and **relation extraction**.
3. Familiarize yourself with more advanced topics, such as web IE and **template filling**.
4. Learn about existing software and data sets for IE.

## INTRODUCTION

Concrete pieces of information, such as names of entities or organizations, or the relations between them, are often buried in unstructured text. Consider, for instance, the following sentence: "Virgin America CEO David Cush said Thursday that there will be 'continued fare wars' as American Airlines and Delta fight back against the discounters." Despite being so short, this text includes mentions of several entities—for example, organization names, Virgin America, American Airlines, and Delta; a person's name, David Cush; and a time entity of Thursday. We can also identify the "CEO-of" relation between David Cush and Virgin America. An event is also described in the text: "fight back against the discounters." As this example illustrates, there are several pieces of structured information that can be extracted from this unstructured text, including entities, events, and relations.

IE (information extraction) is the task of extracting structured information from unstructured data. The type of information to be extracted is usually predefined—for example, entities such as people or locations, events such as airline fair increases, or relations such as "capital of" relations between cities and countries. More recently, systems aiming at "open IE" (or web IE), where the information to be extracted is not predefined, have also started to gain attention.

IE systems have many practical applications, which usually aim at organizing information in a way that is useful for further analysis tools or for people. IE systems can, for instance, be used to obtain names of diseases, symptoms, or drugs; companies and their CEOs; professor names and the universities where they teach; and so on.

In this chapter, we review the main directions of research focusing on the development of IE methods and tools. Specifically, we address in detail the topics of entity and relation extraction, we overview recent work in web IE, and also discuss the task of template filling that combines multiple information extractors together.

# BASIC CONCEPTS

*Information extraction (IE)* is the task of extracting structured information such as entities, events, or relations from unstructured data.

*Entity extraction* is a subtask of IE that targets the identification of instances of a specific type, including named types, such as people or locations, or general semantic types, such as animals or colors.

*Relation extraction* is another subtask of IE that aims to identify relationships between entities such as "capital of," sibling, and so forth.

*Web (open) information extraction (IE)* is a recently defined task that aims to perform IE at scale, without the need to predefine the entities or relationships that are being extracted.

## ENTITY EXTRACTION

An important goal of IE is to identify instances of specific types in text, where a "type" could range from a person's name or a location, to all the entities that fall under a semantic category such as "animal" or "color" or to any specific events such as "rock concerts."

A well-defined and studied subclass of IE is **named entity recognition (NER)**, which aims to identify proper names that can be classified under a certain type. Common NER tasks are the recognition of persons, locations, and organizations, but there are also other more specialized tasks such as the recognition of composer names, or computer science organizations. For instance, Table 12.1 shows examples of named entities, along with their type.

One approach to NER is to first compile a set of representative seeds for the type to be identified in text—for example, Microsoft, Bloomberg, and Reuters are possible examples of organization names. Alternatively, and perhaps more commonly, one can start with a collection of texts manually annotated with the target named entity—for example, a collection of documents where all the organization names are explicitly labeled. A list of seeds can then be compiled from this labeled data set by extracting all the entities marked in the text. Given this starting point, one can locate the seeds inside new unannotated text and therefore learn rules that are good indicators of the presence of these seeds, such as "___, Inc." or "___ company" or "work at ___," which are patterns that are associated with the occurrence of organization names. These patterns in turn can be used to identify additional organization examples—for example, an occurrence such as "I work at Google" will identify Google as a new example of an organization, and it will be added to the list of organization names. The enlarged set of examples can once again be applied on text to learn new patterns, and so on. This is referred to as a **bootstrapping** process, where a list of organization names (or another named entity) and a list of patterns or rules to identify such organization names are incrementally learned from text. This process is similar to the one represented in Figure 13.3.

One danger with such bootstrapping methods is the infiltration of erroneous examples, which can lead to erroneous patterns, and consequently result in even more errors. The solution often used to address this is a scoring mechanism applied both to named entity examples and to patterns on a prelabeled collection. For instance, assuming the availability of a collection of texts previously labeled with all the named entities of interest, when learning a new pattern one can measure how many times that pattern correctly identifies the target named entities versus how many times that same pattern identifies other fragments of text. The patterns are then ranked in reverse order of their score, and only those that pass a certain threshold of "correctness" are allowed in the bootstrapping process.

| TABLE 15.1  ■  Examples of Named Entities | | |
| --- | --- | --- |
| **Type** | **Category examples** | **Examples** |
| PERSON | individuals, small groups | John Smith, Mrs. Jay |
| ORGANIZATION | companies, religious groups, political parties | Microsoft, Democratic Party |
| LOCATION | countries, cities, rivers | Romania, Washington, D.C. |

Similar to this NER process, one can also build IE systems that learn semantic classes—for example, learn all the occurrences of animals or colors in a text (Riloff & Jones, 1999). Unlike NER, this IE task does not have some of the surface clues that named entities would have (e.g., spelling with an uppercase). Instead, the learning of semantic classes can benefit from the availability of dictionaries that include extensive word lists (e.g., WordNet or *Roget's*, which include examples of animals, colors, etc.), which can be used as starting seeds for the bootstrapping process. Moreover, a similar bootstrapping approach can be used to identify events in text, such as rock concerts.

An alternative approach for IE is to use machine learning to automatically classify whether a word is at the beginning (B), inside (I), or outside (O) a piece of relevant information that is to be extracted. Once again, this approach presumes the availability of a collection of documents that have been previously annotated for the information to be extracted. For instance, given the text "I saw Mr. Jones at the market," and assuming we want to extract people names—that is, "Mr. Jones" in our example, the word *Mr.* will be labeled as B (i.e., it is at the beginning of the sequence "Mr. Jones"); the word *Jones* will be labeled as I; and all the other words will be labeled as O. With this formulation, we have a typical classification problem, where we need to assign a label to each word in a text. This classifier will implicitly learn the words that are often found inside relevant information (e.g., "Mr.") and the words that are found in the immediate context (the patterns surrounding the relevant information). While in principle, any machine-learning algorithm could be used to perform this classification (see Chapter 9), the method that was generally found to work best is conditional random fields (CRFs; McCallum & Li, 2003).

The evaluation of such entity extractors is often done by applying the IE system on a collection of texts that have been manually annotated for the entities of interest. On such a data set, one can measure the accuracy, precision, and recall of the system. For more information on these measures, see Chapter 9.

Alternatively, when IE targets the extraction of semantic classes, which consist of finite even if large sets of words, one can use extensive listings of such words from existing resources (e.g., a listing of all the animals as appearing in places such as WordNet or *Roget's*) and perform accuracy, precision, and recall evaluations against these listings.

## RELATION EXTRACTION

Entities are often connected by relations—for example, "company X is located in city Y," which reflects a "location" relation between X and Y, or "X is the sister of Y," which reflects a sibling relation between X and Y. The process of identifying these relationships between entities is called relation extraction, and it is another facet of IE.

The typical formulation of this problem assumes that two entities have been already identified, and the question is whether a certain relation holds between them. While the problem may seem simpler, as we mainly label a pair of entities as either yes (there is a relation) or no (there is not), in reality relation extraction is more difficult than **entity extraction** as it encompasses a larger number of factors that contribute to a decision.

Similar to entity extraction, a common approach to relation extraction is to first annotate a collection of documents with the relations of interest and then train a machine-learning system to identify these relations. In addition to attributes that characterize each of the entities in the relation—for example, the tokens that are part of the entities, or their syntactic/semantic roles—there are also attributes that describe the connection between the entities, usually obtained by extracting the links from a syntactic parse tree or other graphical representation of the text. Given these attributes that model all the candidate pairs of entities (perhaps constrained by a maximum acceptable distance between them), some of which are connected by relations, and some of which are not, a classifier can be trained to automatically determine if a relation exists between two given entities.

## WEB INFORMATION EXTRACTION

The web has brought both challenges and opportunities for the task of IE. Importantly, the very large scale of web data is both an asset, in terms of providing large amounts of instances to train and bootstrap IE systems and in terms of providing data redundancy for quality verification, as well as a drawback as the web brings a significant amount of noise in the form of errors, ill formed texts, heterogeneous formats, and so on.

There are several web scale IE systems that have been built to date. For the purpose of illustration, we briefly describe two of them.

The first system is KnowItAll (Etzioni et al., 2004), which extracts facts and relations from the web. The system is seeded with information obtained from an ontology, along with a few generic templates, which it then uses to create text extraction rules. For instance, the general template "NounPhrase1 such as NounPhraseList" can be applied on text together with some seeds such as Paris and London are cities to infer a generic syntactic patterns of the form "cities such as <?>" that can be used to extract additional city names. Note that the template rules are generic and domain independent and therefore can be automatically instantiated for the extraction of various entities (e.g., cities, countries, colors). Queries formed from its text extraction rules are run against a search engine, and the information obtained is validated by a statistical module in KnowItAll that assesses the correctness likelihood for each piece of IE. The information is then stored in a database for further analysis. While the initial version of KnowItAll included a little over 50,000 facts, follow-ups such as ReVerb (Fader, Soderland, & Etzioni, 2011) and TextRunner (Banko, Cafarella, Soderland, Broadhead, & Etzioni, 2007) had significantly larger coverage including more than 3 million entities and 600,000 relation extractions, among other knowledge pieces.

The second web system is Never-Ending Language Learning (NELL; Carlson et al., 2010), which is another **web (open) information extraction (IE)** system that creates candidate "beliefs" by processing a very large number of webpages, and it then automatically assesses the confidence of these beliefs before committing them to a database. A characteristic of NELL is that it uses bootstrapping to improve its own performance over time, by using information it learned to build even more accurate information extractors. Examples of relations learned by NELL are "WWCS is a radio station" or "haori is a kind of clothing." At the time of this writing, the system has accumulated close to 50 million facts, out of which it has high confidence in almost 3 million facts.

## TEMPLATE FILLING

There are many situations when the pieces of information being extracted are related to one another in that they represent different aspects of the same type of situation or event. For instance, if we speak about a terrorist attack, relevant information would consist of location of the attack, the date and time of the attack, the group behind the attack, the number of victims, and so on. These aspects of an event are often referred to as slots, and they form a template for that event. The process of finding the values for each of the slots is called slot filling, and the overall process of filling in the values for all the aspects in a template is called template filling.

In most cases, separate IE algorithms can be trained following the same set of steps as outlined before: One first annotates a set of documents with the information of interest (i.e., each of the slots marked explicitly in text) or identifies a set of seed values for each slot. A classifier is then trained to recognize patterns that are associated with these slot occurrences, finally followed by a bootstrapping process that automatically grows the lists of patterns and possible values for each slot.

Recent work has also considered the joint application of the IE algorithms for the individual slots, with the idea that there might be some dependencies between the slots. For instance, the location of terrorist attacks might have some association with the groups behind the attacks and so forth. This is referred to as joint aspect learning, or joint slot filling (Mukherjee & Liu, 2012).

## SOFTWARE AND DATA SETS FOR INFORMATION EXTRACTION

GATE (General Architecture for Text Engineering) is a collection of open source tools for natural language processing (NLP), including an extensive component for information extraction (IE) called ANNIE. The suite also includes specialized IE tools for biomedical text or tweets (https://gate.ac.uk).

ReVerb is an implementation of open IE tools (http://reverb.cs.washington.edu).

DeepDive is an open source system that extracts entities and relations from unstructured input (http://deepdive.stanford.edu).

MITIE is a collection of tools for IE, including pre-trained tools for named entity recognition (NER) and relation extraction, as well as tools for training custom extractors (https://github.com/mit-nlp/MITIE).

## Conclusion

IE is one of the core tasks in text mining, used to transform unstructured text into structured data. While some of the most common tools for IE focus on a few entity types for which large amounts of training data are available (e.g., locations), the existing methods for IE can easily be customized to new types. Importantly, many of the approaches that have been proposed to address this task are amenable to bootstrapping, which requires only small amounts of annotated examples coupled with large amounts of unlabeled data. This chapter overviewed the main approaches for IE, covering methods for entity extraction and relation extraction, as well as approaches aimed to process information on a large-scale, often referred to as web (open) IE.

## Key Terms

Bootstrapping   201

Entity extraction   203

Information
    extraction (IE)   199

Relation extraction   199

Template filling   199

Web (open) information
    extraction (IE)   204

## Highlights

- IE is the task of extracting structured information from unstructured data. The type of information to be extracted typically consists of entities, events, or relations and are often predefined.

- IE systems have many practical applications, which usually aim at organizing information in a way that is useful for further analysis tools or for people.

- Entity extraction aims to identify instances of a specific type, including named types, such as people or locations, or general semantic types, such as animals or colors.

- Relation extraction is another facet of IE and aims to identify relationships between entities.

- Scaling up IE has resulted in web (open) IE, where the entities and relationships between entities are not predefined but rather discovered in an unsupervised way.

## Discussion Topics

- Describe the patterns that an IE could learn for the goal of extracting (a) animal names, (b) programming language names, and (c) birthday years of famous people.

- Discuss the advantages and disadvantages of web IE with respect to traditional IE.

- Consider the following research project: We want to identify the symptoms and treatments of a given set of illnesses. How would you go about constructing a solution for this project? (Hints: Think about the data sets required. Think about how to use IE on these data sets.)

# 16

# ANALYZING TOPICS

## LEARNING OBJECTIVES

The goals of Chapter 16 are to help you to do the following:

1. Describe the theoretical foundations of topic modeling methods.
2. Understand the statistical methods used in **topic models**.
3. Discover how social scientists have used topic models in their research.
4. Explore topic modeling software tools.

## INTRODUCTION

Conversations can be analyzed in terms of narratives (see Chapter 10), themes (see Chapter 11), and metaphors (see Chapter 12). Conversations can also be analyzed in a more straightforward way not in terms of *how* people are talking but rather in terms of *what* it is that they are talking about in the first place. For example, consider how the topics covered in newspapers change over time. As events unfold, different news outlets with different audiences, news formats, and business strategies will discuss different topics, choosing to emphasize some over others. Influential news outlets, as well as powerful individuals such as politicians and celebrities, are able to influence the topics that are covered in the news. In turn, the topics covered by the media will influence the opinions and attitudes of readers and viewers. And the public's opinions and attitudes will inform their voting behaviors and the decisions made by elected officials.

As another example of the importance of conversation topics, imagine that after graduating college you were to accept a job offer from a marketing company. To be successful in your new job, you will not only have to learn the technical requirements of the position. You will also have to fit in with your new coworkers, and that process of fitting in will require a change in the topics you customarily talk about. As a university student socializing with your friends, you may have discussed topics like music, movies, classes, assignments, professors, relationships, and parties. But in your new job, some of these topics will change; inevitably, when socializing with your coworkers you will talk about topics such as work projects, careers, clients, supervisors, vacation plans, mortgages, and all sorts of other topics, some of which are related to the topics you discussed in your student days and some of which are new and different. Your skill in discussing the topics that circulate in your work environment will be related to your previous life experiences in school and other settings, and this skill is of interest to social scientists interested in careers, professions, and inequality.

How can we be confident that we know what topics are being discussed within a community or social group? Reading thousands of newspaper articles or interview transcripts is too time-consuming for most researchers. And because it depends on subjective interpretation of texts, reading alone is seen as too open to biased interpretations to be considered scientifically valid. Instead of simply reading large collections of texts to determine the topics that are discussed in them, researchers have in recent years turned to topic models, which are statistical models for identifying what combinations of topics are discussed within a social group and how the topics discussed change over time. This chapter provides an overview of the theory and practice of topic modeling, which has recently caught on with a wide range of researchers in the social sciences and humanities.

## WHAT ARE TOPIC MODELS?

Topic modeling involves automated procedures for coding collections of texts in terms of meaningful categories that represent the main topics being discussed in the texts. Topic models assume that meanings are relational (Saussure, 1959) and that the meanings associated with a topic of conversation can be understood as a set of word clusters. Topic models treat texts as what linguists call a **bag of words**, capturing word **co-occurrences** regardless of syntax, narrative, or location within a text. A topic can be thought of as the cluster of words that tend to come up in a discussion and, therefore, to co-occur more frequently than they otherwise would, whenever the topic is being discussed.

Topic modeling is generally more inductive than are most other approaches to text mining (see Chapters 4 and 5). Instead of starting with predefined codes or categories

# BASIC CONCEPTS

*Topic models* are statistical models for coding texts in terms of categories that represent the main topics discussed in the texts.

Topic models treat a text as a *bag of words* in which word order, syntax, and location within a text are irrelevant.

*Chimera topics* are bogus topics that can occur because of factors related to the data structure and interpretation.

derived from theory, researchers using topic models begin by specifying $k$, the number of topics they wish their topic modeling algorithm to find. How to go about setting $k$ is a highly technical issue discussed by Greene, O'Callahan, and Cunningham (2014) and in many online forums. Selecting too few topics can produce results that are overly broad, while selecting too many leads to too many small, redundant topics. But once $k$ is set, software identifies the specified number of topics, returns the probabilities of words being used in a topic, and provides an accounting of the distribution of those topics across the texts.

Topic modeling is an instance of probabilistic modeling, and the most widely used probabilistic model for topic modeling is **latent Dirichlet allocation (LDA)**, which is a statistical model of language introduced by Blei, Ng, and Jordan (2003). LDA is based on the idea that every text within a text collection is akin to a bag of words produced according to a mixture of topics that the author or authors intended to discuss. Each topic is a distribution over all observed words in the texts such that words that are strongly associated with the text's dominant topics have a higher chance of being included within the text's bag of words. Based on these distributions, authorship is conceptualized as an author repeatedly picking a topic and then a word and placing them in the bag until the document is complete. The objective of topic modeling is to find the parameters of the LDA process that has generated the final text or text collection, a process referred to as "inference" in the LDA literature. Among the outputs of the inference is a set of per-word topic distributions associating a probability with every topic–word pair and a similar set of per-topic text distributions describing the probability of choosing a particular topic for every specific text.

A second probabilistic model used in topic modeling is **latent semantic analysis (LSA)**. LSA was first introduced as a distinct information retrieval technique for library indexing (Dumais, 2004). It is based on the similarity of meaning of words appearing in texts or passages (Landauer, Foltz, & Laham, 1998) and presents words and texts using vector space modelling that compiles textual data into a term-by-document matrix, showing the weighted frequency of terms to represent the documents in the term space. LSA is based on singular value decomposition (SVD), which is closely associated with factor analysis, and represents terms and documents in a space of principal factors (Berry, Dumais, & O'Brien, 1995; Deerwester, Dumais, Furnas, Landauer, & Harshman, 1990; Landauer, 2002). LSA employs a unique form of SVD, truncated SVD, which modifies term frequencies to include only terms of great importance in order to highlight underlying dimensions of the data. This process is very similar to principal component analysis, which is widely used in the social sciences.

In addition to LDA and LSA, computer scientists and statisticians have developed a number of other probabilistic models for identifying topics such as nonnegative matrix factorization (see Lee & Seung, 1999; Pauca, Shahnaz, Berry, & Plemmons, 2004). A different but related approach is employed in the text analysis software **Alceste**. Originally developed by Max Reinert (1987), Alceste was designed to measure what Reinert termed *lexical worlds*, which he conceptualized as "mental rooms" that speakers successively inhabit, each with its own characteristic vocabulary. Alceste analyzes the

---

## Probabilistic Models Used in Topic Modeling

Latent Dirichlet Allocation

In latent Dirichlet allocation (LDA), each topic is a distribution over all observed words in the texts such that words that are strongly associated with the text's dominant topics have a higher chance of being included. Among the outputs of the LDA procedure is a set of per-word topic distributions associating a probability with every topic–word pair and a similar set of per-topic text distributions describing the probability of choosing a particular topic for every specific text.
Advantages: greater accuracy

Latent Semantic Analysis

A model based on the similarity of meaning of words appearing in texts, latent semantic analysis (LSA) presents words and texts using vector space modelling, compiling textual data into a term-by-document matrix. The weighted frequency of terms represent the documents in the term space. LSA is based on singular value decomposition (SVD), which represents terms and documents in a space of principal factors (similar to factor analysis).
Advantages: consistency of results, speed

distribution of words in a collection of texts based on the concepts of *statements*, *words*, and *similarity*. Statements are approximated natural sentences or natural fragments of sentences delimited by punctuation so as to have similar length. Alceste constructs a dictionary of lemmatized *words* referred to as "lexemes." To assess similarity between statements, Alceste constructs a matrix that crosses statements and words where the cells signal the presence or absence of a word (lexeme) within a statement. Alceste then performs a descending classification on this matrix, which produces classes of similar context units. Alceste's descending classification technique maximizes the similarity between statements in the same class and maximizes the difference between the classes. In the end, the user is provided with a series of classes and typical words, statements, and authors that provide a basis for interpreting the classes as lexical worlds, much as LDA and LSA interpret texts in terms of topics (see Brugidou et al., 2000). Alceste has been applied in sociology (Rousselière & Vezina, 2009; van Meter & de Saint Léger, 2014), psychology (Lahlou, 1996; Noel-Jorand, Reinert, Bonnon, & Therme, 1995), political science (Bicquelet & Weale, 2011; Brugidou, 2003; Schonhardt-Bailey, 2013; Weale, Bicquelet, & Bara, 2012), management studies (Illia, Sonpar, & Bauer, 2014), and many other fields.

The use of topic models and Alceste within social science research projects brings with it a number of challenges. Social scientists need to be able to make sense of the topic word clusters that are produced by topic modeling software and to recognize when topics derived from algorithms are worthless or misleading. Ideally, topics will make sense to a subject area specialist or well-informed observer. Topic models require interpretive work, but they

## SPOTLIGHT ON THE RESEARCH
### Comparing the Language of Politicians and the Public

Brugidou, M. (2003). Argumentation and values: An analysis of ordinary political competence via an open-ended question. *International Journal of Public Opinion Research*, *15*(4), 413–430.

In this study from 2003, the political scientist Brugidou analyzed answers to an open-ended question to demonstrate the argumentative competence of "laymen" in public debates over the future of nuclear power. Brugidou hypothesized that ordinary citizens use the same types of rhetorical devices that politicians do. He used Alceste to identify homogeneous subsets of verbatims on the basis of their lexical profile. The classes of answers collected were characterized by the available sociological variables in the survey, including sociodemographic and attitudinal variables.

Specialized software used:

Alceste

www.image-zafar.com/Logicieluk.html

differ from other social science research methods in that in topic modeling interpretive work occurs mainly *after* data are collected and analyzed. Topic models "shift the locus of subjectivity within the methodological program—interpretation is still required, but from the perspective of the actual modeling of the data, the more subjective moment of the procedure has been shifted over to the post-modeling phase of the analysis" (Mohr & Bogdanov, 2013).

In using topic models, there is a significant risk of "chimera topics" (Schmidt, 2012), which are bogus topics that can occur because of various factors related to the data structure and interpretation. Most social scientists and humanities scholars are not yet using sophisticated diagnostics packages on their topic models (see Schmidt, 2012). And yet despite the challenges involved in modeling topics in large text collections and integrating topic models into deductive or abductive research designs, today topic models are being used by researchers in the humanities, political science, sociology and other fields who often work collaboratively with computational linguists and other computer scientists.

# SPOTLIGHT ON THE RESEARCH
## Studying Psychological Adaptation to Extreme Environments

Noel-Jorand, M.-C., Reinert, M., Bonnon, M., & Therme, P. (1995). Discourse analysis and psychological adaptation to high altitude hypoxia. *Stress Medicine, 11*(1), 27–39.

This Alceste psychology study by the medical researcher Noel-Jorand and her colleagues is a contribution to the study of psychological adaptation to extreme environments. Noel-Jorand and her team conducted a discourse analysis on 10 European lowlanders during a 3-week scientific expedition under survival conditions at the top of Mount Sajama in Bolivia. Their discourse analysis was part of a large scientific investigation involving 12 scientific and medical research procedures on human adaptation to high altitude chronic hypoxia. The research team analyzed several freely delivered oral accounts of the survival experience using Alceste to determine the main word distribution patterns and to identify the repetitive language patterns most frequently used. They found three different types of discourse that did not change during exposure to extreme environmental conditions and were not correlated with the events but referred only to the speakers themselves. The three types of discourse were focused on experiences of anxiety, fear, and extreme fear or anguish. In response to these experiences, the research participants used various psychological strategies to escape or to face the situation in different ways. These strategies were revealed by the terms used within the different discourse types.

Specialized software used:

Alceste

www.image-zafar.com/Logicieluk.html

# HOW TO USE TOPIC MODELS

Topic models are easiest to use inductively as a tool for exploring data. But they can also be used in deductive and abductive research projects. For instance, the sociologist Mützel (2015) used topic modeling for empirical research projects on the field of breast cancer therapeutics and on the gastronomic field of the city of Berlin. Based on her firsthand experience with topic models, she discussed how it is critical for researchers to have an idea about how many topics a corpus consists of and the ability to recognize when a set of topics matches with the researcher's knowledge of the field. For Mützel, topic modeling does not do away with qualitative interpretation but shifts it to a later phase of the analysis. The analyst, who should have knowledge of the field being studied in order to interpret the topics, can use topic models to gain "macroscopic insights into the development of entire fields" (Mützel, 2015, p. 2). In Mützel's studies of the fields of breast cancer therapeutics and Berlin gastronomy, results from the LDA procedure allowed her to describe and trace developments over long periods of time. Her results also allowed her to zoom in on particular moments in time to conduct qualitative analysis of her texts. This would seem to be a useful model for social scientists to use topic models while acknowledging their limitations and the need for substantive interpretation.

---

**Using Topic Models in Historical Research**

Qualitative Exploration

*Develop a research question, case selection, repeated reading of texts, take extensive notes, and estimate number of topics in texts.*

Topic Modeling

*Choose latent semantic analysis (LSA) or latent Dirichlet allocation (LDA), and compare results to estimates from qualitative exploration.*

Qualitative Interpretation

*Review notes from your qualitative exploration, and consider implications of your topic models for your research question or questions.*

# EXAMPLES OF TOPIC MODELING

## Digital Humanities

Topic models have been embraced by many researchers in the humanities, and the field of digital humanities is dominated by topic modeling methods. The explosion of interest in topic models among humanists began in 2010 with widely circulated blog posts by Jockers (2010) on topic modeling and Blevins (2011) on a late 18th-century diary. Then, in 2010, several advocates of topic models introduced the method to many humanities scholars for the first time. Since then, humanities scholars have used topic models in studies of themes in 19th-century literature (Jockers & Mimno, 2013), the history of literary scholarship (Goldstone & Underwood, 2012), and many other subjects.

## Journalism Research

Journalism researchers Günther and Quandt (2016) provided a road map of text mining tools available for journalism research, covering rule-based approaches, dictionaries, supervised machine learning, document clustering, and topic models. An example of text mining journalism research is a 2016 study by Jacobi, van Atteveldt, and Welbers, who use LDA topic modeling. Jacobi and colleagues (2016) conducted a case study of the *New York Times* coverage of nuclear technology from 1945 to 2016, partially replicating a study by the sociologists Gamson and Modigliani (1989). Jacobi and colleagues (2016) showed that LDA is a useful tool for analyzing news content in large digital news archives relatively quickly.

## Political Science

Political scientists have used topic models to study a number of different categories of political phenomena. For instance, Quinn, Monroe, Colaresi, Crespin, and Radev (2010) used R to analyze topics in Senate floor speeches delivered between 1997 and 2004 using a database of over 118,000 speeches from the *Congressional Record*. Their method estimates the substance of topics, the keywords that identify topics, and the hierarchical nesting of topics.

Grimmer (2010) used topic models to develop the "expressed agenda model," which measures the attention senators allocate to press releases. His model simultaneously estimates the topics in the texts and the attention political actors allocate to the estimated topics.

Gerrish and Blei (2012) have developed several predictive models linking legislative sentiment to legislative texts and have used these models to predict specific voting patterns with high levels of accuracy.

Roberts, Stewart, and Airoldi (2016) introduced a semiautomated approach to the collection and analysis of open-ended survey responses, the structural topic model (STM; Roberts et al., 2016). Their approach to topic models incorporates information about the document, such as the author's gender, political affiliation, and treatment assignment if an experimental and experimentalists.

Soroka, Stecula, and Wlezien (2015) used topic models to analyze how media reflect economic trends and whether they influence, or are influenced by, public economic perceptions. This article explores the economy, media, and public opinion, focusing in particular on whether media coverage and the public react to changes in or levels of economic activity, and the past, present, or future economy. Analyses rely on content-analytic data drawn from 30,000 news stories over 30 years in the United States. Results indicate that coverage reflects change in the future economy and that this both influences and is influenced by public evaluations. These patterns make more understandable the somewhat surprising finding of positive coverage and public assessments in the midst of the Great Recession. They also may help explain previous findings in political behavior.

## Sociology

Sociologists have used topic models mainly for analysis of historical data from newspaper and scholarly archives. For example, DiMaggio, Nag, and Blei (2013) used LDA to investigate controversies that erupted over federal funding of the arts in the United States during the 1980s and 1990s. They coded almost 8,000 newspaper articles selected from five newspapers in order to analyze "frames," defined as sets of "discursive cues" that suggested a "particular interpretation of a person, event, organization, practice, condition, or situation" (DiMaggio et al., 2013, p. 593). DiMaggio and colleagues found that different media frames were promoted by different institutional actors as a way to try to influence the course of public discourse and political debate. Of the 12 topics identified in their analysis, several clearly reflect politicized frames, such as the 1990s' "culture wars" and National Endowment for the Arts grant controversies.

Levy and Franklin (2013) used topic models to examine political contention in the U.S. trucking industry. Their data were online archives of public comments submitted during agency rulemakings, which they mined from the online portal regulations.gov. They used topic modeling to identify latent themes in a series of regulatory debates about electronic monitoring, finding that different types of commenters use different interpretive frames. Comments submitted by individuals were more likely to frame the electronic monitoring debate in terms of broader logistical problems plaguing the industry, such as long wait times at shippers' terminals. Organizational stakeholders were more likely to frame their comments in terms of technological standards and language relating to cost–benefit analysis.

Light and Cunningham (2016) used topic models to analyze Nobel Peace Prize acceptance speeches, which they found were increasingly associated with globalization and neoliberalism rather than earlier Christian and "global institutional schemas" (p. 43). McFarland and his colleagues (2013) produced a series of studies employing various types of topic models as well as other text mining methodologies. In one study, they analyzed dissertation abstracts from 1980 to 2010 drawn from the ProQuest database of 240 U.S. research universities to identify intellectual movements and trends. Finally, the sociologists Törnberg and Törnberg (2016) used topic models in a critical discourse analysis (CDA; see Chapter 1) project on discursive connections between Islamophobia and antifeminism in an online forum. Törnberg and Törnberg analyzed the shift from traditional media to user-driven social media based on a corpus of over 50 million online posts. Topic modeling allowed the researchers to produce a content map of the corpus and to identify topics within it.

# SOFTWARE FOR TOPIC MODELING

In the digital humanities and social sciences, the Java-based package **MALLET (Machine Learning for Language Toolkit)** is widely used for topic modeling. MALLET performs statistical natural language processing (NLP), document classification, clustering, topic modeling, information extraction, and other machine-learning applications. Because MALLET requires using the command line, it is most appropriate for users with at least moderate programming experience. But it typically uses only a small number of commands over and over so is relatively easy to learn (http://mallet.cs.umass.edu/index.php).

MALLET uses an implementation of Gibbs sampling, a statistical technique meant to quickly construct a sample distribution, to create its topic models. MALLET is also available as a package for R users, who can also use the packages TOPICMODELS and latent Dirichlet allocation (LDA).

Python offers the topic modeling package gensim (https://radimrehurek.com/gensim).

Alceste is a widely used alternative to topic modeling. Alceste stands for Analyse des Lexèmes Co-occurents dans les Énnoncés Simples d'un Texte (Analysis of the co-occurring lexemes within the simple statements of a text). The program is available only in a French language version in which all menus, commands, and outputs are in French, but it can be used on texts in English and other languages. It is available from the company Image (http://www.image-zafar.com/Logicieluk.html).

Alceste is not free, but an open-source reproduction of Alceste is available in the Iramuteq interface for R (www.iramuteq.org).

## Conclusions

Although using topic models requires familiarity with R or other programming environments, the barriers to learning to use topic models are not especially onerous. As such, it is not surprising that topic models are being used across the social sciences as well as in digital humanities research. They are a viable option for researchers interested in data exploration as well as for adding precision and rigor to qualitative research.

## Key Terms

Alceste   210
Bag of words   208
Co-occurrences   208

Latent Dirichlet allocation
   (LDA)   209
Latent semantic analysis
   (LSA)   209

MALLET (Machine
   Learning for Language
   Toolkit)   216
Topic models   207

## Highlights

- Topic models are statistical models for identifying what combinations of topics are discussed within a social group and how the topics discussed change over time.

- Topic models assume that meanings are relational and that the meanings associated with a topic of conversation can be understood as a set of word clusters.

- Topic models treat texts as what linguists call a bag of words, capturing word co-occurrences regardless of syntax, narrative, or location within a text.

- Topic modeling is an instance of probabilistic modeling, and the most widely used probabilistic models for topic modeling are LDA and LSA.

- Social science research using topic models is generally, but not necessarily, inductive.

- Topic models are increasingly popular in journalism research, political science, and sociology, and in digital humanities scholarship.

## Review Questions

- How do different social sciences use topic models differently?

- What are the advantages and disadvantages of using topic models rather than qualitative approaches such as thematic analysis?

## Developing a Research Proposal

Review the topic modeling papers surveyed in this chapter and choose one that is most similar to the research project you are developing. Use research databases such as Google Scholar, Web of Science, or JSTOR to access the study and a few high-quality studies that cite it. Read all of the studies you download carefully, focusing on their research design and methods. Write down some ways your own study can build from the studies you have read, either by applying their methods to new data, by making changes to their methods, or both.

## Internet Resources

Topic Modeling: A Basic Introduction

Megan R. Brett

http://journalofdigitalhumanities.org/2-1/topic-modeling-a-basic-introduction-by-megan-r-brett

The purpose of this post is to help explain some of the basic concepts of topic modeling, introduce some topic modeling tools, and point out some other posts on topic modeling. The intended audience is historians, but it is useful for social sciences students and experienced researchers as well.

## Further Reading

DiMaggio, P., Nag, M., & Blei, D. (2013). Exploiting affinities between topic modeling and the sociological perspective on culture: Application to newspaper coverage of U.S. government arts funding. *Science Direct*, *41*(6), 570–606.

Günther, E., & Quandt, T. (2016). Word counts and topic models: Automated text analysis methods for digital journalism research. *Digital Journalism*, *4*(1), 75–88.

Mohr, J. W., & Bogdanov, P. (2013). Introduction—Topic models: What they are and why they matter. *Poetics*, *41*(6), 545–569.

# Writing and Reporting Your Research

# 17

# WRITING AND REPORTING YOUR RESEARCH

## INTRODUCTION: ACADEMIC WRITING

Writing is a part of virtually every step of a text mining research project, from jotting down research ideas to taking notes on themes found in texts and writing out research hypotheses. But writing up and reporting your research as a term paper or possibly an article for publication in a research journal (e.g., in an undergraduate research journal such as those listed at the end of this chapter) demands specialized writing skills.

There are many resources for students who wish to improve their academic writing, particularly when it comes to grammar, style, conventions, citations, and

**references**. Proper spelling and grammar are critical because mistakes in these areas can detract from your argument. Most word processing programs have corrective tools that should always be used, and for more complex grammar issues, there are many online resources and the classic *Elements of Style* by Strunk and White (1999). Osmond's 2016 *Academic Writing and Grammar for Students* is a more comprehensive resource, which includes chapters on academic writing conventions, conciseness and clarity, and proofreading. And in *Stylish Academic Writing*, the literature scholar and poet Sword (2012a) argued that her book's title is in fact not an oxymoron and that academic writing should be vivid and accessible to nonspecialists. She also has a website, The Writer's Diet (http://writersdiet.com/?page_id=4), where you can paste in a sample of your own academic writing, and the program will diagnose it from "fit" to "flabby" (readers who score poorly on The Writer's Diet can take heart in knowing that a sample of the first author's paragraphs were found to "need toning," and a few were flat-out "flabby").

All academic writing experts agree on several features of good academic writing. These include providing clarity, avoiding jargon, using the active voice, engaging the reader, varying words used, and omitting needless words. There are also some specific errors that are especially common in social science writing, including the unnecessary creation of new and unfamiliar verbs from nouns and nouns from verbs.

---

## Writing With Clarity

Academic writers would do well to value clarity above virtually all else, avoid "over-writing," and omit all unneeded words. It helps if you don't worry about appearing "smart" by using exotic words in long sentences. In his 1992 essay "In Defense of Creative Writing Classes," the poet Hugo wrote that in much academic writing, "clarity runs a poor second to invulnerability." The creative writing professor Toor (2012) picked up on Hugo's invulnerability theme. Comparing celebrities and academics, she wrote this:

> Listening to academics, I pick up a different set of concerns: Am I making a convincing case? Have I mentioned everything everyone else has said about this topic and pointed out the ways that they are (sort of) wrong? Do you see how much I've read? Have I dropped enough important names? Does my specialized language prove I deserve to be a member of your club? Am I right? At the end, I hear hope disguised as an attitude that asks: Am I smart?

So in a nutshell, don't worry about appearing brilliant, and try to express your ideas and write as clearly as possible. Your readers will be thankful you did.

# EVIDENCE AND THEORY

The principle features of good academic writing apply to all areas of academic research, from the social sciences and humanities to the physical and life sciences and engineering. But there are special challenges, and also special conventions, associated with writing in social science disciplines such as anthropology, communications, economics, political science, psychology, and sociology. While each of these disciplines has its own idiosyncratic writing conventions, there are particular features that characterize most social science writing that relate to what constitutes valid social scientific knowledge. Among the most important of these characteristics are the requirement that writers support their arguments with evidence—particularly evidence that is the product of systematic and rigorous research—and the use of theory to construct explanations about how the social world works.

Evidence is important in social science writing because it is used to support or question beliefs, propositions, and hypotheses about the social world. For example, your research question may be whether members of two ethnic groups interpret the same medical diagnoses differently based on their culture and language (see the study by Schuster, Beune, & Stronks, 2011; see Chapter 12). This forms an initial question but one that is too vague to explore as it stands. More precise questions might be about whether the two groups express different emotions (see Chapter 14), use different metaphors (see Chapter 12), or discuss different topics (see Chapter 16). To answer these kinds of questions, the researcher will need to formulate more specific claims that can be systematically and rigorously explored. Such claims could be formulated in the following terms. *In the Netherlands, (white) Dutch participants will use more metaphors that construct the human body and its organs as machines or parts of machines, while participants of Hindustani and Creole descent will use more metaphors that represent hypertension as an unknown enemy* (Schuster et al., 2011). These claims can now be subjected to systematic research. In other words, the researcher will gather evidence for and against each claim—evidence that she or he will seek to evaluate. This process of evaluation will tend to support or refute the original claim, but it may be inconclusive and may also generate further questions and new or different theoretical concepts (see Chapter 4 on abductive inference).

---

## Resist the Urge to "Verb"

Any noun can be "**verbed**," and so can many adjectives. We neaten our desk, prettify a room, google things we'd like to know, and "Facebook" our friends. Executives greenlight projects, social science research impacts society (or so we like to think), we fax, text message, e-mail, download, upload, dialogue, enable bad behavior, and parent children. While some of these new verbs formed from nouns are useful in everyday language, most do not belong in academic research papers. As a rule of thumb, check the dictionary before using a noun or an adjective as a verb in your academic writing.

Generally, in social science writing, you are expected to identify and evaluate evidence from existing research findings and to find and evaluate evidence for and against any claim. Theory is important in social science writing because the theoretical orientation of the researcher will tend to inform the types of question she or he asks, the specific claims tested, the ways in which evidence is identified and gathered, and the manner in which this evidence is interpreted and evaluated (see Chapter 4). In other words, the theoretical orientation of the social scientist is likely to influence the forms of knowledge she or he will produce.

Consider as an example a research question such as how best to explain the popularity of Politician X. A researcher trained in critical discourse analysis (CDA) or Foucauldian analysis (see Chapter 1) may analyze Politician X's speeches with reference to other political speeches and different kinds of texts circulating in contemporary society, while one trained in topic modeling (see Chapter 16) may ask whether there is something unique about the topics discussed by Politician X, and a researcher trained in sentiment analysis may ask about sentiment expressed in Politician X's public statements (see Chapter 14). These three researchers might look at the same texts and each come to a different **conclusion**, perhaps that Politician X's rhetoric is, or is not, unique.

As we discussed in Chapter 4, there is considerable debate within the social sciences about the exact relationship between theory and evidence. To simplify somewhat, some social scientists argue that evidence can be used to support or invalidate the claims investigated by research and thereby produce theoretical accounts of the social world that are

---

## Avoid These: "Zombie Nouns"

Nouns formed from other parts of speech are called nominalizations. For example, you can create a noun from an adjective like *vulnerable*, which becomes *vulnerability*, or from a verb like *orient*, which becomes *orientation*. Although they are widely used by academics, lawyers, bureaucrats, and business writers, nominalizations should be avoided whenever possible. Perhaps most common in academic writing is the suffix *-ism*, which forms nominalizations such as constructionism, globalism, relativism, formalism, and positivism.

At their best, nominalizations help writers express complex ideas concisely, but at their worst, they can impede clear communication and create artificial distance between academic discourse and how ordinary people speak. Sword (2012b) called them **zombie nouns** because they "cannibalize active verbs, suck the lifeblood from adjectives, and substitute abstract entities for human beings." Use of nominalizations (such as *heteronormativity*, *interpellation*, and *taxonomization*) can also send the dangerous message to your reader that you think people who use big words are smarter than those who do not.

more or less accurate. Others argue that our theoretical orientations and the philosophical assumptions and value judgments they contain condition processes of social scientific inquiry so that we can never claim to produce universally true or accurate accounts of social phenomena. In any event, the point to take away from this **discussion** is simply that the theories we use inform both the questions we ask and **methods** we apply in our research and that social science writing should in most cases carefully and explicitly address theoretical issues.

# THE STRUCTURE OF SOCIAL SCIENCE RESEARCH PAPERS

A social science research paper is an argument. A good argument does not have to be wildly controversial, but it does have to state a position and support it with evidence in a clear and logical fashion.

In presenting and supporting their main arguments, most papers written in the social sciences, life sciences, business, education, and related fields follow the same basic structure and use APA (American Psychological Association) style (www.apastyle.org). We recommend that for your own research project you use APA or another widely accepted style such as Chicago. Although these areas of research may be very different, their methods of writing, presenting evidence, and explaining the research process are generally similar. Most quantitative (and many qualitative and mixed methods) papers use the same organization and order, including the following: (1) introduction, (2) literature review, (3) methods, (4) **results**, (5) discussion, (6) conclusion, (7) references, and (8) appendices (if needed).

## Introduction

The **introduction** should be used to provide a kind of road map for the rest of your paper, and you should give your reader guideposts along the way to help them follow your line of reasoning. In the introduction, you should state the problem you are going to address and pose the research question as well. Briefly discuss what is already known about the subject within your own and other disciplines. In writing your introduction, it is critical that you put your study into context in terms of why it matters and to whom. Who is your intended audience, and why should they be interested in your project? What does your argument mean for some broader issue? The context of your study does not have to be too broad; a narrower and more specific context is often preferable to a broader one. You should have in mind some potential consequences of your study for readers. Keep the larger context of your study in mind throughout the process of writing up your research, and return to a consideration of this broader context in the paper's conclusions section.

Be sure to avoid logical fallacies in your introduction and throughout the paper. Common logical fallacies, which will weaken your argument, include *argument by assertion*, which is simply stating that something is true or obvious when this does not make it so. *Begging the question* is merely restating your thesis in different words without providing supporting evidence. And *ad hominem arguments* appeal to personal considerations rather than logic, reason, or evidence. For example, showing that a particular argument was made by an individual you dislike does not in itself make that argument incorrect.

At the end of your paper's introduction, state the principle results of your study and the principle conclusions you have reached. What did you do to get to this conclusion? The rest of your paper will discuss your findings and add to the information summarized in the introduction.

## Literature Review

The **literature review** is a detailed discussion of what is already known about the subject of your study. This may include developed discussions of theoretical schools of thought, conceptual definitions, and the history of particular research fields. The best literature reviews do not simply review all the studies that have been conducted that are relevant in some way to your study. Instead, they are structured so that they make connections between similar research and discuss contradictions, disagreements, and gaps in scientific knowledge. A thorough, structured literature review establishes for your reader that you understand the topic and that your contribution is valuable. The object of this portion of your paper is to explain the research thoroughly enough to allow your audience to understand the material without having to do any additional reading but to provide relevant citations so that the reader can further investigate (see Osmond, 2016).

It may help to think of your literature review not as a list of published papers and books but as a tree with roots and branches. The roots are the first major published studies on your research topic. Although these may be many decades old, it is a good idea to start your literature with a few sentences summarizing these studies. Next, describe the main branches that have grown from these roots. What are the main approaches to your research topic in the social sciences? What are the seminal studies within each approach? Then move on to the newer, greener branches: recent studies published in the past 5 to 10 years. Given all that has been learned from older and newer research, how can your study make a new contribution? Is there something missing from our knowledge about the topic? Are there new theories or research methodologies that could be applied to the topic?

## Citations: Why and How

In social science writing, all assertions should be supported with evidence. Whenever you use an idea or a fact that is not your own as evidence, you must cite its source. Citing sources is important not only to give credit where credit is due but also to allow your readers to track down your sources if they are interested. In social science papers, in-text citations and the bibliography should be presented in a consistent format, whether MLA (Modern Language Association), ASA (American Sociological Association), Chicago, or another format, although APA (American Psychological Association) format is the most widely used (see www.apastyle.org).

## Methods

The methods section should explain what you did in your research so that anyone who reads it can replicate your exact process. Precision is essential in the methods section; you must describe in detail your methods for choosing subjects and collecting and analyzing data. You are expected to discuss the type of study you chose to perform and why, who or what you chose to study, and why you chose them and not someone or something else (see Chapter 5 on case selection and sampling). You must also explain ethical precautions taken in your study (see Chapter 3) and whether or not your study was approved by your institution's institutional review board (IRB). If it was not submitted for review to your IRB, justify why approval was not needed.

The methods section is where you discuss the precise details of your data selection and/or sampling strategies. How did you identify your data? How did you identify your sample? What tools did you use to collect data (see Chapters 2 and 6)? How did you select or construct these tools? You should describe your process for collecting data in as close to chronological order as possible and describe the statistical or data analysis procedures that you used. Also be sure to discuss problems or limitations with your research method. For example, if your sample is not representative of a larger population or is biased in some way, be sure to discuss these limitations of your study here. If you choose to include additional data in an **appendix**, you should mention this in the methods section.

## Results

The results (or findings) section is where you present the answers that your research produced. The results section is not a presentation of raw data but of the numbers or facts determined from the analysis. Evidence presented in the results section can take many forms, including facts, figures, selections from interview transcripts, or summaries of data

---

### How to Write About Your Data

Conducting social science research involves making hundreds of decisions related to selecting, sampling, and analyzing data. The methods section is where you walk your reader through these decisions. The goal of the methods section of a text mining paper should be to explain the major decisions made regarding data, such as where and how you acquired your data (see Chapter 2), your sampling procedures (see Chapter 5), text preparation (see Appendix B), and analysis. Minor data-related decisions should be included in footnotes, and data samples should be included in appendices. For instance, in the main text of your methods section you should discuss the *criteria* you developed for including or excluding words and phrases from your data in your analysis. Decisions about whether to remove *specific* words or phrases from your data belong in the footnotes or endnotes, and you may consider including an appendix, listing words excluded from the analysis. It is acceptable to explain some of the major data-related decisions made in terms of practical concerns such as cost and having limited time to conduct the study.

---

that anticipate or refute counterarguments. When presenting evidence in a results section, make sure the evidence supports your thesis, make it clear to the reader how the evidence supports your thesis, and make sure the presentation of evidence is well organized. If you are using hypotheses, this is where you state whether you accept or reject each hypothesis. Tables, charts, and other forms of data visualization (see Appendix G) that display your results can make this a very short but very effective section. It is not always necessary to repeat in the text what you show in a chart. Instead, the text should lead the reader to the chart, table, or other visualization rather than repeat what can already be seen.

## Discussion

In the discussion section, you should avoid repeating what you showed in the results section and instead consider what your results mean. Offer generalizations, principles, or relationships. Develop each paragraph in this section based on a theme or trend revealed in the findings. Discuss unexpected results and exceptions to the trends or patterns you have identified. Discuss how your research agrees or disagrees with previous studies.

## Conclusion

A good conclusion should restate your answer to your research question, hypotheses, or primary claim based on the results of your study. It should return to the themes from your paper's introduction and also make recommendations for further studies or changes that should be made in research practice. In applied research projects, it is appropriate to discuss practical implications of your research findings in the conclusion.

## Oral Presentations

Social scientists often present their research at conferences in the form of oral presentations. These presentations typically involve a member of the research team talking in front of a slide deck designed with Microsoft PowerPoint, Google Slides, or other presentation software. Academic oral presentations generally last about 20 minutes and include no more than 20 slides. When presenting your research in class or at a conference, it is good practice to follow these guidelines:

- Use a slide design with a dark background and white or light-colored font.
- Keep the text in the slides to a minimum. The slides are an outline and should include few full sentences.
- Focus on one main idea per slide.
- Legends and axis labels on your charts should be easy to read and understand.
- As in all academic writing, avoid technical jargon. If you must use technical language, explain the terms you are using.
- Your first slide should include your presentation title, name, course title (if applicable), and university name.
- The second slide should give an overview of your study using two to three bullet points.
- The order of your slides should follow the outline of your paper.
- When discussing your data, include excerpts (anonymized) to familiarize your audience with the data.
- Practice your presentation, and especially its timing, alone in front of a mirror, by recording yourself, or with a friend.

## References

For most social sciences papers, your reference page should follow the guidelines of APA (www.apastyle.org). However, disciplines often prefer other styles, such as ASA (American Sociological Association; www.asanet.org/documents/teaching/pdfs/Quick_Tips_for_ASA_Style.pdf), Chicago (www.chicagomanualofstyle.org/tools_citationguide.html), or MLA (Modern Language Association; https://www.mla.org/MLA-Style). Citations and a bibliography are important so that the reader knows where you found your evidence and can check whether you are using it appropriately. In-text citations and the bibliography should be presented in a consistent format, whether MLA, APA, ASA, Chicago, or another format.

## Appendices

A research paper's appendices section includes tables, charts, figures, or samples of raw data that may not be critically important to your study but may be of interest to readers who want further evidence relevant to your hypotheses, predictions, or primary claim. It is appropriate to place very fine-grained discussions of specific methodological procedures in an appendix and refer to them in the methods section.

## Conclusion

In this chapter, we have reviewed basic principles of academic writing and discussed specific skills needed for social science writing. Writing up and reporting text mining research projects presents special challenges to you as a writer, partly because of the multiple forms of inferential logic that can be used (see Chapter 4). And the interdisciplinary nature of text mining research places demands on you as an author to review research literature from multiple disciplines. Thus, just as is discussed at the end of Chapter 5 on designing your own research project, as you write and report your research project it would be a mistake to rely exclusively on this chapter. A better strategy would be to use published research as a template. Use the citations and references in this book, along with research databases such as Google Scholar (https://scholar.google.com), Web of Science (https://www.webofknowledge.com), ResearchGate (https://www.researchgate.net), and Academia. edu (https://www.academia.edu) to find exemplary published research that resembles your project in terms of it methods used or theoretical framework. Then, using this chapter as a guide, pay close attention to how the authors have chosen to write up their study as you make decisions about how best to write up and report your own research.

## Key Terms

Appendix   229

Conclusion   226

Discussion   227

Introduction   227

Literature review   228

Methods   227

References   224

Results   227

"Verbed"   225

Zombie nouns   226

## Highlights

- Writing is a part of virtually every step of a text mining research project, from taking notes about your texts to writing for publication.

- Write as clearly as you can, and avoid jargon and unnecessary words.

- It is possible to publish your research in print or online undergraduate research journals (see the Undergraduate Research Journals section).

## Web Resources

- The Social Science Writing Project (www.csun.edu/sswp)

- "What Is a Social Science Essay?" (www.sagepub.com/sites/default/files/upm-binaries/39896_9780857023711.pdf)

- "In Defense of Creative-Writing Classes" by Richard Hugo (http://adilegian.com/PDF/HugoDefenseCreativeWriting.pdf)

- "Becoming a 'Stylish' Writer: Attractive Prose Will Not Make You Appear Any Less Smart" by Rachel Toor (www.chronicle.com/article/Becoming-a-Stylish-Writer/132677)

## Undergraduate Research Journals

*General Undergraduate Research Journals*

*American Journal of Undergraduate Research*

www.ajuronline.org

*American Journal of Undergraduate Research (AJUR)* is a national, independent, peer-reviewed, open-source, no-cost-to-authors, quarterly, multidisciplinary student research journal established in 2002. *AJUR* publishes undergraduate research conducted at any accredited university.

*(Continued)*

(Continued)

*Inquiries Journal*

www.inquiriesjournal.com

*Inquiries Journal* is an open-access online academic journal focused on publishing the work of university students from around the world in a wide range of academic disciplines. Established in 2009 by students at Northeastern University in Boston, Massachusetts, the journal has no official affiliation and is financially independent. *Inquiries Journal* accepts submissions from undergraduates at all accredited academic institutions.

*International Social Science Review*

https://www.pigammamu.org/international-social-science-review.html

The *International Social Science Review (ISSR)* is the peer-reviewed journal of the Pi Gamma Mu International Honor Society in Social Sciences (www.pigammamu.org). Published semiannually, the ISSR invites the submission of manuscripts in history, political science, sociology, anthropology, economics, international relations, criminal justice, social work, psychology, social philosophy, history of education, and geography. *ISSR* accepts submissions only from Pi Gamma Mu members.

*Journal of Integrated Social Sciences*

http://jiss.org

The *Journal of Integrated Social Sciences (JISS)* is a web-based, peer-reviewed social science journal that encourages submissions from undergraduate students and their faculty advisers. The *JISS* publishes undergraduate research conducted at any accredited university.

*Journal of Student Research*

www.jofsr.com/index.php/path

*Journal of Student Research (JOFSR)* is an electronic, academic, multidisciplinary peer-reviewed journal.

*Journal of Student Research*

https://www.stu.edu/JSR

The *Journal of Student Research (JSR)* at St. Thomas University is a digital, international, multidisciplinary journal devoted to publishing research articles in the areas of business, communication, education, law, science, and technology. *JSR* provides a venue for students to publish their research that tests, extends, or builds theory. *JSR* is published twice each year, in fall and spring of each academic year, and accepts submissions from undergraduates at all accredited universities.

*Journal of Undergraduate Research*

http://cornerstone.lib.mnsu.edu/jur

The *Journal of Undergraduate Research (JUR)* is interdisciplinary and accepts submissions that would meet the standard of excellence for students in diverse fields of study. Although most submissions are made by students from Minnesota State University, submissions from any undergraduate student will be considered for publication. *JUR* is published annually as an online journal.

*Journal of Undergraduate Research and Scholarly Excellence*

http://jur.colostate.edu

The *Journal of Undergraduate Research and Scholarly Excellence (JUR)* is a peer-reviewed undergraduate journal registered with the Library of Congress that accepts submissions at any time on any subject from any undergraduate institution.

*Journal of Young Investigators*

www.jyi.org

The *Journal of Young Investigators (JYI)* is dedicated to representing undergraduate research in biological and biomedical sciences, physical sciences, mathematics and engineering, psychology, and social sciences. This journal accepts submission from undergraduates from any accredited institution.

*Lethbridge Undergraduate Research Journal*

https://lurj.org

The *Lethbridge Undergraduate Research Journal (LURJ)* is an online journal for undergraduate students run by and for undergraduate students. *LURJ* is international in scope and welcomes papers from all undergraduates. Papers are accepted at all times, and new issues are released approximately three times annually.

*Midwest Journal of Undergraduate Research*

http://research.monm.edu/mjur

The *Midwest Journal of Undergraduate Research (MJUR)* is a peer-reviewed journal produced under the direction of student editors and a faculty advisory board. Founded in 2011, *MJUR* is dedicated to the publication of outstanding scholarship by undergraduates. The journal accepts submissions from all academic disciplines and from all accredited undergraduate institutions (although the majority of manuscripts are submitted by students from colleges and universities in the U.S. Midwest). The *MJUR* acceptance rate is about 25%.

*(Continued)*

(Continued)

*Pittsburgh Undergraduate Review*

www.pur.honorscollege.pitt.edu

The review process of the *Pittsburgh Undergraduate Review (PUR)* is structured after that of professional academic journals. An editorial board composed of undergraduates evaluates each submission, and papers meeting the board's standards are sent to two faculty referees. *PUR* was founded in the early 1980s as a vehicle through which undergraduates could contribute to the academic community. Its national accolades include publication of George Stephanopoulos's work in 1982 and recognition by the *New York Times* in 2001. This journal accepts submissions from any academic institution located anywhere in the world.

*Pursuit—The Journal of Undergraduate Research at the University of Tennessee*

http://trace.tennessee.edu/pursuit

Founded in 2009, *Pursuit* is dedicated to publishing the scholarly work of undergraduates and is supported by the University of Tennessee Office of Research and the Chancellor's Honors Program. The editors and review board members are undergraduate students who consider and review submissions and work with select faculty and staff to publish *Pursuit*. *Pursuit* accepts submissions from all accredited undergraduate institutions.

*Reinvention: An International Journal of Undergraduate Research*

www2.warwick.ac.uk/fac/cross_fac/iatl/reinvention

*Reinvention* is an peer-reviewed online journal dedicated to the publication of undergraduate student research. The journal welcomes academic articles from all disciplinary areas and all academic institutions. All articles in this journal undergo rigorous peer review based on initial editor screening and refereeing by two anonymous referees. The journal is produced, edited, and managed by students and staff at Monash University and the University of Warwick and is published biannually.

Undergraduate Research Journal for the Human Sciences

www.kon.org/CFP/cfp_urjhs.html

The *Undergraduate Research Journal for the Human Sciences* is an annual, peer-reviewed online journal dedicated to the publication of undergraduate student research. Submissions are accepted for review on an ongoing basis. Papers may represent a full range of research design, including experiments, surveys, case studies, and documentary research. Themes of research may include, but are not limited to, integrative cross-specialization research, service learning research, and traditional research in the specializations. The journal accepts submissions from undergraduates at all accredited academic institutions.

*Anthropology Undergraduate Research Journals*

*AnthroJournal*

http://anthrojournal.com

AnthroJournal, a sister publication to *Popular Archaeology* magazine (http://popular-archaeology .com), provides a venue for college students or recent graduates to publish academic papers for a global audience. Submissions are free, and all students whose papers are selected may receive a free 1-year premium subscription to *Popular Archaeology*.

*Journal of Undergraduate Anthropology*

http://anthrojournal.binghamton.edu

The mission of this journal is to provide a medium for undergraduates nationwide to share their anthropological research and experiences. Editing is largely done by undergraduate students. The *Journal of Undergraduate Anthropology* was founded in the fall of 2010 by Binghamton University students. While this journal accepts submissions from all undergraduate institutions, associate editors are all from the State University of New York system. The *Journal of Undergraduate Anthropology* has been published annually since the spring of 2011.

*Lambda Alpha Journal*

http://soar.wichita.edu/handle/10057/782

The *Lambda Alpha Journal* is an annual publication of student papers by members of the Lambda Alpha National Collegiate Honors Society for Anthropology that is published at the Wichita State University Department of Anthropology. This journal welcomes professional, avocational, and student manuscripts as well as book reviews. The *Lambda Alpha Journal* accepts submissions from all Lambda Alpha members.

*NEXUS: The Canadian Student Journal of Anthropology*

https://journals.mcmaster.ca/nexus

*Nexus* is a graduate student-run publication from the Department of Anthropology, McMaster University, Hamilton, Ontario, Canada, that provides a forum for quality student work in anthropology from Canadian and international colleges and universities. As an online journal, *Nexus* is not constrained to physical printing limitations and encourages the use of technology and multimedia projects that may not be suited for traditional print materials. GIS, 3D modeling, and audio/video media files are welcomed.

*(Continued)*

(Continued)

*Student Anthropologist: Journal of the National Association of Student Anthropologists*

https://studentanthropologist.wordpress.com

*Student Anthropologist* is the flagship peer-reviewed journal of the National Association of Student Anthropologists (NASA; the largest organization of anthropologist students in the world). *Student Anthropologist* journal publishes peer-reviewed, original ethnographic or theoretical student research and accepts submissions from undergraduates at all accredited academic institutions.

*Political Science Undergraduate Research Journals*

*Pi Sigma Alpha Undergraduate Journal of Politics*

www.psajournal.org

Founded in 2001, the *Pi Sigma Alpha Undergraduate Journal of Politics* welcomes submissions related to politics from undergraduates in any major enrolled at any accredited university.

*Journal of Politics & Society*

www.helvidius.org

The *Journal of Politics & Society* (created by the Helvidius Group at Columbia University) focuses on undergraduates and interdisciplinary coverage of public policy and law. This journal is the only scholarly publication of its kind. It is commercially distributed nationwide and accepts submissions from undergraduates at any accredited university.

*Psychology Undergraduate Research Journals*

*Journal of Interpersonal Relations, Intergroup Relations and Identity*

http://jiriri.ca/en

The *Journal of Interpersonal Relations, Intergroup Relations and Identity (JIRIRI)* is a social psychology journal created at Université de Montréal. An international scientific, peer-reviewed journal for undergraduate students, *JIRIRI*'s goal is to promote creative and original ideas in social psychology and related fields, produced by undergraduate students worldwide.

*Journal of Psychological Inquiry*

www.fhsu.edu/psych/jpi

The *Journal of Psychological Inquiry (JPI*; Fort Hays State University) is devoted to undergraduate psychology research. *JPI* encourages undergraduate students to submit manuscripts for consideration. Manuscripts may include empirical studies, literature reviews, and historical articles and may cover any topical area in the psychological sciences.

*Journal of Psychology and Behavioral Sciences*

http://view2.fdu.edu/academics/becton-college/psychology-and-counseling/jpbs/

The *Journal of Psychology and Behavioral Sciences (JPBS)* is an annual periodical published by the Psychology and Counseling Department of Fairleigh Dickinson University. The responsibility for review and contact resides with the undergraduate and graduate journal student officers. *JPBS* offers undergraduate and graduate students, as well as faculty, an opportunity to publish in a recognized academic journal. However, the undergraduate student, and not faculty members or graduate students, must be the first author of any accepted submission. The *JPBS* accepts submissions from undergraduates in accredited academic institution.

*Journal of Undergraduate Ethnic Minority Psychology, Alabama State University*

www.juempsychology.com

The *Journal of Undergraduate Ethnic Minority Psychology (JUEMP*; Alabama State University) is an edited and refereed online journal devoted to publishing empirical research (extended abstracts as well as quantitative and qualitative full-length manuscripts) authored by university undergraduate students. *JUEMP* invites empirical research submissions that incorporate ethnic minority perspectives or that concern the thoughts and behaviors of ethnic minority populations.

*Modern Psychological Studies*

www.utc.edu/psychology/mps

*Modern Psychological Studies (MPS)* is a psychological journal devoted exclusively to publishing manuscripts by undergraduate students. *MPS* considers manuscripts in any area of psychology. Although *MPS* focuses primarily on experimental research, this journal also publishes theoretical papers, literature reviews, and book reviews. Although based at the University of Tennessee at Chattanooga, *MPS* accepts submissions from undergraduates at any accredited academic institution.

*Psi Chi Journal of Psychological Research*

www.psichi.org/?page=journal_main#.WRBojxiZOql

The *Psi Chi Journal of Psychological Research* supports professional development and disseminates psychological science. Psi Chi is the International Honor Society in psychology. This journal accepts submissions from all Psi Chi members. Submissions are accepted for review throughout the year. Although manuscripts are limited to empirical research, they may cover any topical area in the psychological sciences. Replication studies are also welcome.

*(Continued)*

(Continued)

*Yale Review of Undergraduate Research in Psychology*

http://campuspress.yale.edu/yrurp

The *Yale Review of Undergraduate Research in Psychology* is an annual journal that showcases the best and most original research in psychology conducted by undergraduates from around the world. They publish research in all areas of psychology, including clinical, developmental, cognitive, and social psychology. This journal's goal is to contribute to the scientific advance by encouraging serious, quality research early in students' academic careers.

### Sociology Undergraduate Research Journals

*Eleven: The Undergraduate Journal of Sociology*

http://eleven.berkeley.edu

*Eleven* publishes sociological papers written by current and recent University of California, Berkeley, undergraduates as well as undergraduates from across the nation and countries such as Canada and Norway. In the spirit of Marx's "Eleventh Thesis on Feuerbach" that mandates one to engender constructive change, the journal offers opportunities for an intellectual space that encourages critical engagement with the world.

*Sociological Insight*

https://repositories.lib.utexas.edu/handle/2152/11227

*Sociological Insight* is a fully refereed undergraduate research journal sponsored by the University of Texas at Austin. It is the longest running undergraduate research journal in sociology that caters to undergraduate researchers. The journal publishes undergraduate research around the world on topics with sociological relevance, broadly defined. Around seven academic manuscripts are published annually at the end of the spring academic semester. Each academic manuscript is reviewed by at least a faculty member, a graduate student, and an undergraduate student who are selected from all over the United States. *Sociological Insight* also features research notes and reviews of recent books in the social sciences. The first issue of *Sociological Insight* was published in May 2009.

## Further Reading

Osmond, A. (2016). *Academic writing and grammar for students*. Thousand Oaks, CA: Sage.

Sword, H. (2012). *Stylish academic writing*. Cambridge, MA: Harvard University Press.

# APPENDIX A

## Data Sources for Text Mining

---

## THE AMERICAN PRESIDENCY PROJECT

www.presidency.ucsb.edu

The American Presidency Project is one of the most comprehensive collections of web resources on the American presidency, including documents, public papers, executive orders, addresses, press conferences, debates, election data, and approval ratings data. The American Presidency Project was established in 1999 as a collaboration between John T. Woolley and Gerhard Peters at the University of California, Santa Barbara. The archives contain 116,994 documents related to the study of the presidency.

## arXiv BULK DATA ACCESS

https://arxiv.org/help/bulk_data

This is a continuously updated list of high-quality open data sets in public domains.

## CATEGORY:DATASET

http://wiki.urbanhogfarm.com/index.php/Category:Dataset

A community effort, Category:Dataset seeks to aggregate public data sets related to social media and online communities.

## CMU MOVIE SUMMARY CORPUS

www.cs.cmu.edu/~ark/personas

This page provides links to a data set of movie plot summaries and associated metadata collected by David Bamman, Brendan O'Connor, and Noah A. Smith at the Language Technologies Institute and Machine Learning Department at Carnegie Mellon University.

# CONGRESSIONAL AND FEDERAL GOVERNMENT WEB HARVESTS

https://webharvest.gov

Since 2006, the U.S. National Archives and Records Administration has harvested Congressional websites at the end of each Congress. They also did a harvest of all federal websites for the 2004 presidential transition.

# CONGRESSIONAL RECORD

https://www.gpo.gov/fdsys/browse/collection.action?collectionCode=CREC

The *Congressional Record* is the official record of the proceedings and debates of the U.S. Congress. The *Congressional Record* began publication in 1873 and is still published today. It is published daily when Congress is in session, and its documents are available as ASCII text and in Adobe PDF.

# CONSUMER COMPLAINT DATABASE

https://catalog.data.gov/dataset/consumer-complaint-database

From the Consumer Financial Protection Bureau, these are complaints received about financial products and services available as comma-separated values (CSV) files and in other formats as well.

# CORPUS OF CONTEMPORARY AMERICAN ENGLISH

http://corpus.byu.edu/coca

The Corpus of Contemporary American English (COCA) is the largest public access corpus of English and the only large and balanced corpus of American English. The corpus contains more than 520 million words of text and is equally divided among spoken, fiction, popular magazines, newspapers, and academic texts.

# DOCUMENTCLOUD

https://www.documentcloud.org

DocumentCloud runs every document you upload through Thomson Reuters OpenCalais, which tags the people, places, companies, facts, and events in the document.

# EBSCO NEWSPAPER SOURCE

https://www.ebscohost.com/public/newspaper-source

This database provides full text for over 400 national (United States), international, and regional newspapers. It also offers television and radio news transcripts from major networks.

# GLOWBE: CORPUS OF GLOBAL WEB-BASED ENGLISH

http://corpus.byu.edu/glowbe

The Corpus of Global Web-Based English (GloWbE), created by Mark Davies of Brigham Young University, is composed of 1.9 billion words from 1.8 million web-pages in 20 different English-speaking countries. The corpus was released in 2013 and is related to other large corpora including the 520 million-word Corpus of Contemporary American English (COCA) and the 400 million-word Corpus of Historical American English (COHA). Together, these three corpora allow research-ers to examine variation in English by dialect, genre, and over time. Data in GloWbE comes in three formats including tables for relational databases, word/lemma/part of speech, or text.

# HATHITRUST

https://www.hathitrust.org/datasets

HathiTrust is a partnership of major research institutions and libraries working to ensure that the cultural record is preserved and accessible long into the future.

HathiTrust's documents include non-Google-digitized volumes, which are freely available, and Google-digitized volumes, which are available through an agreement with Google. Within each category, there is a distinction between public domain works available only in the United States and public domain works available anywhere in the world. The non-Google-digitized volumes include approximately 550,000 public domain volumes as of March 2015, which are primarily English-language materials published prior to 1923. The Google-digitized volumes include approximately 4.8 million public domain volumes as of March 2015, representing a wide variety of languages, subjects, and dates.

## INTERNET ARCHIVE

https://archive.org

Founded in 1996 and located in San Francisco, the Internet Archive is a nonprofit organization that was founded to build an Internet library. Its purposes include offering permanent access for researchers, historians, scholars, people with disabilities, and the general public to historical collections that exist in digital format. Internet Archive contains millions of free books, movies, software, and music.

## JSTOR FOR RESEARCH

http://dfr.jstor.org

JSTOR is a popular digital library of academic journals, books, and primary sources. JSTOR's Data for Research service is a free service for researchers wishing to analyze content on JSTOR through a variety of lenses and perspectives.

## LEXISNEXIS ACADEMIC

https://www.lexisnexis.com/hottopics/lnacademic

LexisNexis Group is a corporation providing computer-assisted legal research as well as business research and risk management services. Their news database includes news from over 10,000 sources.

# OBSERVATORY ON SOCIAL MEDIA

https://osome.iuni.iu.edu

The Observatory on Social Media (also known as Truthy) is an informal nickname associated with a research project of the Center for Complex Networks and Systems Research at the Indiana University School of Informatics and Computing. The project aims to study how information spreads on social media, such as Twitter. The project has focused on domains such as news, politics, social movements, scientific results, and trending social media topics. Researchers develop theoretical computer models and validate them by analyzing public data, mainly from the Twitter streaming application programming interface (API). Social media posts available through public APIs are processed without human intervention or judgment to visualize and study the spread of millions of memes. An important goal of the project is to help mitigate misuse and abuse of social media by helping us better understand how social media can be potentially abused.

# OPENLIBRARY

https://openlibrary.org/data

Open Library is an open, editable library catalog building toward a webpage for every book ever published.

# PUBLIC.RESOURCE.ORG

https://public.resource.org

Public.Resource.Org contains bulk downloadable content harvested from government websites and other sources.

# PUBMED

https://www.ncbi.nlm.nih.gov/pubmed

PubMed includes more than 25 million citations for literature from biomedical fields. Some citations include links to full-text content.

## ROBOTS READING *VOGUE*

http://dh.library.yale.edu/projects/vogue

This project from Yale University is based on the ProQuest *Vogue* Archive (www .proquest.com/products-services/vogue_archive.html). *Vogue* is an American lifestyle magazine that has been continuously published for over a century. The archive contains over 2,700 covers, 400,000 pages, and six TB of data.

## TEXT CREATION PARTNERSHIP

www.textcreationpartnership.org

The primary goal of the Text Creation Partnership is to create standardized, accurate XML/SGML encoded electronic text editions of early printed books. The partnership transcribes and encodes the page images of books from ProQuest's Early English Books Online, Gale Cengage's Eighteenth Century Collections Online, and Readex's Evans Early American Imprints. The resulting text files are jointly funded and owned by more than 150 libraries worldwide.

## the @unitedstates PROJECT

https://theunitedstates.io

The @unitedstates project is a shared commons of data and tools for the United States that features work from people with the Sunlight Foundation, GovTrack.us, the *New York Times*, and the Electronic Frontier Foundation.

## UNIVERSITY OF OXFORD TEXT ARCHIVE

https://ota.ox.ac.uk

The University of Oxford Text Archive develops, collects, catalogs, and preserves electronic literary and linguistic resources for use in research, teaching, and learning. The Oxford Text Archive also gives advice on the creation and use of these resources and is involved in the development of standards and infrastructure for electronic language resources.

# YAHOO WEBSCOPE PROGRAM

https://webscope.sandbox.yahoo.com/#datasets

The Yahoo Webscope Program data sets are a reference library of interesting and scientifically useful data sets for noncommercial use by academics and other scientists.

# APPENDIX B

## Text Preparation and Cleaning Software

Text data are not always in a format that can be used for social science research. In many cases, you will need to clean your data, eliminating nonwords such as URLs, advertisements, and copied text (such as in e-mail chains). In some text mining projects, you will need to eliminate stop words (see Chapter 8) such as *and* and *the*. While there is no one standard list of English stop words, an Internet search will yield several such lists that you can use.

There are several tools and methods that can be used for cleaning texts, including simple Find and Replace commands in word processors and spreadsheets, regular expressions (regexes), and software.

## FIND AND REPLACE

The most basic tool for cleaning texts is the Find and Replace text editor command in word processors such as Microsoft Word and Google Docs. To use Find and Replace effectively, you must know your data well, keeping your eyes on patterns and repetitions in your files. Before trying Replace All, start by replacing unwanted text one at a time until you are certain you are not replacing important content. Work around the parts that don't repeat, and use the existing structure of the data to your advantage.

## REGEXES

When there are patterns in a text file but not exact character matches, you can use regular expressions, or regexes. Microsoft Word, Google Docs, and Google Sheets all have regex functionality, which can be a tremendous time saver when working with large files.

In Microsoft Word, regex Find and Replace commands use wildcard characters, which are keyboard characters that can represent one or many characters. For instance, the asterisk (*) typically represents one or more characters, and the question mark (?) typically represents a single character. Regexes are combinations of literal and wildcard characters that you use to find and replace patterns of text. The literal text characters indicate text that must exist in the target string of text, and the wild-card characters indicate the text that can vary in the target string.

https://support.office.com/en-us/article/Find-and-replace-text-by-using-regular-expressions-Advanced-eeaa03b0-e9f3-4921-b1e8-85b0ad1c427f

In Google Docs, the command REGEXREPLACE allows you to replace part of a text string with a different text string using regular expressions. If you are using Google Sheets, you can use REGEXMATCH. You can learn more about Google's regular expressions here:

https://support.google.com/docs/answer/3098244

Regexes require some memorization and practice, but if you need to clean large documents and document collections they are a powerful and inexpensive option.

# SOFTWARE

While Find and Replace and regular expressions are useful tools for cleaning data, there are many software packages available that can help you clean, organize, and manage your document collections.

## Adobe Acrobat

https://acrobat.adobe.com/us/en/acrobat.html

The full version of Adobe Acrobat (not Adobe Reader) allows you to convert PDF files into plain text quickly as well as perform top of the line optical character recognition (OCR). If you are having trouble with texts with formatting issues, you may consider trying Acrobat.

## BBEdit

http://www.barebones.com/products/bbedit

BBEdit is a professional HTML and text editor for Mac designed for web authors and software developers. BBEdit's features include regular expression (regex) pattern matching, search and replace across multiple files, project definition tools, function navigation and syntax coloring for numerous source code languages, code folding, FTP and SFTP open and save, AppleScript, Mac OS X Unix scripting support, text and code completion, and a complete set of HTML markup tools.

## OpenRefine

http://openrefine.org

OpenRefine (formerly Google Refine) is a free, open source tool for cleaning data and transforming it from one format into another.

## TextCleanr

www.textcleanr.com

TextCleanr is a simple-to-use web-based tool for fixing and cleaning up text when copying and pasting between applications. It is able to remove e-mail indents, find and replace, and clean up spacing and line breaks.

## TextPipe

www.datamystic.com/textpipe

This software suite for text processing makes it easy to write filters to strip documents of HTML tags or other similar formatting tasks.

## TextSoap

https://www.unmarked.com/textsoap

TextSoap automatically removes unwanted characters and can fix messed up carriage returns. It features over 100 built-in cleaners and has regular expression support.

## Trifacta Wrangler

https://www.trifacta.com/products/wrangler

Originally known as Data Wrangler, Trifacta Wrangler is a text cleaning and formatting tool that can automatically find patterns in your data based on things you select and can even make suggestions as to what to do with those patterns. It also learns over time, so it is constantly improving the suggestion system.

## UltraEdit

http://ultraedit.com

UltraEdit is a powerful Windows-based tool that can load and work with extremely large text files.

# APPENDIX C

## General Text Analysis Software

For students who prefer to use commercial or free software rather than programming environments like Python or R, in this appendix we provide an overview of general text mining and text analysis software that has been used in social science research. The software packages include Leximancer, Linguistic Inquiry and Word Count (LIWC), RapidMiner, TextAnalyst, and WordStat.

## LEXIMANCER

https://info.leximancer.com

Leximancer, originally created at the University of Queensland in Australia, includes concept mapping and sentiment analysis tools. In Leximancer, a text block is the unit of analysis, and the software is Bayesian-based in that it "learns" from an uploaded data set that it reads iteratively. For concept mapping, it creates a network of concepts defined in text blocks of about a paragraph in size. For sentiment analysis, Leximancer maps the frequency and co-occurrence of concepts with a built-in thesaurus of sentiment terms (positive versus negative).

Leximancer has been used by the health researchers Bell, Campbell, and Goldberg (2015) in their Foucauldian analysis of nurses' professional identities and by the psychologists Colley and Neal (2012) in their study of organizational safety.

## LINGUISTIC INQUIRY AND WORD COUNT

http://liwc.wpengine.com

Based on psychological research by James Pennebaker, Linguistic Inquiry and Word Count (LIWC) is a text analysis program that counts words based on psychological categories. It has been used in numerous studies of attentional focus, emotionality, social relationships, thinking styles, and personality differences (see Tausczik & Pennebaker,

2010). It has also been used in computer science studies (e.g., Danescu-Niculescu-Mizil, Lee, Pang, & Kleinberg, 2012).

# RAPIDMINER

http://rapidminer.com

RapidMiner is an open source system for data mining available as a stand-alone application for data analysis and as a data mining engine. It is used for business and commercial applications as well as for research and education and supports all steps of the data mining process including data preparation, validation, and results visualization.

# TEXTANALYST

http://megaputer.com/site/textanalyst.php

TextAnalyst maps out semantic relationships between specific terms within a document or set of documents to highlight thematic structures within the text. It quantifies terms based on their overall relevance to the text as a whole as well as their relationships to each other, generating a semantic network of the interrelated themes within a text document through the application of linguistic rules and an "artificial neural network" program that approximates human cognition. TextAnalyst has been used by the sociologists Adams (2009), Roscigno (Adams & Roscigno 2005), and Ignatow (2009).

# WORDSTAT

https://provalisresearch.com/products/content-analysis-software

WordStat works with QDA Miner (see Appendix D) and offers keyword-in-context, keyword retrieval, dictionary building, machine learning, and visualization capabilities.

## RESEARCH IN THE SPOTLIGHT
Using *TextAnalyst* to Study Collective Identity

Adams, J. (2009). Bodies of change: A comparative analysis of media representations of body modification practices. *Sociological Perspectives*, *52*(1), 103–129.

The sociologist Adams examined how mainstream media represent cosmetic surgery, tattooing, and body piercing by analyzing 72 newspaper articles using TextAnalyst. Adams found that cosmetic surgery and tattooing are positively presented as consumer lifestyle options, while piercing is often negatively framed as an unhealthy and problematic practice. The risks associated with cosmetic surgery and tattooing are frequently downplayed, as are tattooing's associations with deviance, while the potential risks related to body piercing are overemphasized. Gender is also a prominent framing device, often used to reinforce normative appearance expectations.

Adams, J., & Roscigno, V. (2005). White supremacists, oppositional culture and the world wide web. *Social Forces*, *84*(2), 759–778.

As in the 2009 study of body modification by Josh Adams, in this study from 2005 Adams and the sociologist Roscigno used TextAnalyst to investigate how white supremacist organizations use the Internet. Specifically, Adams and Roscigno investigated how these groups recruit members, build collective identities, and organize their activities. The authors used TextAnalyst to construct semantic network graphs (see Appendix G on concept maps) of thematic content from major white supremacist websites and to delineate patterns and thematic associations relative to three aspects of social movement culture: identity, interpretational framing of cause and effect, and political efficacy. They found that nationalism, religion, and definitions of responsible citizenship are interwoven with race to create a sense of collective identity for members of these groups as well as for potential recruits. These groups use interpretative frameworks that simultaneously identify threatening social issues and provide corresponding recommendations for social action. Adams and Roscigno discussed how the Internet has been integrated into white supremacist groups' tactical repertoires.

# APPENDIX D

## Qualitative Data Analysis Software

---

Narrative analysis (see Chapter 10), thematic analysis (see Chapter 11), metaphor analysis (see Chapter 12), and other forms of qualitative and mixed method text analysis can be performed without the help of highly specialized software (beyond word processors and spreadsheets). But specialized software can help to expand the scope, methodological sophistication, and rigor of text analysis research. The most popular software used for text analysis is known as computer-assisted qualitative data analysis software (CAQDAS, or qualitative data analysis software [QDAS] for short). QDAS packages are tools for organizing collections of documents so that they can be more efficiently and effectively analyzed qualitatively, although as we will see several QDAS packages include modules for statistical analysis and data visualization. Such software is widely used in psychology, sociology, and marketing research, and typically includes tools for content searching, coding or labeling text, linking text units, querying, writing and annotation, and visualizing results as maps, networks, or word clouds (see Appendix G).

Versions of QDAS have been around since the 1980s and have been used to assist content analysis, discourse analysis, grounded theory analysis, and mixed method projects. The first version of the QDAS program NUD*IST was released in 1981, and ATLAS and WinMAX were released in 1989. These software packages subsequently evolved into more developed forms: WinMAX into MAXQDA, ATLAS into ATLAS.ti, and NUD*IST into NVivo.

QDAS packages perform several interrelated functions for researchers. First and foremost they allow researchers to code and retrieve samples of text. They also allow researchers to use coded text to build theoretical models of the social, psychological, cognitive, and linguistic processes that are thought to have generated the text. Their interfaces also allow for relatively easy text retrieval and for management of and navigation within large document collections. In addition to these core functions, as we will see, many software packages allow for visualization and statistical analysis of the interrelationships between coded textual units.

A central feature of QDAS is the ability to set up rules to apply labels to texts. QDAS packages offer a variety of text coding techniques that allow for code and retrieve functionality, including *in vivo coding*, an inductive method where a word or short phrase taken from the text itself is the code or label (King, 2008). Other forms of coding include *free coding*, which involves assigning any code to arbitrary sequences of data; *contextual coding*, in which users label text in such a way as to allow them to quickly navigate to view the labeled text in context; *automatic coding*, which involves assigning codes automatically to search results; and even artificial intelligence-based *software-generated coding*, in which the software suggests codes based on its own analysis of the text.

QDAS packages feature a number of different types of text search tools, including simple searches; Boolean searches using the Boolean operators AND, OR, and NOT; placeholder searches that allow you to use placeholders for certain characters; and proximity searches that allow you to retrieve combinations of two or more text strings and/or codes that occur in a definable proximity to each other. Fuzzy searches, or "approximation searches," are as of this writing exclusive to NVivo. These allow you to perform searches that retrieve textual data even if the data contain typographic errors. Combination searches involve combinations of some of the previously mentioned types of searches.

In addition to coding and searching texts, QDAS packages provide a variety of different tools for annotation (e.g., memo writing and storage) and for producing output in different formats, from variable diagrams and network diagrams for visualizing theoretical models, to word clouds. Most software allows users to export data on code and word frequencies to allows for statistical analysis with appropriate statistical packages such as SPSS or STATA, or else include statistical tools for analyzing word frequencies, cross-tabulations, clusters, and word co-occurrence matrices.

Although you may be tempted to use the software that is most familiar or available to you, it is worth investing some time in carefully calculating the benefits and disadvantages of the various software tools that might be used for your project. Because the learning curve for some of these packages is steep and the time commitment involved substantial, it is important to choose the best tool for the job.

Different types of research projects require QDAS packages with different sets of features. Some qualitative data analysis software packages feature dashboards that are especially easy to use, others have more powerful project management and data organization tools, while still others allow users to easily explore and interact with their data.

While QDAS packages are popular and widely used in several disciplines, the value of using software in qualitative analysis has been vigorously debated. Coffey, Holbrook, and Atkinson (1996), Macmillan (2005), and Goble, Austin, Larsen, Kreitzer, and Brintnell (2012) are good places to start for critical appraisals of QDAS (see the Further Reading section).

Loughborough University's QDAS site provides some useful guidelines for matching software to research project requirements. They recommend MaxQDA or QDA Miner for mixed methods projects; NVivo and ATLAS.ti for discourse analysis (see Chapter 1); and ATLAS.ti, HyperRESEARCH, or Qualrus for virtual ethnography (see Chapter 1). It is, of course, important to refer to the software websites to keep up to date on new features, as new versions of both commercial and open source software are released frequently.

# COMMERCIAL SOFTWARE

## ATLAS.ti

http://atlasti.com

One of the first and most highly developed QDAS tools, it allows coded data to be exported for analysis with statistical packages such as SPSS.

## Dedoose

www.dedoose.com

A web-based qualitative and mixed methods research application, Dedoose builds on tools available in its predecessor, EthnoNotes. Dedoose is specifically designed to support the concurrent analysis of large amounts of mixed data by teams of geographically dispersed researchers.

## f4analyse

http://www.audiotranskription.de/english/f4-analyse

This is a basic, competitively priced QDAS tool from Germany that is easy to use.

## HyperRESEARCH

http://www.researchware.com/products/hyperresearch.html

HyperRESEARCH is a QDAS for the Mac OS featuring advanced multimedia capabilities.

## Kwalitan

http://www.kwalitan.nl

Designed to assist in the development of grounded theories, this software from the Netherlands enables hierarchical coding and the navigation of data with Boolean searches.

## MAXQDA

http:// maxqda.com

MAXQDA is a sophisticated package with statistical and visualization add-ons available.

## NVivo

http://www.qsrinternational.com/product

NVivo features relatively elaborate organizing functions that allow users to link together text data in a variety of ways.

## QDA Miner

https://provalisresearch.com/products/qualitative-data-analysis-software

A sophisticated QDAS tool that integrates with SimStat, a statistical data analysis module, and WordStat, a quantitative content analysis and text mining module.

## Qualrus

http://qualrus.com

Qualrus is a QDAS tool that is "portable" for use on multiple platforms (Mac, Windows).

## Quirkos

https://www.quirkos.com

Quirkos is an easy-to-use and competitively priced QDAS tool from the University of Edinburgh.

Although free trial versions of most commercial QDAS packages are available, the full versions can be expensive, particularly for single users who do not have access to a group license. So you may want to explore some of the many free and open source QDAS tools that may meet their needs. If you already use the programming language R, or are considering using it for quantitative analysis, you can use the RQDA package to combine text coding with the statistical power of R. RQDA is probably the most advanced of all the free QDAS packages. It allows users to perform word cloud analysis (see Appendix G), create queries for complex cross-coding retrieval, program auto-coding commands, plot the relationship between codes, and export data as spreadsheets. RQDA also features a very intuitive user interface.

# FREE AND OPEN SOURCE QUALITATIVE DATA ANALYSIS SOFTWARE

There are dozens of free and open source QDAS/CAQDAS tools available, including QDA Miner Lite, which is a free version of QDA Miner with limited features for both PC and Mac, Open Code (PC only), Saturate (cloud), and Coding Analysis Toolkit (CAT; cloud). Some of these packages are quite sophisticated: Text Analysis Markup System (TAMS), and RQDA allow both inductive and deductive coding as well as coding memos, can support hierarchical or structured coding, provide basic coding statistics, and perform text and coding retrieval. For quick and simple coding, Open Code and Saturate are easy to use, although they only allow one code per predefined text segment. Saturate is particularly well suited for coding with more than one analyst.

## AQUAD

www.aquad.de/en

Aquad is a German open source QDAS package with sophisticated features including Boolean search.

## Cassandre

www.cassandre.ulg.ac.be

Cassandre is a free QDAS package for Windows, Mac, and Linux from Belgium. Most documentation is in French.

## Coding Analysis Toolkit

http://cat.textifer.com

Coding Analysis Toolkit (CAT) is a free web-based tool from the University of Pittsburgh. CAT was designed to use mainly keystrokes rather than the mouse for coding and can import an ATLAS.ti project for quantitative analysis, though it has a coding mechanism built into itself as well.

## CATMA

http://www.catma.de

CATMA is software for Windows, Mac OS, and Linux developed at the University of Hamburg mainly for humanities researchers.

## Compendium

http://compendium.open.ac.uk/institute

Compendium is a general purpose sharing and collaboration tool from the Open University in the United Kingdom.

## FreeQDA

http://freeqda.sourceforge.net

FreeQDA is an open source QDAS tool.

## libreQDA

http://www.libreqda.edu.uy

This is a free Spanish-language QDAS tool developed in Uruguay.

## Open Code

http://www.phmed.umu.se/english/units/epidemiology/research/open-code

Free from Umea University in Sweden, Open Code was originally developed for use with grounded theory but now is a general-purpose qualitative data analysis tool.

## QDA Miner Lite

https://provalisresearch.com/products/qualitative-data-analysis-software/freeware

QDA Miner Lite is an easy-to-use version of QDA Miner that offers basic QDAS features.

## RQDA

http://rqda.r-forge.r-project.org

RQDA is a package for the popular programming language R. Used with R, it performs both qualitative and quantitative analysis.

## Saturate

http://onlineqda.hud.ac.uk/Step_by_step_software/Saturate

Saturate is an online QDAS tool from the University of Huddersfield in the United Kingdom.

### Text Analysis Markup System

https://sourceforge.net/projects/tamsys

Text Analysis Markup System (TAMS) is an open source QDAS tool.

### Text Analysis Markup System Analyzer

http://tamsys.sourceforge.net

Text Analysis Markup System (TAMS) Analyzer works with TAMS to allow users to efficiently assign codes to text passages.

# QDAS TIPS

- Different packages are best suited to different types of research projects. Don't rush when selecting a package.

- Check that the package you select can output codes in formats you can use at later stages of your research—for example, for statistical analysis or visualization.

# INTERNET RESOURCES

### CAQDAS Networking Project

https://www.surrey.ac.uk/sociology/research/researchcentres/caqdas

### Loughborough University's CAQDAS Site

www.restore.ac.uk/lboro/research/software/caqdas_comparison.php

# Further Reading

Coffey, A., Holbrook, B., & Atkinson, P. (1996). Qualitative data analysis: Technologies and representations. *Sociological Research Online*, *1*(1). Retrieved from http://www.socresonline.org.uk/1/1/4.html

Goble, E., Austin, W., Larsen, D., Kreitzer, L. E., & Brintnell, S. (2012). Habits of mind and the split-mind effect: When computer-assisted qualitative data analysis software is used in phenomenological research. *Forum: Qualitative Social Research*, *13*(2). Retrieved from http://www.qualitative-research.net/index.php/fqs/article/view/1709

Macmillan, K. (2005). More than just coding? Evaluating CAQDAS in a discourse analysis of news texts. *Forum: Qualitative Social Research*, *6*(3). Retrieved from http://www.qualitative-research.net/index.php/fqs/article/view/28/59

# APPENDIX E

## Opinion Mining Software

Opinion mining (sentiment analysis) can be performed with Python or in other programming environments, but there are also many opinion mining software packages available. While these are designed mainly for business intelligence, a few have been used for social science research.

## LEXICODER

www.lexicoder.com

Lexicoder is a Java-based, multiplatform package for automated content analysis of text that is freely available for academic use. Lexicoder features a sentiment dictionary designed to capture sentiment in political texts.

## OPINIONFINDER

http://mpqa.cs.pitt.edu/opinionfinder

OpinionFinder is a system that processes documents and automatically identifies subjective sentences as well as various aspects of subjectivity within sentences, including agents who are sources of opinion, direct subjective expressions and speech events, and sentiment expressions. OpinionFinder was developed by researchers at the University of Pittsburgh, Cornell University, and the University of Utah.

## RAPIDMINER SENTIMENT ANALYSIS

https://rapidminer.com/solutions/sentiment-analysis

RapidMiner is an analytics platform for web crawling and mining (see Appendix C) that provides an integrated environment for machine learning, data mining, text mining, predictive analytics, and business analytics.

# SAS SENTIMENT ANALYSIS STUDIO

https://www.sas.com/en_us/software/analytics/sentiment-analysis.html

SAS is widely used in business but is not widely used in the social sciences due to its high cost.

# APPENDIX F

## Concordance and Keyword Frequency Software

As is discussed briefly in Chapter 1, concordancing arose out of a practical need for biblical scholars to be able to alphabetize and cite words and passages in the bible. Linguists began using computers to create concordances in the 1950s, and literary scholars as well as library and information scientists began working with computer-generated concordances that analyzed keywords in context (KWIC) in the 1970s. The term *corpus linguistics* did not come into common usage until the early 1980s, and social scientists did not begin to use corpus linguistics tools until the 1990s, when Fairclough and other critical discourse analysis (CDA) researchers (see Chapter 1) began to experiment with them.

## ADELAIDE TEXT ANALYSIS TOOL

https://www.adelaide.edu.au/carst/resources-tools/adtat

The Adelaide Text Analysis Tool (AdTAT) is a cross-platform tool that can conduct basic word and phrase searches and searches for associated words and phrases. It provides frequency lists of words appearing both left and right of search terms, can print and save results, and can assist in constructing corpora.

## AntConc

www.laurenceanthony.net/software/antconc

AntConc is a free corpus analysis toolkit for concordancing and text analysis. It works on multiple platforms and includes a concordancer, word and keyword frequency generators, tools for cluster and lexical bundle analysis, and a word distribution plot. AntConc also offers the choice of simple wildcard searches or regular expression (regex) searches (see Appendix B) and features an intuitive user interface.

# SIMPLE CONCORDANCE PROGRAM

www.textworld.com/scp

Simple Concordance Program is a free concordance and word-listing program for Windows and Mac that lets you create word lists and search natural language text files for words, phrases, and patterns. It is able to read texts written in English, French, German, Polish, Greek, Russian, and other languages. In her 2014 book on social movements and social class, the sociologist Leondar-Wright used Simple Concordance Program to analyze class speech differences.

# TextSTAT

http://neon.niederlandistik.fu-berlin.de/en/textstat

TextSTAT is a simple program that reads plain text files and HTML files directly from the Internet and produces word frequency lists and concordances from these files. It allows you to use regular expressions (regexes; see Appendix B) and can cope with many different languages and file encodings. Social science studies using TextSTAT include a 2010 study by the communications researchers Hellsten, Dawson, and Leydesdorff that used semantic maps (see Appendix G) to analyze newspaper debates on artificial sweeteners published in the *New York Times* between 1980 and 2006.

# WMATRIX

http://ucrel.lancs.ac.uk/wmatrix

Wmatrix is a web-based software package that features corpus annotation tools and standard corpus linguistic methodologies such as frequency lists and concordances.

# WORDSMITH

www.lexically.net/wordsmith

WordSmith is a popular package for Windows that offers tools for analyzing keywords in context (KWIC), analyzing word co-occurrences, and building dictionaries. Published by Lexical Analysis Software and Oxford University Press since 1996, it has been used by CDA (see Chapter 1) researchers including Fairclough (2006). It has also been used by media researchers (e.g., Ensslin & Johnson, 2006).

# APPENDIX G

## Visualization Software

Software tools for visualization of patterns of word use and themes in texts are increasingly popular in the social sciences. In this appendix, we survey visualization tools that can be used with qualitative data analysis software (QDAS) packages (see Appendix D) as well as in combination with other types of software.

While the field of visualization is developing rapidly and exciting new tools for visualizing patterns in texts are introduced regularly, you should recognize that these tools have some limitations. The majority of visualization techniques ultimately transform qualitative data into quantifiable segments, an approach to analysis that may be antithetical to the goals of qualitative research methods (see Biernacki, 2014). If done poorly, visualizations may distract from the meaning and power of your analysis. Visual transformation of texts may result in a loss of emotional tone and nuances of meaning and may also lead to the impression that an analysis is less ambiguous and contradictory than it actually is. Thus, in addition to visualizations, you should consider including text excerpts or longer narratives to explore your texts and communicate your findings to your readers.

There are many software tools available to visually represent words and themes in texts (see Henderson & Segal, 2013), including correspondence analysis (LeRoux & Rouanet, 2010), path and network diagrams (Durland & Fredericks, 2005), decision trees (Ryan & Bernard, 2010), and tools for visualization of sentiment analysis (Gregory et al., 2006). In this appendix, we survey several of the most accessible visualization tools for text mining and text analysis including word clouds, word trees and phrase nets, and matrices and maps.

## WORD CLOUDS

Word clouds provide a visual display of word counts from one or more texts. The more frequently a word appears, the larger the word is displayed in a word cloud visual (Viégas & Wattenberg, 2008). It has been only relatively recently that word counts have become easy to display visually in word or tag clouds through popular online applications such as Wordle (http:// wordle.net) or TagCrowd (http://tagcrowd.com), and word cloud tools have been added to many QDAS packages including NVivo, ATLAS.ti, Dedoose, and MAXQDA (see Appendix D). Although word cloud software creates dramatic visuals, significant concerns have been brought up about its use. One concern is that word clouds rely entirely on word frequency and do not provide context for readers to understand how words are used within a text (Harris, 2011). Word clouds are unable to differentiate between words with positive or negative connotations, and they can be visually misleading because longer words take more space within the cloud (Viégas & Wattenberg, 2008, p. 51). Despite these concerns, word clouds' ease of use can make them a practical tool for social scientists if they are used sparingly and their limitations are acknowledged. Although not very useful for complex analysis, they can be used in a project's early phases to help researchers identify keywords in texts or compare multiple corpora or documents (Weisgerber & Butler, 2009). For example, two or more word clouds can be shown together to contrast word usage across corpora or documents (e.g., Uprichard, 2012). Advanced word cloud visualizations such as parallel tag clouds (Collins, Viégas, & Wattenberg, 2009) and SparkClouds (Lee, Riche, Karlson, & Carpendale, 2010) are recent developments that allow users to compare multiple word clouds. Finally, when coupled with written analysis and explanation, word clouds can be used to illustrate ideas or themes for lay audiences.

# WORD TREES AND PHRASE NETS

The two main tools for visualizing texts in terms of sentences and short phrases (rather than single words as in word clouds) are word trees and phrase nets. These tools were originally developed as part of IBM's project Many Eyes but are now available in NVivo and other QDAS packages. Word tree software allows researchers to see how a particular word is used in sentences or phrases and provides visual displays of the connection of an identified word or words to other words in a corpus through a branching system (Viégas & Wattenberg, 2008). These systems allow the researcher to have the tree branch to words that come either before or after the identified word, providing some context for words, which is an improvement over word clouds. For example, Henderson and Segal (2013) examined the relationship between a research university and local community organizations and found that the understandings and goals of research varied for the two groups. A word tree created from the study's documents displayed all the sentences that contain the word *research* to provide a better understanding of how this word was used and the variation of its use. Although they resemble word trees, phrase nets differ from word trees in that they focus on connections of word pairs rather than whole sentences (see van Ham, Wattenberg, & Viégas, 2009).

Although sentence visualization tools provide more contextual information than single word analysis, they are best suited for exploratory data analysis (Weisgerber & Butler, 2009) rather than for complex analysis or hypothesis testing. By focusing on keywords within sentences, word trees and phrase maps allow social scientists to quickly identify patterns of word use within corpora and whether words are being used in divergent ways within or across texts.

## MATRICES AND MAPS

Matrices and maps are tools for the visualization of themes (rather than words or sentences) in texts. Since the process of identifying themes requires at least an initial analysis of the texts (see Chapter 11), visualization of themes is more valuable in the analysis and reporting phases of a project than in exploratory phases. Because researchers can rank themes or place them into nonordinal categories, visualizing a corpus at the thematic level offers more options and dimensions for visual representations than at the word or sentence level.

Matrices are sets of numbers arranged in rows or columns. In text analysis, a matrix involves "the crossing of two or more dimensions . . . to see how they interact" (Miles & Huberman 1994, p. 239). Matrices are very useful for organizing textual data and for visualizing the relationships between and among categories of data, examining how categories relate to theoretical concepts, and searching for propositions linking categories of data. Similar to a cluster heat map (Wilkinson & Friendly, 2009) or an ethnoarray (Dohan, Abramson, & Miller, 2012), a benefit of matrices is that they provide an overview of thematic patterns within corpora and allow for comparison between corpora. As with QDAS packages' increased capabilities with word clouds, most qualitative software packages have the ability to create a matrix based on theme frequency with links to the corresponding text within the program. However, because matrices do not provide the stories or context behind the themes they organize, ideally, when creating matrices or other visualizations, researchers should link the individual boxes to quotes that support reader understanding of the theme.

Matrices, mind maps, and concept maps (Trochim, 1989; Wheeldon & Ahlberg, 2012) focus on the connections and relations between themes. In mind maps and concept maps, arrows indicate the direction of influence and can be made different thicknesses to signify the degree of connection if that information is available. Maps can be easily created for data analysis and reporting with standard or specialized software such as ATLAS.ti, MAXQDA, and NVivo. For example, Trochim, Cook, and Setze (1994) used concept mapping to develop a conceptual framework of the views of 14 staff members of a psychiatric rehabilitation agency's views of a program of supported employment for individuals with severe mental illness. And Wheeldon and Faubert (2009) showed how concept maps can be used in data collection in an exploratory study of the perceptions of four Canadians.

# INTERNET RESOURCES

### The Collaboration Site of Viégas and Wattenberg

http://hint.fm

### "Visualizing the Future of Interaction Studies"

www.cios.org/ejcpublic/019/1/019125.HTML

### The Word Tree, an Interactive Visual Concordance

http://hint.fm/papers/wordtree_final2.pdf

### Wordle

www.wordle.net

### TagCrowd

http://tagcrowd.com

# APPENDIX H

## List of Websites

## GENERAL TEXT MINING WEBSITES

### The DiRT Directory

http://dirtdirectory.org

The DiRT (Digital Research Tools) Directory is a registry of digital research tools for scholarly use. DiRT makes it easy for scholars conducting digital research to find and compare research tools including content management systems, optical character recognition software, statistical analysis packages, and visualization software.

### Loughborough University's CAQDAS Site

www.restore.ac.uk/lboro/research/software/caqdas_comparison.php

This site offers a comparative overview of computer-assisted qualitative data analysis software (CAQDAS) packages (see Appendix D). The site is ordered by product functions rather than by software products.

### The National Centre for Text Mining

www.nactem.ac.uk

The National Centre for Text Mining (NaCTeM) is the first publicly funded text mining center in the world. Operated by the University of Manchester, the site links to text mining services provided by NaCTeM, software tools, text mining groups seminars, general events, conferences, workshops, tutorials, demonstrations, and text mining publications.

### The QDAS Networking Project

https://www.surrey.ac.uk/sociology/research/researchcentres/caqdas

This site, operated by the University of Surrey, provides practical support, training, and information in the use of a range of software programs designed to assist qualitative data analysis. It features platforms for debates concerning the methodological and epistemological issues arising from the use of such software packages.

## Text Analysis Portal for Research

http:// tapor.ca

The Text Analysis Portal for Research (TAPoR) is a gateway to the tools used in text mining and text analysis. The project is led by Rockwell, Sinclair, Uszkalo, and Radzikowska and housed at the University of Alberta. The site features software reviews and recommendations and links to papers, articles, and other sources of information about specific software tools.

# SOCIAL SCIENCE ETHICS WEBSITES

### Ethical Decision-Making and Internet Research: Recommendations From the AoIR Ethics Working Committee

http://aoir.org/reports/ethics2.pdf

### The American Psychological Association Report Psychological Research Online: Opportunities and Challenges

www.apa.org/science/leadership/bsa/internet/internet-report.aspx

### The British Psychological Society's Ethics Guidelines for Internet-Mediated Research

www.bps.org.uk/system/files/Public%20files/inf206-guidelines-for-internet-mediated-research.pdf

### The Davis–Madsen Ethics Scenarios From the Academy of Management Blog Post "Ethics in Research Scenarios: What Would YOU Do?"

http://ethicist.aom.org/2013/02/ethics-in-research-scenarios-what-would-you-do

### The Ethicist Blog From the Academy of Management

http://ethicist.aom.org

**The Office of Research Integrity, U.S. Department of Health and Human Services**

http://ori.hhs.gov

## SOCIAL SCIENCE WRITING WEBSITES

**The Social Science Writing Project**

http://www.csun.edu/sswp

**"What Is a Social Science Essay?"**

www.sagepub.com/sites/default/files/upm-binaries/39896_9780857023711.pdf

**"Becoming a 'Stylish' Writer: Attractive Prose Will Not Make You Appear Any Less Smart"**

Rachel Toor

http://chronicle.com/article/Becoming-a-Stylish-Writer/132677

## OPEN ACCESS JOURNAL ARTICLES

**"Opening up to Big Data: Computer-Assisted Analysis of Textual Data in Social Sciences"**

Gregor Wiedemann

www.qualitative-research.net/index.php/fqs/article/view/1949

http://nbn-resolving.de/urn:nbn:de:0114-fqs1302231

**"Hypertextuality, Complexity, Creativity: Using Linguistic Software Tools to Uncover New Information about the Food and Drink of Historic Mayans"**

Rose Lema

www.qualitative-research.net/index.php/fqs/article/view/1852

## "Text Mining Tools in the Humanities: An Analysis Framework"

Geoffrey Rockwell, John Simpson, Stéfan Sinclair, Kirsten Uszkalo, Susan Brown, Amy Dyrbye, and Ryan Chartier

http://journalofdigitalhumanities.org/2-3/text-mining-tools-in-the-humanities-an-analysis-framework

## "Mapping Texts: Visualizing American Newspapers"

Andrew J. Torget and Jon Christensen

http://journalofdigitalhumanities.org/1-3/mapping-texts-project-by-andrew-torget-and-jon-christensen

http://mappingtexts.org

# APPENDIX I

## Statistical Tools

Statistical analysis is traditionally performed on data organized in table (spreadsheet) format. In spreadsheets, data are arrayed in tables where each row represents a record and each column a variable, which is a feature of the record. Text mining data in tables contain two types of variables: (1) quantitative or numeric variables such as word frequency and (2) nominal or categorical variables such as codes for different words or phrases.

Statistical software packages such as STATA, SPSS, SAS, and R are often used to analyze data in tabular format from text mining projects. There are several statistical measurements and operations that are typically taught in social science statistics courses that are used in text mining and text analysis research, including reliability coefficients, analysis of variance (ANOVA), chi-square tests, and multiple regression (for general overviews, see Field, 2013; Field & Miles, 2012).

## RELIABILITY COEFFICIENTS

In statistics, interrater reliability (or interrater agreement) is the degree of agreement among raters. Interrater reliability is useful for determining if a particular scale is appropriate for measuring a particular variable; if multiple raters do not agree, either the scale is defective or the raters need retraining.

A number of statistics can be used to determine interrater reliability, with different statistics being appropriate for different types of measurement. Some options are joint probability of agreement, Cohen's kappa, Fleiss's kappa, interrater correlation, the concordance correlation coefficient, and intraclass correlation. But for text analysis and content analysis methods such as metaphor analysis, narrative analysis, and thematic analysis, the communications researcher and statistician Krippendorff's (2013, pp. 221–250) alpha coefficient is one of the most widely used statistical measure of interrater agreement. An advantage of Krippendorff's alpha is that it can deal with missing entries because it does not require the same number of raters for each item. Alpha can be calculated with software including SPSS and SAS (Hayes & Krippendorff, 2007) or in the statistics package R with the *kripp.alpha()* function in the interrater reliability package (https://www.rdocumentation.org/packages/irr/versions/0.70/topics/kripp.alpha).

Let's take a look at the use of reliability coefficients in the study of coverage of women's and men's sports in the *NCAA* (National Collegiate Athletic Association) *News*. In this 2004 study, the sport science researchers Cunningham, Sagas, Satore, Amsden, and Schellhase (2004) had two coders independently code each of 5,745 paragraphs in their sample of magazine issues for gender and for the paragraph's location within the magazine and content. Prior to this coding process, three pilot tests had been conducted using previous issues not included in the main analyses. The pilot tests allowed the research team to clarify the definitions for each category to improve consistency in the rating process. The research team read randomly selected coded paragraphs out of the context of the article to ensure that the coding was consistent with the information in each paragraph. The researchers then used Cohen's kappa to estimate the reliability, which they found was high for the coding of the paragraphs' gender ($\kappa = .912$, $p < .001$), content ($\kappa = .964$, $p < .001$), and location ($\kappa = .997$, $p < .001$). The reliability as measured by the Pearson product moment correlation for length ($r = .995$) was also high. When differences in the coding did occur, the researchers met to discuss the differences until agreement was reached.

## ANALYSIS OF VARIANCE

Developed by the statistician and evolutionary biologist Fisher, ANOVA is a collection of statistical models used to analyze variation between groups. In its simplest form, ANOVA provides a statistical test of whether or not the means of several groups are equal. ANOVAs are useful for comparing the means of three or more groups or variables.

There are two main types of analysis of variance models: (1) fixed-effects and (2) random-effects models. The fixed-effects ANOVA model applies to situations in which an experimenter applies one or more treatments to the subjects of the experiment to see whether the response variable values change. Random-effects models are used when a study's various factor levels are sampled from a larger population.

Let's return to the study by Cunningham and his colleagues (2004) to understand why and how they used an ANOVA for comparing groups, as the goal of their study was to examine whether their text collection (issues of the magazine *NCAA News*) contained equitable distributions of content about men and women's sports teams. For such a study, a random-effects ANOVA makes sense, and Cunningham and colleagues (2004) used the ANOVA procedure to compare average paragraph length for stories about men's sports teams versus stories about women's teams. They did not find a significant difference between the two (M = 2.25, SD = 2.17 for men's teams; M = 2.25, SD = 2.42 for women's teams), $F(1, 4063) = .01$, $p = .94$, where M and SD are the mean and the standard deviation for each group, respectively, and the

F statistic represents the difference between the variance between groups (in this case men's versus women's sports teams) over the variance within groups in an ANOVA. Unlike in a t-test, the ANOVA procedure can be used to calculate the differences between groups larger than two. In this case, the p statistic of 0.94 shows that the F statistic is not statistically significant for the compared groups. In addition to comparing paragraph length, Cunningham and his colleagues (2004) also ran ANOVAs for gender differences in the size of the photographs featured in the magazine (see also Hirschman, 1987).

## CHI-SQUARE TESTS

Where the ANOVA procedure is used to compare means across two or more groups, the chi-square statistic is used to compare word frequencies across documents or groups of documents that may differ in size. A statistical goodness-of-fit test originally suggested by the mathematician and biostatistician Pearson, the chi-square test is calculated based on the observed (actual) frequency $O_i$, the expected (averaged) frequency $E_i$, and the total frequency $N_i$ in corpus i. The null hypothesis of the chi-square goodness-of-fit test is that there is no difference between the observed frequencies of a word in the two corpora. Even if the null hypothesis is not rejected, it cannot be concluded that it is true. The chi-square statistic is typically calculated on a $2 \times 2$ table to compare frequencies of words or other variables between two corpora.

Let's return to Cunningham and colleagues' (2004) study of the *NCAA News* for an example of the use of a chi-square test. Why did Cunningham and colleagues (2004) perform a chi-square test in addition to an ANOVA? First, they used a chi-square analysis to establish that the amount of coverage allotted to women's teams did not differ from 1999 to 2001, $\chi^2(1) = 3.65$, p = .06, where the p value of over 0.05 indicates that the difference in the *proportions* of coverage of women's to men's sports had not changed to a statistically significant degree. Where an ANOVA would allow for a comparison of means either across genders or over time, the chi-square allows for a comparison of the proportion of women to men for the two periods. These proportions can be easily visualized as a $2 \times 2$ table with gender on one axis and time on the other. In addition to their comparison of men's sports versus women's sports over time, Cunningham and colleagues (2004) compared their paragraphs in terms of information related to athletics versus information not related to athletics, for stories on men's teams and women's teams. Results indicate that paragraphs focused on women and women's teams were just as likely to contain information related to athletics (70.4%) as were paragraphs focused on men and men's teams (69.3%), $\chi^2(1) = .57$, p = .45. They also used a chi-square to compare the proportion of women featured in photographs by year (see Ignatow, 2003, p. 12, for another example of the use of chi-square for comparing word frequency proportions).

# REGRESSION

Multiple regression is widely used in the social sciences to isolate the effects of one or more factors (*independent variables*) on some outcome of interest (a *dependent variable* or variables). Multiple regression, which is based on vector calculus, is a basic procedure featured in all statistical software packages used in the social sciences (see Field, 2013). In text mining and text analysis applications, regression, like ANOVA and chi-square, is used after data has been coded and univariate statistics (word frequencies and averages across groups) have been calculated. Regression models can be fitted to text data when the research question involves some factor, such as the speaker's age, gender, or number of friends, having an independent positive or negative effect on an outcome such as a frequency count or sentiment score (see Chapter 14 and Appendix E).

An example of the use of multiple regression is the study reviewed in Chapter 12 by management researchers Gibson and Zellmer-Bruhn. Gibson and Zellmer-Bruhn (2001) analyzed the relationship between metaphor use and employee attitudes in four countries. Their theoretical framework explained variance in the concept of teamwork across national and organizational cultures. Deriving five different metaphors for teamwork from team members' language used during interviews in four different geographic locations of six multinational corporations, they used the qualitative data analysis software QSR NUD*IST and TACT (see Appendix D) to analyze the frequency of the use of metaphors. For hypothesis testing, Gibson and Zellmer-Bruhn (2001) used a multinomial logit regression model (p. 293) where the dependent variable was the choice of teamwork metaphor from among the five possible types and the independent variables in their model were three dummy variables (binary variables that are coded either 1 [true] or 0 [false]) for country and five dummy variables for organization, representing the organizations in the study. Their models included control variables (independent variables that are not related to the research question or questions) for gender, team function, and the total number of words in each interview. Multiple regression allowed the researchers to control for (hold constant) gender, functional background, and total words in an interview. This revealed significant interaction effects that indicated that use of teamwork metaphors varied across countries and organizations net of other factors (for more detail, see Gibson & Zellmer-Bruhn, 2001, pp. 293–296).

# GLOSSARY

**Abduction** A type of inferential logic in which the conclusion is a hypothesis that can then be tested with a new or modified research design, abduction is a forensic logic that is commonly use in social science research but also in natural science fields such as geology and astronomy where experiments are rarely performed.

**Alceste** Software originally developed by Reinert in the 1980s, Alceste measures what Reinert termed *lexical worlds*, which he conceptualized as "mental rooms" that speakers successively inhabit, each with its own characteristic vocabulary.

**Analogy** A form of metaphorical language that involves comparison between two things, typically on the basis of their correspondence or partial similarity

**Analysis of variance (ANOVA)** Developed by the statistician and evolutionary biologist Fisher, analysis of variance (ANOVA) refers to statistical models for analyzing differences among group means and other statistics related to variation among groups.

**Anonymize** In almost all text mining research, social scientists are required to anonymize (use pseudonyms for) users' user names and full names.

**Appendix** Located at the end of social science research papers, the appendices are optional sections, typically lettered A, B, C, etc., that contain information that may be useful to the reader but is not a critical component of the paper's scientific contribution. An appendix may contain raw data, supplementary analysis, or other material.

**Background metaphors** Widely used metaphors in a community or group that can be collected from sources such as encyclopedias, journals, and specialist and generalist book according to Schmitt's (2005) method of comparative metaphor analysis

**Bag of words** In topic modeling, the treatment of a text as combinations of word co-occurrences regardless of syntax, narrative, or location within a text

**Bootstrapping** A list of organization names (or another named entity) and a list of patterns or rules to identify such organization names are incrementally learned from text

**Case selection** Strategies and procedures used in ethnographic and historical research for selecting data sources

**Characters** In narrative theory, characters are brought together with actions in a plotline that involves change over time.

**Cognitive linguistics** The research field in which cognitive metaphor theory, which provides a conceptual foundation for most contemporary metaphor analysis methodologies, developed.

**Cognitive metaphor theory (CMT)** Pioneered by cognitive linguists Lakoff and Johnson (1980), the basic claim of cognitive metaphor theory (CMT) is that language is structured by metaphor at a neural level and that metaphors used in natural language reveal cognitive schemas and associated patterns of neural connections shared by members of social groups.

**Coherence theory** A major philosophical position that has influenced social science in which truth, knowledge, and theory must fit within a coherent system of propositions that may be applied to specific cases only in accordance with properties of the general system

**Collocation** Closely related to linguistic co-occurrence, in corpus linguistics collocation refers to a sequence of words or terms that co-occur more often than would be expected by chance.

**Collocation identification** Automatically identifying sequences of words that have a special meaning when taken as a phrase

**Conceptual metaphors** In cognitive metaphor theory, natural language is characterized by the presence of conventional metaphorical expressions organized around prototypical metaphors, which Lakoff and Johnson (1980) have referred to as conceptual metaphors.

**Conclusion**  The final section of a research paper (although before the references and appendices), the conclusion section summarizes the main points made in the paper and makes suggestions for future research.

**Concordance(s)**  A list of the principal words used in a text, listing every instance of each word with its immediate context

**Constructionism**  Philosophical position based on questioning belief in an external reality that emphasizes how different groups construct their beliefs (see Gergen, 2015)

**Content analysis**  Research method for using systematic and generally quantitative tools to make inferences from recorded human communication (see Krippendorff, 2013)

**Contextual level**  Text analysis conducted at this level of analysis involves focusing on the immediate social context in which texts are produced and received, including situational contexts and the characteristics of the texts' authors.

**Conversation analysis**  An approach to the study of social interaction that began with a focus on casual daily conversation but expanded to include task- and institution-centered interactions such as those occurring in offices, courts, and educational settings

**Co-occurrences**  Often interpreted as an indicator of semantic proximity and related to, but distinct from, linguistic collocation, co-occurrence refers to the above-chance occurrence of two terms from a text corpus located in close proximity to each other in a certain order.

**Correspondence theory**  Traditional model of knowledge and truth associated with scientific positivism, correspondence theory considers that there exists a correspondence between truth and reality and that notions of truth and reality correspond with things that actually exist in the world.

**Crawlers**  Automatic processes that browse the web to collect data

**Critical case**  A case selected because of its strategic importance to the research question

**Critical discourse analysis (CDA)**  Based on Fairclough's (1995) concept of "intertextuality," which is the idea that people appropriate from discourses circulating in their social space whenever they speak or write, CDA is a qualitative text analysis method that involves seeking the presence of features from other discourses in the text or discourse to be analyzed.

**Critical metaphor analysis**  A qualitative methodology developed by Charteris-Black (2009, 2012, 2013) that draws on methodologies and perspectives developed in cognitive linguistics, corpus linguistics, and critical linguistics that has been used to examine metaphors in political rhetoric, press reporting, and religion

**Critical realism**  Combining the realism of correspondence theory with the sociocultural reflexivity of social constructionism, in critical realism, some objects are understood to be more socially constructed than others.

**Data mining**  Analyzing large quantities of data inductively in search of trends and patterns

**Data sampling**  Refers to statistical techniques for selecting and analyzing a representative subset of data from a larger data set to identify trends and patterns in the larger data set

**Decision trees**  Structures that look like flowcharts; each internal node represents a test on one of the features and the nodes represent classification decisions

**Deduction**  The form of inferential logic most closely associated with the scientific method, deduction starts with theoretical abstractions, derives hypotheses from those theories, and then sets up research projects that test the hypotheses on empirical data.

**Deep learning**  One of the newest branches of machine learning, it consists of algorithms that aim to learn high-level representations of the data that can be used for effective learning

**Dictionary**  An alphabetical list of the words in a language, which may include information such as definitions, usage examples, etymologies, translations, etc.

**Digital archives**  Collections of digital information, such as newspaper archives or archives of digitized historical documents, that are often accessible online and generally compatible with text mining research methods

**Disambiguation**  A text mining process that involves the use of contextual clues to decide where words refer to one or another of their multiple meanings

**Discourse analysis** Involves seeking the presence of features from other discourses in the text or discourse to be analyzed based on the idea that people appropriate from discourses circulating in their social space whenever they speak or write

**Discourse positions** Typical discursive roles that people adopt in their everyday communication practices, the analysis of discourse positions is a (generally qualitative) way of linking texts to the social spaces in which they have emerged.

**Discussion** The discussion section of a research paper is located after the results (findings) but before the conclusions. The discussion section typically includes consideration of the meaning and implications of the results relative to the hypotheses/predictions and main argument.

**Emplotment** In narrative theory, the process of bringing together characters and actions into a plot that involves change over time

**Entity extraction** A subtask of information extraction (IE) that targets the identification of instances of a specific type, including named types, such as people or locations, or general semantic types, such as animals or colors.

**Enumeration** A first element in any sampling strategy, enumeration involves assigning numbers to or comprehensively listing the units within a population.

**Epistemology** Involves assumptions made in social science research about the nature of knowledge

**Ethical guidelines** Generally published by academic and professional associations as well as by universities, these are guidelines for ethical social science research that cover issues such as informed consent and privacy.

**Extreme case** Cases chosen for research that are thought to reveal more information because they activate more actors and more basic mechanisms in the situation studied

**Feature ablation** A way to compare the performance of different features, by running the classifier using one feature at a time (forward ablation) or removing from the full feature set one feature at a time (backward ablation)

**Feature vector** Collections of such properties, used to represent an instance of an event

**Feature weighting** A technique used to indicate the role played by individual features in a classifier

**Features (or attributes)** Measurable properties of an event being observed

**Foucauldian analysis** A text analysis methodology that involves referring to the discourses that circulate in the social space in which the text is produced and received

**Free clause** In Labov's (1972) narrative theory, a clause within a narrative that does not have a temporal component and can therefore be moved freely within the text without altering the text's meaning (see also *Minimal narrative*)

**Functional approach** An approach to narrative pioneered by the psychologist Bruner (1990), who argued that humans' ordering of experience occurs in two modes: (1) a *paradigmatic, or logico–scientific mode*, which attempts to fulfill the ideal of a formal, mathematical system of description and explanation, and (2) a *narrative mode* in which events' particularity and specificity as well as people's involvement, accountability, and responsibility in bringing about specific events are centrally important

**General Inquirer project** A long-running, large-scale content analysis project housed at Harvard University that involves developing a lexicon attaching syntactic, semantic, and pragmatic information to part-of-speech tagged words

**Grand theory** Highly abstract and formal social theories that are broad in scope

**Grounded theory** Systematic theory developed inductively based on observations that are grouped into conceptual categories (see Bryant & Charmaz, 2010)

**Heaps' law** Models the number of words in the vocabulary as a function of the corpus size

**Hypotheses** In deductive research, a proposition or set of propositions set forth as an explanation for the occurrence of a group of phenomena

**Idiographic approaches** Approaches to causal explanation that emphasize concrete sequences of events, thoughts, and actions that lead to specific outcomes

**Indigenous categories** Local terms that are used in unfamiliar ways and that can provide insights into themes and subthemes of the community being investigated

**Induction** Involves making inferences that take empirical data as their starting point and work upward to theoretical generalizations

**Inference** The process of deriving conclusions reached on the basis of evidence and reasoning

**Inference to the best explanation** A type of inferential reasoning closely related to abduction

**Information extraction (IE)** The task of extracting structured information such as entities, events, or relations from unstructured data

**Informed consent** A core principle of human research ethics, established in the aftermath of the Second World War, that requires that research subjects explicitly agree to be participants in a research project based on a comprehensive understanding of what will be required of them

**Instance-based learning** Form of lazy learning that includes algorithms such as $k$-nearest neighbors (KNN) and kernel machines

**Institutional review board (IRB)** A university committee that has been formally designated to review, approve, and monitor social science and biomedical research involving humans

**Intellectual property (IP)** Referring to intellectual creations for which a monopoly is assigned to their designated owners by law, common types of intellectual property rights are trademarks, copyright, and patents.

**Introduction** In social science research papers, the introduction section includes background information about the phenomenon under investigation, review of relevant research literature, and the paper's research question or questions.

**Language models** Probabilistic representations of language

**Latent Dirichlet allocation (LDA)** Based on the idea that every text within a text collection is akin to a bag of words produced according to a mixture of topics that the author or authors intended to discuss, latent Dirichlet allocation (LDA) is a statistical model of language introduced by Blei, Ng, and Jordan (2003) for topic modeling.

**Latent semantic analysis (LSA)** Based on the similarity of meaning of words appearing in texts or passages, a probabilistic model used in topic modeling that presents words and texts using vector space modelling that compiles textual data into a term-by-document matrix, showing the weighted frequency of terms to represent the documents in the term space

**Learning curve** A graphical representation of the increase in learning performance ($y$-axis) with the amount of training data ($x$-axis)

**Lemmatization** The process of identifying the base form (or root form) of a word

**Levels of analysis** A term used in the social sciences to point to the scope or scale of the social phenomenon or phenomena to be studied

**Linguistic markets** Also known in sociolinguistics and sociology as linguistic marketplaces, this concept refers to the symbolic markets in which linguistic exchanges occur. It is generally assumed that more standard language has higher value (prestige) in linguistic markets than nonstandard language (based on accent, vocabulary, and other factors).

**Literature review** Literature review is sometimes included within a paper's introduction but is often its own section. Rather than simply reviewing the history of previous research on a particular topic, a good literature review is structured so that it highlights how the study stands to contribute to the literature by resolving a contradiction, solving a puzzle, or opening a new line of inquiry.

**Logico–scientific mode** In Bruner's (1990) functional theory of narrative, the mode of organizing experience that attempts to fulfill the ideal of a formal, mathematical system of description and explanation (see also *Paradigmatic mode*)

**Machine learning** A field in artificial intelligence that has had a very significant impact on a large number of problems in a diverse set of domains, ranging from information management to linguistics to astrophysics and many others

**MALLET (Machine Learning for Language Toolkit)** A popular Java-based package used for topic modeling in the social sciences and humanities

**Meso theory** Less sweeping and abstract than grand theory, and more closely connected to the practice of empirical research, meso theory draws on empirically supported substantive theories and models.

**Metaphors** While metaphorical language takes a number of grammatical forms, including analogy, simile, and synecdoche, in all cases it involves figures of speech that make implicit comparisons in which a word or phrase ordinarily used in one domain is applied in another.

**Metatheory** Reflection on the role of theory within social science research

**Methods** The methods section of a social science paper includes a discussion of the method of analysis chosen and performed by the researchers. It typically includes discussion of why the method chosen is the best choice among all available methods as well as the details of how the method was used to analyze the data used in the paper.

**Minimal narrative** In Labov's (1972) narrative theory, any sequence of two clauses that are temporally ordered (see also *Free clause*)

**Mixed methods** Research methodologies that include both quantitative and interpretive elements

**Modality analysis** A mixed method of narrative analysis intended for cross-cultural and cross-linguistic comparative research that evaluates languages by analyzing modal clauses in multiple large collections of text in multiple languages in order to identify what activities the users of each language treat as possible, impossible, inevitable, or contingent (see Roberts, 2008)

**Naive Bayes** A classification technique based on Bayes theorem

**Named entity recognition (NER)** Refers to tools for identifying proper names that can be classified under a certain type

**Narrative analysis** A form of qualitative analysis that focuses on how people tell stories to make sense of everyday experiences and events in their lives (see Holstein & Gubrium, 2011)

**Narrative clauses** In the narratologist Labov's (1972) terminology, narrative clauses are clauses within a story that have a temporal component (rather than providing background information). Movements of narrative clauses with a story change the story's meaning.

**Narrative mode** In Bruner's (1990) functional theory of narrative, the mode of organizing experience in which events' particularity and specificity as well as people's involvement, accountability, and responsibility in bringing about specific events are centrally important.

**Natural language processing (NLP)** The process or ability of a machine or program to understand natural (or human) text or speech

**Netnography** The use of ethnographic methods to study online communities (see also *Virtual ethnography*)

**Network techniques** Text analysis methods that model statistical associations between words to infer the existence of mental models shared by members of a community

**N-fold cross-validation** A technique to evaluate a machine-learning classifier by partitioning the data into N folds and repeatedly training the classifier on ($N$−1) folds and testing it on the remaining fold

**Nomothetic approaches** Approaches to causal explanation that emphasize common influences on a number of cases or events

**Normalization** The process of transforming text into a canonical form (e.g., by expanding abbreviations, by correcting misspellings)

**Ontology** Involves assumptions about the nature of reality

**Opinion mining** The task of identifying such private states in language; it has two main subtasks: (1) subjectivity analysis and (2) sentiment analysis

**OpinionFinder** Includes words and phrases that are indicators of subjectivity, along with a polarity markup

**Paradigmatic mode** In Bruner's (1990) functional theory of narrative, the mode of organizing experience that attempts to fulfill the ideal of a formal, mathematical system of description and explanation (also referred to as the *logico–scientific mode*)

**Part-of-speech tagging** The task of assigning each word in an input text with its correct syntactic role, such as noun, verb, and so forth

**Password-protected data** Because users posting in password-protected websites are likely to have expectations of privacy, there is widespread agreement that websites that require registration and password-protected data should be considered to be in the private domain.

**Philosophy of social science** An academic research area that lies at the intersection of philosophy and social science, philosophy of social science involves the development and critique of concepts that are foundational to the practice of social science research.

**Plagiarism** A major ethical concern in social science research that involves the wrongful appropriation of another researcher's language or ideas and the representation of them as one's own original work

**Plotline** In theories of narrative, the narrative's structure in which characters and actions are brought together and change over time

**Pointwise mutual information (PMI)** A measure of (word) association stemming from information theory

**Polarity label** Indicates whether the corresponding word or phrase is positive, negative, or neutral

**Pragmatism** Approaches to the philosophy of social science in which truth is defined as those tenets that prove useful to the believer or user, and truth and knowledge are verified through experience and practice

**Preprocessing** A sequence of basic text processing steps applied in advance of more complex processing, typically consisting of tokenization, lemmatization, and normalization

**Privacy** A major ethical concern for text mining researchers that is treated somewhat differently in different national contexts (e.g., in the European Union versus the United States) and in academic and professional associations' ethical guidelines

**Probability sample** Involves taking someone else's research or ideas and passing them off as one's own

**Prompted data** Collecting users' textual data after actively manipulating the online environment as a stimulus intended to assess reactions or responses

**Public domain** Data in the public domain can be used freely by text mining researchers, although many websites and social media platforms have privacy policies that set expectations for users' privacy and can be used as guidelines for whether it is ethical to treat the site's data as in the public domain or whether informed consent may be required.

**Public stories** Narratives that circulate in popular culture

**Purposive sampling (see also Relevance sampling)** A research-question-driven, nonprobabilistic sampling technique in which the researcher learns about a population of interest and then gradually reduces the number of texts to be analyzed based on the texts' relevance to the research question

**Qualitative analysis** Text analysis methodologies based on human interpretation of texts

**Quantitative analysis** Text analysis methodologies based on mathematical and statistical techniques

**Random sample** A sampling strategy that reduces sample bias by using a randomization device such as software or an online random number generator to select items of data from an enumerated data set

**References** Reference sections of social science papers include all the publications (papers, books, book chapters, conference proceedings, websites) cited in the paper. Several different reference formats are widely used in the social sciences, including APA (American Psychological Association) and Chicago formats.

**Registration** Websites that require user registration and password-protected data are generally considered to be in the private domain.

**Regression (multiple regression)** A collection of statistical techniques used to predict the value of one variable (a "dependent" variable) based on the value of two or more other variables ("independent" variables)

**Relation extraction** A subtask of information extraction (IE) that aims to identify relationships between entities, such as "capital of," sibling, and so forth

**Relevance sampling (see Purposive sampling)** A research question-driven, nonprobabilistic sampling technique in which the researcher learns about a population of interest and then gradually reduces the number of texts to be analyzed based on the texts' relevance to the research question

**Repeated reading** This is the first step in thematic analysis where the researcher acquires a collection of texts and reads them repeatedly while searching for themes and taking extensive notes (see Braun & Clarke, 2006).

**Representative case** Data that are representative of a larger population that are selected when the objective of a project is to achieve the greatest possible amount of information about a phenomenon

**Research design** The phase of research concerned with the basic architecture of research projects and designing projects that allow theory, data, and method to interface in such a way as to maximize a project's ability to achieve its goals

**Results** The results section includes the results of the analysis performed. Results are presented in a straightforward manner, generally with a high level of technical detail but little interpretation of their meaning.

**Rocchio classifier** Builds upon the ideas of the vector-space model used in information retrieval

**Sample bias** A major disadvantage of Internet-accessed data samples is that it is very difficult to draw inferences about the larger population that the sampled data are claimed to represent. This is due to sample bias based on factors such as level of Internet access, level of Internet skill, and specific characteristics (such as comment moderation strategies) of websites and social media platforms.

**Sampling** Involves the selection of a subset of data from within a statistical population to estimate characteristics of the whole population

**Scientific method** A formal method of research that involves identification of a problem, collection of relevant data, formulation of hypotheses, and empirical testing of hypotheses

**Scrapers** Automatic processes for extracting data from websites

**Semantic networks** A network that defines the semantic relations between words

**Semantic relations** Relations that exist between word meanings

**Semantic techniques** Sometimes referred to as hermeneutic or hermeneutic structuralist techniques, these include a variety of methods designed to recognize latent meanings in texts.

**Semantic triplet** In Franzosi's approach to narrative, a fundamental semantic structure involving an actor, action, and object of action

**Sentiment analysis** Use of software to discern subjective material and extract various forms of attitudinal information such as sentiment, opinion, mood, and emotion

**SentiWordNet** A resource for opinion mining built on top of WordNet, which assigns each synset in WordNet with a score triplet, indicating the strength of each of these three properties for the words in the synset

**Simile** A form of metaphorical language that involves the comparison of one thing with another thing of a different kind, used to make a description more emphatic or vivid

**Snowball sampling** A widely used iterative sampling technique in which a researcher starts with a small sample and then repeatedly applies a sampling criterion until a sample size limit is reached

**Sociological approaches** Approaches to narrative that focus on the cultural, historical, and political contexts in which particular stories are, or can be, told by particular narrators to particular audiences

**Sociological level** A level of analysis at which attempts are made to identify causal relations between texts and the social contexts in which they are produced and received

**Source domain** In cognitive metaphor theory, perceptual and sensory experiences from an embodied source domain, such as pushing, pulling, supporting, balance, straight–curved, near–far, front–back, and high–low, are used to represent abstract entities in a target domain.

**Stemming** A processing step that uses a set of rules to remove inflections

**Story grammar** In structural narrative analysis, a basic narrative structure that is repeated across many diverse narrative genres

**Stratified sampling** A sampling strategy that involves sampling from within subunits ("strata") of a population

**Structural approaches** Approaches to narrative analysis pioneered by Propp (1968) and Labov (1972) that center on story grammars and other basic structural features of narratives that are found in narratives from diverse sources

**Subjectivity analysis** Identifies if a text contains an opinion and correspondingly labels the text as either subjective or objective

**Substantive theory** Theory derived from data analysis that involves rich conceptualizations of specific social and historical situations

**Supervised learning** Consists of using an automatic system to learn from a history of occurrences of a certain "event" and consequently make predictions about future occurrences of that event

**Support vector machines (SVMs)** Supervised learning machine algorithms that identify the hyperplane that best separates the training data

**Synecdoche** A form of metaphorical language involving a figure of speech in which a part is made to represent the whole or vice versa

**Syntactic parsing** Within computational linguistics, syntactic parsing refers to the use of software to formally analyze a sentence or other string of words in terms of its constituents, resulting in a parse tree showing words' and phrases' syntactic relations to each other.

**Systematic sampling** A sampling strategy that involves sampling every $k$th unit from an enumerated list

**Target domain** In cognitive metaphor theory, the target domain is the relatively abstract or complex entity that is represented by perceptual and sensory experiences drawn from an embodied source domain. For instance, the relatively abstract concept of *argument* can be a target domain where *battle* would be a possible source domain. In this way, *argument* is understood to have many of the qualities (e.g., the existence of a winner and a loser) of a battle.

**Template filling** The overall process of filling in the values for all the aspects in a template

**Text analysis** In the social sciences, text analysis refers to methods of systematically analyzing word use patterns in texts that often combine formal statistical methods and less formal, more humanistic interpretive techniques.

**Text classification** The process of assigning texts to one or more predefined categories

**Text clustering** The process of grouping texts into clusters of texts based on their similarity

**Text mining** The use of digital research tools to derive high-quality information from textual data

**Textual level** A level of analysis at which attempts are made to characterize or determine the composition and structure of the text itself

**Thematic analysis** A method of text analysis for identifying, analyzing, and reporting patterns of themes within texts (see Boyatzis, 1998)

**Thematic coding** Within thematic analysis, the process of systematically labeling texts based on predetermined or emergent categories

**Thematic techniques** Text analysis techniques that are focused on manifest meanings in texts and include methods commonly used in business as well as the social sciences such as topic modeling

**Theoretical models** Simplified, often schematic representations of complex social phenomena that are used in almost all social science research but particularly in research that is done in a positivist mode of inquiry

**Thesauruses** Databases that group the words in a language according to similarities

**Tokenization** The process of separating the punctuation from the words while maintaining their intended meaning

**Topic models** Involve automated procedures for coding collections of texts in terms of meaningful categories that represent the main topics being discussed

**Transformation** In narratology, transformation refers to changes in characters over time that result from events and characters' actions.

**Traversal strategies** Methods that define the sequence of steps that a web crawler will take; typical traversal strategies are depth-first and breadth-first

**Units of analysis** For texts, the unit of analysis can be conceived in many ways, including in terms of hierarchies in which one level includes the next, or as sequentially ordered events, or as networks of intertextual relationships.

**Unstructured data** Free-form text data are considered to be unstructured data because they are not organized in a predefined manner (such as in a matrix with rows and columns).

**Unsupervised learning** A type of machine-learning algorithm that makes inferences using unlabeled data

**URL** The address of a webpage

**Varying probability sampling** A sampling strategy used to sample proportionately from data sources with different sizes or levels of importance, such as newspapers with different circulation levels

**"Verbed"** It refers to the widespread tendency in academic writing to turn nouns into unfamiliar and sophisticated-sounding verbs. It should be avoided whenever possible.

**Virtual ethnography** The use of ethnographic methods to study online communities (see also *Netnography*)

**Web crawling** Use of Internet bots to systematically browse the World Wide Web for the purpose of web indexing

**Web (open) information extraction (IE)** A recently defined task that aims to perform information extraction (IE) at scale, without the need to predefine the entities or relationships that are being extracted

**Web scraping** A computer software technique of extracting information from websites, usually with programs that simulate human exploration of the World Wide Web

**Word sense disambiguation** Maps input words to dictionary senses and is used to identify the meaning of a word as a function of its context

**Word similarity** A measure that reflects the semantic closeness between two words

**WordNet-Affect** Another extension of WordNet, it includes affective labels assigned to word senses; the six emotion categories of specific interest are (1) anger, (2) disgust, (3) fear, (4) joy, (5) sadness, and (6) surprise.

**Zipf's law** Models the distribution of terms in a corpus and provides a mathematical way to answer this question: How many times does the $r$th most frequent word appear in a corpus of N words?

**Zombie nouns** Often formed with the suffix *-ism*, zombie nouns are nouns formed from other parts of speech such as adjectives and verbs. Like "verbed," the formation of zombie nouns should be avoided.

# REFERENCES

Acerbi, A., Lampos, V., Garnett, P., & Bentley, A. (2013, March 20). The expression of emotions in 20th century books. *PLOS ONE*. Retrieved from http://journals.plos.org/plosone/article?id=10.1371/journal.pone.0059030

Adams, J. (2009). Bodies of change: A comparative analysis of media representations of body modification practices. *Sociological Perspectives*, *52*(1), 103–129.

Adams, J., & Roscigno, V. (2005). White supremacists, oppositional culture and the World Wide Web. *Social Forces*, *84*(2), 759–778.

Albergotti, R., & Dwoskin, E. (2014, June 30). Facebook study sparks soul-searching and ethical questions. *Wall Street Journal*.

Alder, K. (2007). *The lie detectors: The history of an American obsession*. New York, NY: Simon & Schuster.

Alm, C. O., Roth, D., & Sproat, R. (2005). Emotions from text: Machine learning for text-based emotion prediction. *Proceedings of the Conference on Human Language Technology and Empirical Methods in Natural Language Processing* (pp. 579–586). Stroudsburg, PA: Association for Computational Linguistics.

Andersen, D. (2015). Stories of change in drug treatment: A narrative analysis of "whats" and "hows" in institutional storytelling. *Sociology of Health & Illness*, *37*(5), 668–682.

Asher, K., & Ojeda, D. (2009). Producing nature and making the state: Ordenamiento territorial in the Pacific lowlands of Colombia. *Geoforum*, *40*(3), 292–302.

Asplund, T. (2011). Metaphors in climate discourse: An analysis of Swedish farm magazines. *Journal of Science Communication*, *10*(4), 1–10.

Attard, A., & Coulson, N. (2012). A thematic analysis of patient communication in Parkinson's disease online support group discussion forums. *Computers in Human Behavior*, *28*(2), 500–506.

Ayers, E. L. (1999). *The pasts and futures of digital history*. Retrieved June 17, 2015, from http://www.vcdh.virginia.edu/PastsFutures.html

Bail, C. (2012). The fringe effect: Civil society organizations and the evolution of media discourse about Islam since the September 11th attacks. *American Sociological Review*, *77*(6), 855–879.

Baker, P., Gabrielatos, C., Khosravinik, M., Krzyzanowski, M., Mcenery, T., & Wodak, R. (2008). A useful methodological synergy? Combining critical discourse analysis and corpus linguistics to examine discourses of refugees and asylum seekers in the UK press. *Discourse & Society*, *19*(3), 273–306.

Balog, K., Mishne, G., & de Rijke, M. (2006). Why are they excited? Identifying and explaining spikes in blog mood levels. *Proceedings of the Eleventh Meeting of the European Chapter of the Association for Computational Linguistics*. Stroudsburg, PA: Association for Computational Linguistics.

Bamberg, M. (2004). Form and functions of "slut bashing" in male identity constructions in 15-year-olds. *Human Development*, *47*(6), 331–353.

Banerjee, S., & Pedersen, T. (2002). An adapted Lesk algorithm for word sense disambiguation using WordNet. *Proceedings of the International Conference on Intelligent Text Processing and Computational Linguistics*, Mexico City, Mexico.

Banko, M., Cafarella, M. J., Soderland, S., Broadhead, M., & Etzioni, O. (2007, January). Open information extraction from the web. *Communications of the ACM—Surviving the Data Deluge*, *51*(12), 68–74.

Bastin, G., & Bouchet-Valat, M. (2014). Media corpora, text mining, and the sociological imagination: A free software text mining approach to the framing of Julian Assange by three news agencies. *Bulletin de Méthodologie Sociologique*, *122*, 5–25.

Bauer, M. W., Bicquelet, A., & Suerdem, A. K. (Eds.). (2014). Text analysis: An introductory manifesto. In M. W. Bauer, A. Bicquelet, & A. K. Suerdem (Eds.), *Textual analysis (SAGE benchmarks in social research methods)* (Vol. 1). Thousand Oaks, CA: Sage.

Bauer M. W., Gaskell, G., & Allum, N. (2000). Quantity, quality and knowledge interests: Avoiding confusions. In M. W. Bauer & G. Gaskell (Eds.), *Qualitative researching with text, image and sound* (pp. 3–17). Thousand Oaks, CA: Sage.

Becker, H. S. (1993). How I learned what a crock was. *Journal of Contemporary Ethnography*, *22*, 28–35.

Bednarek, M., & Caple, H. (2014). Why do news values matter? Towards a new methodological framework for analyzing news discourse in critical discourse analysis and beyond. *Discourse & Society*, *25*(2), 135–158.

Beer, F. A., & De Landtsheer, C. L. (2004). *Metaphorical world politics: Rhetorics of democracy, war and globalization*. East Lansing: Michigan State University.

Bell, E., Campbell, S., & Goldberg, L. R. (2015). Nursing identity and patient-centredness in scholarly health services research: A computational text analysis of PubMed abstracts, 1986–2013. *BMC Health Services Research*, *15*(3), 1–16.

Berelson, B. (1952). *Content analysis in communication research*. Glencoe, IL: Free Press.

Berger, P. L., & Luckmann, T. (1966). *The social construction of reality: A treatise in the sociology of knowledge*. Garden City, NY: Doubleday.

Berglund, F. (2001). Facts, beliefs and biases: Perspectives on forest conservation in Finland. *Journal of Environmental Planning and Management*, *44*, 833–849.

Bernard, R., Wutich, A., & Ryan, G. (2016). *Analyzing qualitative data: Systematic approaches*. Thousand Oaks, CA: Sage.

Berry, M., Dumais, S., & O'Brien, G. (1995). Using linear algebra for intelligent information retrieval. *SIAM Review*, *37*(4), 573–595.

Bhaskar, R. (2008). *A realist theory of science*. New York, NY: Routledge. (Original work published 1975)

Bickes, H., Otten, T., & Weymann, L. C. (2014). The financial crisis in the German and English press: Metaphorical structures in the media coverage on Greece, Spain and Italy. *Discourse & Society*, *25*(4), 424–445.

Bicquelet, A., & Weale, A. (2011). Coping with the cornucopia: Can text mining help handle the data deluge in public policy analysis? *Policy and Internet*, *3*(4), 1–21.

Biernacki, R. (2014). Humanist interpretation versus coding text samples. *Qualitative Sociology*, *37*(2), 173–188.

Birke, J., & Sarkar, A. (2007). Active learning for the identification of nonliteral language. *Proceedings of the Workshop on Computational Approaches to Figurative Language*, 21–28.

Birnbaum, M. H. (2000). Decision making in the lab and on the web. In M. H. Birnbaum (Ed.), *Psychological experiments on the Internet* (pp. 3–34). Cambridge, MA: Academic Press.

Blei, D. M., Ng, A. Y., & Jordan, M. I. (2003). Latent Dirichlet allocation. *Journal of Machine Learning Research*, *3*, 993–1022.

Blevins, C. (2011, June 19–22). Topic modeling historical sources: Analyzing the diary of Martha Ballard. *Digital Humanities*, Stanford University, Stanford, CA. Retrieved from http://dh2011abstracts.stanford.edu/xtf/view?docId=tei/ab-173.xml;query=;brand=default

Bolden, R., & Moscarola, J. (2000). Bridging the quantitative-qualitative divide: The lexical approach to textual data analysis. *Social Science Computer Review*, *18*(4), 450–460.

Bollen, J., Mao, H., & Zeng, X.-J. (2011). Twitter mood predicts the stock market. *Journal of Computational Science*, *2*(1), 1–8.

Boroditsky, L. (2000). Metaphoric structuring: Understanding time through spatial metaphors. *Cognition*, *75*(1), 1–28.

Boussalisa, C., & Coan, T. G. (2016). Text-mining the signals of climate change doubt. *Global Environmental Change*, *36*, 89–100.

Bourdieu, P., & Thompson, J. B. (1991). *Language and symbolic power*. Cambridge, MA: Harvard University Press.

Boyatzis, R. E. (1998). *Transforming qualitative information: Thematic analysis and code development*. Thousand Oaks, CA: Sage.

Bradley, J. (1989). *TACT user manual*. Toronto, Canada: University of Toronto Press.

Braun, V., & Clarke, V. (2006). Using thematic analysis in psychology. *Qualitative Research in Psychology*, *3*(2), 77–101.

Brill, E. (1992). A simple rule-based part of speech tagger. *Proceedings of the Third Conference on Applied Natural Language Processing*. Trento, Italy.

Broaddus, M. (2014, July 1). Issues of research ethics in the Facebook "Mood Manipulation" Study: The importance of multiple perspectives. *Ethics and Society*. Retrieved from https://ethicsandsociety.org/2014/07/01/issues-of-research-ethics-in-the-facebook-mood-manipulation-study-the-importance-of-multiple-perspectives-full-text

Brugidou, M. (2003). Argumentation and values: An analysis of ordinary political competence via an open-ended question. *International Journal of Public Opinion Research*, *15*(4), 413–430.

Brugidou, M., Escoffier, C., Folch, H., Lahlou, S., Le Roux, D., Morin-Andréani, P., & Piat, G. (2000). Les facteurs de choix et d'utilisation de logiciels d'Analyse de Données Textuelles. The factors of choice and use of textual data analysis software. In *JADT 2000* (5èmes Journées Internationales d'Analyse Statistique des Données Textuelles).

Bruner, J. S. (1990). *Acts of meaning*. Cambridge, MA: Harvard University Press.

Bryant, A., & Charmaz, K. (Eds.). (2010). *The SAGE handbook of grounded theory*. Thousand Oaks, CA: Sage.

Buchholz, M. B., & von Kleist, C. (1995). *Psychotherapeutische Interaktion—Qualitative Studien zu Konversation und Metapher, Geste und Plan*. Opladen: Westdeutscher Verlag.

Bunn, J. (2012). *The truth machine: A social history of the lie detector (Johns Hopkins studies in the history of technology)*. Baltimore, MD: Johns Hopkins University Press.

Busanich, R., McGannon, K., & Schinke, R. (2014). Comparing elite male and female distance runners' experiences of disordered eating through narrative analysis. *Psychology of Sport and Exercise*, *15*(6), 705–712.

Cameron, L. (2003). *Metaphor in educational discourse*. New York, NY: Continuum.

Carenini, G., Ng, R., & Zhou, X. (2007). Summarizing emails with conversational cohesion and subjectivity. *Proceedings of the Sixteenth International Conference on World Wide Web*. New York, NY: Association for Computing Machinery.

Carlson, A., Betteridge, J., Kisiel, B., Settles, B., Hruschka, E. R., Jr., & Mitchell, T. M. (2010, July). Toward an architecture for never-ending language learning. *Proceedings of the Twenty-Fourth American Association for Artificial Intelligence Conference on Artificial Intelligence* (pp. 1306–1313). Cambridge, MA: AAAI Press.

Carver, T., & Pikalo, J. (2008). *Political language and metaphor: Interpreting and changing the world*. New York, NY: Routledge.

Cerulo, K. A. (1998). *Deciphering violence: The cognitive structure of right and wrong*. New York, NY: Routledge.

Chalaby, J. K. (1996). Beyond the prison-house of language: Discourse as a sociological concept. *The British Journal of Sociology*, *47*(4), 684–698.

Chambers, C. (2014, July 1). Facebook fiasco: Was Cornell's study of "emotional contagion" an ethics breach? *Guardian*. Retrieved from https://www.theguardian.com/science/headquarters/2014/jul/01/facebook-cornell-study-emotional-contagion-ethics-breach

Charteris-Black, J. (2009). Metaphor and political communication. In A. Musolff & J. Zinken (Eds.), *Metaphor and discourse* (pp. 97–115). Basingstoke, England: Palgrave Macmillan.

Charteris-Black, J. (2012). Comparative keyword analysis and leadership communication: Tony Blair—A study of rhetorical style. In L. Helms (Ed.), *Comparative political leadership* (pp. 142–164). Basingstoke, England: Palgrave Macmillan.

Charteris-Black, J. (2013). *Analysing political speeches: Rhetoric, discourse and metaphor*. Basingstoke, England: Palgrave Macmillan.

Chilton, P. (1996). *Security metaphors: Cold War discourse from containment to common house*. New York, NY: Peter Lang.

Church, K. W., & Hanks, P. (1990). Word association norms, mutual information, and lexicography. *Computational Linguistics*, *16*(1), 22–29.

Coffey, A., Holbrook, B., & Atkinson, P. (1996). Qualitative data analysis: Technologies and representations. *Sociological Research Online*, *1*(1). Retrieved from http://www.socresonline.org.uk/1/1/4.html

Cohen, D. J., & Rosenzweig, R. (2005). *Digital history: A guide to gathering, preserving, and presenting the past on the web*. Philadelphia: University of Pennsylvania Press.

Collins, C., Viégas, F. B., & Wattenberg, M. (2009). Parallel tag clouds to explore and analyze faceted text corpora. *IEEE Symposium on Visual Analytics Science and Technology*. Retrieved June 17, 2015, from http://ieeexplore.ieee.org/xpls/abs_all.jsp?arnumber=5333443&tag=1

Collins, M. (2002). Ranking algorithms for named-entity extraction: Boosting and the voted perceptron. *Proceedings of the 40th Annual Meeting on Association for Computational Linguistics* (pp. 489–496). Stroudsburg, PA: Association for Computational Linguistics.

Collins, M. (2003). Head-driven statistical models for natural language parsing. *Computational Linguistics*, *29*(4), 589–637.

Collins, M., & Singer, Y. (1999). Unsupervised models for named entity classification. *Proceedings of the Conference on Empirical Methods in Natural Language Processing*.

Colley, S. K., & Neal, A. (2012). Automated text analysis to examine qualitative differences in safety schema among upper managers, supervisors and workers. *Safety Science*, *50*(9), 1775–1785.

Corley, P., Collins, Jr., P., & Calvin, B. (2011). Lower court influence on U.S. Supreme Court opinion content. *Journal of Politics*, *73*(1), 31–44.

Coulson, N. S. (2005). Receiving social support online: An analysis of a computer-mediated support group for individuals living with irritable bowel syndrome. *CyberPsychology & Behavior*, *8*(6), 580–584.

Coulson, N. S., Buchanan, H., & Aubeeluck, A. (2007). Social support in cyberspace: A content analysis of communication within a Huntington's disease online support group. *Patient Education and Counseling*, *68*(2), 173–178.

Couper, M. P. (2000). Web surveys: A review of issues and approaches. *Public Opinion Quarterly*, *64*(4), 464–494.

Creswell, J. D. (2014). *Research design: Qualitative, quantitative, and mixed methods approaches*. Thousand Oaks, CA: Sage.

Cunningham, G. B., Sagas, M., Sartore, M. L., Amsden, M. L., & Schellhase, A. (2004). Gender representation in the *NCAA News*: Is the glass half full or half empty? *Sex Roles*, *50*(11–12), 861–870.

Curd, M., Cover, J. A., & Pincock, C. (2013). *Philosophy of science: The central issues* (2nd ed.). New York, NY: W. W. Norton.

Danescu-Niculescu-Mizil, C., Lee, L., Pang, B., & Kleinberg, J. (2012, April 16–20). Echoes of power: Language effects and power differences in social interaction. *WWW 2012*. Retrieved March 29, 2016, from http://www.cs.cornell.edu/~cristian/Echoes_of_power_files/echoes_of_power.pdf

Danesi, M. (2012). *Linguistic anthropology: A brief introduction*. Toronto: Canadian Scholars' Press.

Deerwester, S., Dumais, S., Furnas, G., Landauer, T., & Harshman, R. (1990). Indexing by latent semantic analysis. *JASIS*, *41*(6), 391–407.

Denzin, N. K, & Lincoln, Y. S. (2011). Epilogue: Toward a "refunctioned ethnography." *The SAGE Handbook of Qualitative Research* (pp. 715–718). Thousand Oaks, CA: Sage.

DiMaggio, P., Nag, M., & Blei, D. (2013). Exploiting affinities between topic modeling and the sociological perspective on culture: Application to newspaper coverage of U.S. government arts funding. *Science Direct*, *41*(6), 570–606.

Dohan, D., Abramson, C. M., & Miller S. (2012). *Beyond text: Using arrays of ethnographic data to identify causes and construct narratives*. Presentation at the American Journal of Sociology Conference on Causal Thinking and Ethnographic Research. Chicago, IL.

Dumais, S. T. (2004). Latent semantic analysis. *Annual Review of Information Science and Technology*, *38*(1), 188–230.

Durland, M., & Fredericks, K. (2005). An introduction to social network analysis. *New Directions for Evaluation*, *107*, 5–13.

Edley, N., & Wetherell, M. (1997). Jockeying for position: The construction of masculine identities. *Discourse & Society*, *8*(2), 203–217.

Edley, N., & Wetherell, M. (2001). Jekyll and Hyde: Men's construction of feminism and feminists. *Feminism & Psychology*, *11*(4), 439–457.

Ensslin, A., & Johnson, S. (2006). Language in the news: Investigating representations of "Englishness" using WordSmith tools. *Corpora*, *1*(2), 153–185.

Eshbaugh-Soha, M. (2010). The tone of local presidential news coverage. *Political Communication*, *27*(2), 121–140.

Esuli, A., & Sebastiani, F. (2006a). Determining term subjectivity and term orientation for opinion mining. *Proceedings of the Eleventh Conference of the European Chapter of the Association for Computational Linguistics*, Trento, Italy.

Esuli, A., & Sebastiani, F. (2006b). SentiWordNet: A publicly available lexical resource for opinion mining. *Proceedings of the Fifth Conference on Language Resources and Evaluation*, Genova, Italy.

Etzioni, O., Cafaraella, M., Downey, D., Kok, S., Popescu, A. M., Shaked, T., . . . Yates, A. (2004). Web-scale information extraction in KnowItAll: (Preliminary results). *Proceedings of the Thirteenth International Conference on World Wide Web* (pp. 100–110). New York, NY: Association for Computing Machinery.

Evison, J. (2013). Turn openings in academic talk: Where goals and roles intersect. *Classroom Discourse*, *4*(1), 3–26.

Eysenbach, G., & Till, J. E. (2001). Ethical issues in qualitative research on Internet communities. *British Medical Journal*, *323*, 1103–1105.

Fader, A., Soderland, S., & Etzioni, O. (2011). Identifying relations for open information extraction. *Proceedings of the Conference on Empirical Methods in Natural Language Processing* (pp. 1535–1545). Stroudsburg, PA: Association for Computational Linguistics.

Fairclough, N. (1992). Intertextuality in critical discourse analysis. *Science Direct*, *4*(3–4), 269–293.

Fairclough, N. (1995). *Critical discourse analysis: The critical study of language*. London, England: Longman.

Fass, D. (1991). Met*: A method for discriminating metonymy and metaphor by computer. *Computational Linguistics*, *17*(1), 49–90.

Feldman, J. (2006). *From molecule to metaphor*. Cambridge, MA: MIT Press.

Fellbaum, C. (Ed.). (1998). *WordNet: An electronic lexical database*. Cambridge, MA: MIT Press.

Fenton, F. (1911). The influence of newspaper presentations upon the growth of crime and other anti-social activity. *American Journal of Sociology*, *16*(3), 342–371.

Fereday, J., & Muir-Cochrane, E. (2006). Demonstrating rigor using thematic analysis: A hybrid approach of inductive and deductive coding and theme development. *International Journal of Qualitative Methods*, *5*(1), 80–92.

Fernandez, J. W. (1991). *Beyond metaphor: The theory of tropes in anthropology*. Stanford, CA: Stanford University Press.

Field, A. (2013). *Discovering statistics using IBM SPSS statistics* (4th ed.). Thousand Oaks, CA: Sage.

Field, A., Miles, J., & Field, Z. (2012). *Discovering statistics using R*. Thousand Oaks, CA: Sage.

Flyvbjerg, B. (2001). *Making social science matter: Why social inquiry fails and how it can succeed again*. Cambridge, England: Cambridge University Press.

Fors, A., Dudas, K., & Ekman, I. (2014). Life is lived forwards and understood backwards—Experiences of being affected by acute coronary syndrome: A narrative analysis. *International Journal of Nursing Studies*, *51*(3), 430–437.

Foucault, M. (1973). *The order of things: An archaeology of the human sciences*. New York, NY: Vintage Books.

Foucault, M. (1975). *The birth of the clinic: An archaeology of medical perception*. New York, NY: Vintage Books.

Franklin, S. (2002). Bialowieza Forest, Poland: Representation, myth, and the politics of dispossession. *Environment and Planning*, 34, 1459–1485.

Franzosi, R. (1987). The press as a source of socio-historical data: Issues in the methodology of data collection from newspapers. *Historical Methods*, 20(1), 5–16.

Franzosi, R. (2010). *Quantitative narrative analysis*. Thousand Oaks, CA: Sage.

Franzosi, R., De Fazio, G., & Vicari, S. (2012). Ways of measuring agency: An application of quantitative narrative analysis to lynchings in Georgia (1875–1930). *Sociological Methodology*, 42(1), 1–42.

Freud, S. (2011). *From the history of an infantile neurosis—A classic article on psychoanalysis*. Worcestershire, England: Read Books. (Original work published 1918)

Frith, H., & Gleeson, K. (2004). Clothing and embodiment: Men managing body image and appearance. *Psychology of Men & Masculinity*, 5(1), 40–48.

Gamson, W., & Modigliani, A. (1989). Media discourse and public opinion on nuclear power: A constructionist approach. *American Journal of Sociology*, 95(1), 1–37.

Gandy, L., Allan, N., Atallah, M., Frieder, O., Howard, N., Kanareykin, S., . . . Argamon, S. (2013). Automatic identification of conceptual metaphors with limited knowledge. *Proceedings of the Twenty-Seventh AAAI Conference on Artificial Intelligence*. Bellevue, Washington.

Garton, L., Haythornthwaite, C., & Wellman, B. (1997). Studying online social networks. *Journal of Computer Mediated Communication*, 3(1) http://onlinelibrary.wiley.com/doi/10.1111/j.1083-6101.1997.tb00062.x/abstract.

Gatti, L., & Catalano, T. (2015). The business of learning to teach: A critical metaphor analysis of one teacher's journey. *Teaching and Teacher Education*, 45, 149–160.

Gee, J. P. (1991). A linguistic approach to narrative. *Journal of Narrative and Life History*, 1(1), 15–39.

Gergen, K. (2015). *An invitation to social construction*. Thousand Oaks, CA: Sage.

Gerrish, S., & Blei, D. (2012). How they vote: Issue-adjusted models of legislative behavior. *Neural Information Processing Systems*. Retrieved June 26, 2015, from https://www.cs.princeton.edu/-blei/papers/GerrishBlei2012.pdf

Gibbs, R. W. (1994). *The poetics of mind: Figurative thought, language, and understanding*. Cambridge, England: Cambridge University Press.

Gibson, C. B., & Zellmer-Bruhn, M. E. (2001). Metaphors and meaning: An intercultural analysis of the concept of teamwork. *Administrative Science Quarterly*, 46(2), 274–303.

Glaser, B., & Strauss, A. L. (1967). *The discovery of grounded theory: Strategies for qualitative research*. Piscataway, NJ: Transaction Publishers.

Goatly, A. (2007). *Washing the brain: Metaphor and hidden ideology*. Philadelphia, PA: John Benjamins Publishing Company.

Goble, E., Austin, W., Larsen, D., Kreitzer, L., & Brintnell, E. S. (2012). Habits of mind and the split-mind effect: When computer-assisted qualitative data analysis software is used in phenomenological research. *Forum: Qualitative Social Research*, 13(2). Retrieved June 26, 2015, from http://www.qualitative-research.net/index.php/fqs/article/view/1709

Goldstone, A., & Underwood, T. (2012). What can topic models of PMLA teach us about the history of literary scholarship? *The Stone and the Shell*. Retrieved June 27, 2015, from tedunderwood.com/2012/12/14/what-can-topic-models-of-pmla-teach-us-about-the-history-of-literary-scholarship

González-Ibánez, R., Muresan, S., & Wacholder, N. (2011). Identifying sarcasm in Twitter: A closer look. *Proceedings of the Forty-Ninth Annual Meeting of the Association for Computational Linguistics: Human Language Technologies—Short Papers Volume 2*. Stroudsburg, PA: Association for Computational Linguistics.

Goodfellow, I., Bengio, Y., & Courville, A. (2016). *Deep learning*. Cambridge, MA: MIT Press.

Gorard, S. (2013). *Research design: Creating robust approaches for the social sciences*. Thousand Oaks, CA: Sage.

Gorbatai, A., & Nelson, L. (2015). *The narrative advantage: Gender and the language of crowdfunding*. Retrieved from http://

faculty.haas.berkeley.edu/gorbatai/working%20papers%20 and%20word/Crowdfunding-GenderGorbataiNelson.pdf

Gorski, D. (2014, June 30). Did Facebook and PNAS violate human research protections in an unethical experiment? *Science-Based Medicine*. Retrieved from https://sciencebased medicine.org/did-facebook-and-pnas-violate-human-research-protections-in-an-unethical-experiment

Gottschall, J. (2012). *The storytelling animal*. New York, NY: Houghton Mifflin.

Gregory, M., Chinchor, N., Whitney, P., Carter, R., Hetzler, E., & Turner, A. (2006). User-directed sentiment analysis: Visualizing the affective content of documents. *Proceedings of the Workshop on Sentiment and Subjectivity in Text*, Sydney, Australia.

Greene, D., O'Callahan, D., & Cunningham, P. (2014). How many topics? Stability analysis for topic models. In T. Calders, F. Esposito, E. Hüllermeier, & R. Meo (Eds.), *Machine learning and knowledge discovery in databases* (Vol. 87352, pp. 498–513). Berlin, Germany: Springer.

Grimmelmann, J. (2015, May 27). Do you consent? If tech companies are going to experiment on us, they need better ethical oversight. *Slate*. Retrieved from http://www.slate.com/articles/technology/future_tense/2015/05/facebook_emotion_contagion_study_tech_companies_need_irb_review.html

Grimmer, J. (2010). A Bayesian hierarchical topic model for political texts: Measuring expressed agendas in Senate press releases. *Political Analysis*, *18*(1), 1–35.

Grimmer, J., & Stewart, B. M. (2013). Text as data: The promise and pitfalls of automatic content analysis methods for political texts. *Political Analysis*, *21*(3), 267–297.

Günther, E., & Quandt, T. (2016). Word counts and topic models: Automated text analysis methods for digital journalism research. *Digital Journalism*, *4*(1), 75–88.

Haigh, C., & Jones, N. (2005). An overview of the ethics of cyber-space research and the implications for nurse educators. *Nurse Education Today*, *25*(1), 3–8.

Haigh, C., & Jones, N. (2007). Techno-research and cyber ethics: Research using the Internet. In T. Long & M. Johnson (Eds.), *Research ethics in the real world: Issues and solutions for health and social care* (pp. 157–174). Philadelphia, PA: Elsevier Health Sciences.

Hair, N., & Clark, M. (2007). The ethical dilemmas and challenges of ethnographic research in electronic communities. *International Journal of Market Research*, *49*(6). Retrieved from https://www.mrs.org.uk/ijmr/archive#Articles

Hakimnia, R., Holmström, I., Carlsson, M., & Höglund, A. (2014). Exploring the communication between telenurse and caller—A critical discourse analysis. *International Journal of Qualitative Studies on Health and Well-Being*, *9*, 1–9.

Halberstadt, A., Langley, H., Hussong, A., Rothenberg, W., Coffman, J., Mokrova, I., & Costanzo, P. (2016). Parents' understanding of gratitude in children: A thematic analysis. *Early Childhood Research Quarterly*, *36*, 439–451.

Hanna, A. (2013). Computer-aided content analysis of digitally enabled movements. *Mobilization*, *18*(4), 367–388.

Hardy, C. (2001). Researching organizational discourse. *International Studies of Management & Organization*, *31*(3), 25–47.

Harris, J. (2011). Word clouds considered harmful. *Nieman Journalism Lab*. Retrieved June 26, 2015, from http://www.niemanlab.org/2011/10/word-clouds-considered-harmful

Hatzivassiloglou, V., & McKeown, K. (1997). Predicting the semantic orientation of adjectives. *Proceedings of the Thirty-Fifth Annual Meeting of the Association for Computational Linguistics and Eighth Conference of the European Chapter of the Association for Computational Linguistics* (pp. 174–181). Stroudsburg, PA: Association for Computational Linguistics.

Hellsten, I., Dawson, J., & Leydesdorff, L. (2010). Implicit media frames: Automated analysis of public debate on artificial sweeteners. *Public Understanding of Science*, *19*(5), 590–608.

Herrera, Y. M., & Braumoeller, B. F. (2004, Spring). Symposium: Discourse and content analysis. *Qualitative Methods Newsletter*, 15–19. Retrieved from http://www.braumoeller.info/wp-content/uploads/2012/12/Discourse-Content-Analysis.pdf

Hirschman, E. C. (1987). People as products: Analysis of a complex marketing exchange. *Journal of Marketing*, *51*(1), 98–108.

Hardie, A., Koller, V., Rayson, P., & Semino, E. (2007). Exploiting a semantic annotation tool for metaphor analysis. In M. Davies, P. Rayson, S. Hunston, & P. Danielsson (Eds.), *Proceedings of the Corpus Linguistics 2007 Conference*. Retrieved June 27, 2015, from ucrel.lancs.ac.uk/people/paul/publications/HardieEtAl_CL2007.pdf

Hart, C. (2010). *Critical discourse analysis and cognitive science: New perspectives on immigration discourse*. Basingstoke, England: Palgrave Macmillan.

Hayes, A., & Krippendorff, K. (2007). Answering the call for a standard reliability measure for coding data. *Communication Methods and Measures*, *1*(1), 77–89.

Heath, C., & Luff, P. (2000). *Technology in action*. Cambridge, England: Cambridge University Press.

Hempel, C., & Oppenheim, P. (1948). Studies in the logic of explanation. *Philosophy of Science*, *15*(2), 135–175.

Henderson, S., & Segal, E. (2013). Visualizing qualitative data in evaluation research. *New Directions for Evaluation*, *139*, 53–71.

Heritage, J., & Raymond, G. (2005). The terms of agreement: Indexing epistemic authority and subordination in talk-in-interaction. *Social Psychology Quarterly*, *68*(1), 15–38.

Hewson, C. (2014). Qualitative approaches in Internet-mediated research: Opportunities, issues, possibilities. In P. Leavy (Ed.), *The Oxford handbook of qualitative research* (pp. 423–452). New York, NY: Oxford University Press.

Hewson, C., & Laurent, D. (2012). Research design and tools for Internet research. In J. Hughes (Ed.), *SAGE Internet research methods: Volume 1*. Thousand Oaks, CA: Sage.

Hewson, C., Vogel, C., & Laurent, D. (2015). *Internet research methods: A practical guide for the behavioural and social sciences*. Thousand Oaks, CA: Sage.

Hewson, C., Yule, P., Laurent, D., & Vogel, C. (Eds.). (2003). *Internet research methods: A practical guide for the social and behavioural sciences*. Thousand Oaks, CA: Sage.

Hine, C. (2000). *Virtual ethnography*. Thousand Oaks, CA: Sage.

Hoffman, M. (1999). Problems with Peirce's concept of abduction. *Foundations of Science*, *4*(3), 271–305.

Hofstede, G. (1980). *Culture's consequences: International differences in work-related values*. Beverly Hills, CA: Sage.

Holstein, J., & Gubrium, J. (2011). *Varieties of narrative analysis*. Thousand Oaks, CA: Sage.

Howell, K. (2013). *An introduction to the philosophy of methodology*. Thousand Oaks, CA: Sage.

Hu, M., & Liu, B. (2004). Mining and summarizing customer reviews. *Proceedings of the Tenth ACM SIGKDD International Conference on Knowledge Discovery and Data Mining* (pp. 168–177). New York, NY: Association for Computing Machinery.

Hugo, R. (1992). In defense of creative writing classes. *The triggering town: Lectures and essays on poetry and writing* (pp. 53–66). New York, NY: W. W. Norton.

Ignatow, G. (2003). "Idea hjamsters" on the "bleeding edge": Profane metaphors in high technology argon. *Poetics*, *31*(1), 1–22.

Ignatow, G. (2004). Speaking together, thinking together? Exploring metaphor and cognition in a shipyard union dispute. *Sociological Forum*, *19*(3), 405–433.

Ignatow, G. (2009). Culture and embodied cognition: Moral discourses in Internet support groups for overeaters. *Social Forces*, *88*(2), 643–669.

Ignatow, G., & Williams, A. T. (2011). New media and the "anchor baby" boom. *Journal of Computer-Mediated Communication*, *17*(1), 60–76.

Ilieva, J., Baron, S., & Healey, N. M. (2002). Online surveys in marketing research: Pros and cons. *International Journal of Market Research*, *44*(3), 361–376.

Illia, L., Sonpar, K., & Bauer, M. W. (2014). Applying co-occurrence text analysis with Alceste to studies of impression management. *British Journal of Management*, 25 (2), 352–372.

Jacobi, C., van Atteveldt, W., & Welbers, K. (2016). Quantitative analysis of large amounts of journalistic texts using topic modelling. *Digital Journalism*, *4*(1), 89–106.

James, W. (1975). *Pragmatism: A new name for some old ways of thinking*. Cambridge, MA: Harvard University Press. (Original work published 1907)

James, W. (1975). *The meaning of truth*. Cambridge, MA: Harvard University Press. (Original work published 1909)

Jockers, M. L. (2010, March 19). Who's your DH blog mate: Match-making the day of DH bloggers with topic modeling. *Matthew L. Jockers*. Retrieved from http://www.matthewjockers.net/2010/03/19/whos-your-dh-blog-mate-match-making-the-day-of-dh-bloggers-with-topic-modeling

Jockers, M. L., & Mimno, D. (2013). Significant themes in 19th-century literature. *Poetics*, *41*(6), 750–769.

Johnson-Laird, P. N. (1983). *Mental models: Toward a cognitive science of language, inference, and consciousness*. Cambridge, MA: Harvard University Press.

Jones, M. V., Coviello, Y., & Tang, Y. K. (2011). International entrepreneurship research (1989–2009), A domain ontology and thematic analysis. *Journal of Business Venturing*, *26*(6), 632–649.

Jurafsky, D., & Martin, J. (2009). *Speech and language processing*. Upper Saddle River, NJ: Prentice Hall.

Kallus, N. (2014). Predicting crowd behavior with big public data. *WWW '14 Companion Proceedings of the 23rd International Conference on World Wide Web*, 625–630. doi:10.1145/2567948.2579233

Kaplan, D. (Ed.). (2009). *Readings in the philosophy of technology*. Lanham, MD: Rowman & Littlefield.

Kassarjian, H. (1977). Content analysis in consumer research. *Journal of Consumer Research*, *4*(1), 8–18.

Kim, S.-M., & Hovy, E. (2006). Identifying and analyzing judgment opinions. *Proceedings of the Main Conference on Human Language Technology Conference of the North American Chapter of the Association of Computational Linguistics*. Stroudsburg, PA: Association for Computational Linguistics.

King, A. (2008). In vivo coding. In L. Given (Ed.), *The SAGE encyclopedia of qualitative research methods*. Thousand Oaks, CA: Sage.

Klein, D., & Manning, C. D. (2004). Corpus-based induction of synactic structure: Models of dependency and constituency. *Proceedings of the Forty-Second Annual Meeting of the Association for Computational Linguistics*. Stroudsburg, PA: Association for Computational Linguistics.

Kleinman, D., & Moore, K. (2014). *Routledge handbook of science, technology, and society*. New York, NY: Routledge.

Koller, V., & Mautner, G. (2004). Computer applications in critical discourse analysis. *Applying English grammar* (pp. 216–228). London, England: Hodder and Stoughton.

Koppel, M., Argamon, S., & Shimoni, A. R. (2002). Automatically categorizing written texts by author gender. *Literary and Linguistic Computing*, *17*(4), 401–412.

Kovecses, Z. (2002). *Metaphor: A practical introduction*. Oxford, England: Oxford University Press.

Kozinets, R. V. (2002). The field behind the screen: Using netnography for marketing research in online communities. *Journal of Marketing Research*, *39*(1), 61–72.

Kozinets, R. V. (2009). *Netnography: Doing ethnographic research online*. Thousand Oaks, CA: Sage.

Kramer, A., Guillory, J., & Hancock, J. (2014). Experimental evidence of massive-scale emotional contagion through social networks. *Proceedings of the National Academy of Sciences*, *111*(24), 8788–8790.

Krippendorff, K. (2013). *Content analysis: An introduction to its methodology*. Thousand Oaks, CA: Sage.

Krishnamurthy, R. (1996). Ethnic, racial and tribal: The language of racism? In C. R. Caldas-Coulthard & M. Coulthard (Eds.), *Texts and practices: Readings in critical discourse analysis* (pp. 128–149). London, England: Routledge.

Krueger, R. A., & Casey, M. A. (2014). *Focus groups: A practical guide for applied research*. Thousand Oaks, CA: Sage.

Kuckartz, U. (2014). *Qualitative text analysis: A guide to methods, practice, and using software*. Thousand Oaks, CA: Sage.

Labov, W. (1972). *Sociolinguistic patterns*. Philadelphia: University of Pennsylvania Press.

Labov, W., & Waletzky, J. (1967). Narrative analysis. In J. Helm (Ed.), *Essays on the verbal and visual arts* (pp. 12–44). Seattle: University of Washington Press.

Lahlou, S. (1996). A method to extract social representations from linguistic corpora. *Japanese Journal of Experimental Social Psychology*, 35(3), 278–291.

Laird, E. A., McCance, T., McCormack, B., & Gribben, B. (2015). Patients' experiences of in-hospital care when nursing staff were engaged in a practice development programme to promote person-centredness: A narrative analysis study. *International Journal of Nursing Studies*, 52(9), 1454–1462.

Lakoff, G. (1987). *Women, fire, and dangerous things. What categories reveal about the mind*. Chicago, IL: University of Chicago Press.

Lakoff, G. (1996). *Moral politics*. Chicago, IL: University of Chicago Press.

Lakoff, G., & Johnson, M. (1980). *Metaphors we live by*. Chicago, IL: University of Chicago Press.

Lakoff, G., & Johnson, M. (1999). *Philosophy in the flesh*. New York, NY: Basic Books.

Landauer, T. K. (2002). On the computational basis of learning and cognition: Arguments from LSA. *Psychology of Learning and Motivation*, 41, 43–84.

Landauer, T. K., Foltz, P. W., & Laham, D. (1998). An introduction to latent semantic analysis. *Discourse Processes*, 25(2–3), 259–284.

Lasswell, H. (1927). Propaganda technique in the world war. *American Political Science Review*, 21(3), 627–631.

Lazard, A., Scheinfeld, E., Bernhardt, J., Wilcox, G., & Suran, M. (2015). Detecting themes of public concern: A text mining analysis of the Centers for Disease Control and Prevention's Ebola live Twitter chat. *American Journal of Infection Control*, 43(10), 1109–1111.

Lee, B., Riche, N. H., Karlson, A. K., & Carpendale, S. (2010). SparkClouds: Visualizing trends in tag clouds. *Visualization and Computer Graphics, IEEE Transactions on Knowledge and Data Engineering*, 16(6), 1182–1189.

Lee, D. D., & Seung, S. (1999). Learning the parts of objects by non-negative matrix factorization. *Nature*, 401, 788–791.

Leondar-Wright, B. (2014). *Missing class: Strengthening social movement groups by seeing class cultures*. Ithaca, NY: Cornell University Press.

LeRoux, B., & Rouanet, H. (2010). *Multiple correspondence analysis*. Thousand Oaks, CA: Sage.

Lesk, M. (1986). Automatic sense disambiguation using machine readable dictionaries: How to tell a pine cone from an ice cream cone. *Proceedings of the SIGDOC Conference 1986* (pp. 24–26). New York, NY: ACM.

Levenberg, A., Pulman, S., Moilanen, K., Simpson, E., & Roberts, S. (2014). *Predicting economic indicators from web text using sentiment composition*. Retrieved from http://www.robots.ox.ac.uk/~parg/pubs/sentiment_ICICA2014.pdf

Levina, N., & Arriaga, M. (2012). Distinction and status production on user-generated content platforms: Using Bourdieu's theory of cultural production to understand social dynamics in online fields. *Information Systems Research*, 25(3), 468–488.

Levy, K., & Franklin, M. (2013). Driving regulation: Using topic models to examine political contention in the U.S. trucking industry. *Social Science Computer Review*, 32(2), 182–194.

Light, R., & Cunningham, J. (2016). Oracles of peace: Topic modeling, cultural opportunity, and the Nobel Peace Prize, 1902–2012. *Mobilization: An International Quarterly*, 21(1), 43–64.

Lindseth, A., & Norberg, A. (2004). A phenomenal hermeneutical method for researching lived experience. *Scandinavian Journal of Caring Sciences*, 18(2), 145–153.

Lipton, P. (2003). *Inference to the best explanation*. New York, NY: Routledge.

Liu, B., & Mihalcea, R. (2007). *Of men, women, and computers: Data-driven gender modeling for improved user interfaces*. Paper presented at the Proceedings of the International Conference on Weblogs and Social Media, Boulder, CO.

Lloyd, L., Kechagias, D., & Skiena, S. (2005). Lydia: A system for large-scale news analysis. *Processing and Information Retrieval*, 3372, 161–166.

Maas, A. L., Daly, R. E., Pham, P. T., Huang, D., Ng, A. Y., & Potts, C. (2011). Learning word vectors for sentiment analysis. *Proceedings of the Forty-Ninth Annual Meeting of the Association for Computational Linguistics: Human Language Technologies.* Stroudsburg, PA: Association for Computational Linguistics.

Macmillan, K. (2005). More than just coding? Evaluating CAQDAS in a discourse analysis of news texts. *Forum: Qualitative Social Research, 6*(3). Retrieved June 27, 2015, from qualitative-research.net/index.php/fqs/article/view/28

Magnini, B., & Cavaglia, G. (2000). Integrating subject field codes into WordNet. *Proceedings of the Conference on Language Resources and Evaluations (LREC-2000)* (pp. 1413–1418). Athens, Greece.

Maguire, S., Hardy, C., & Lawrence, T. (2004). Institutional entrepreneurship in emerging fields: HIV/AIDS treatment advocacy in Canada. *Academy of Management Journal, 47*(5), 657–679.

Mairesse, F., Walker, M., Mehl, M., & Moore, R. (2007). Using linguistic cures for the automatic recognition of personality in conversation and text. *Journal of Artificial Intelligence Research, 30,* 457–501.

Marcus, M. P., Marcinkiewicz, M. A., & Santorini, B. (1993). Building a large annotated corpus of English: The Penn Treebank. *Computational Linguistics, 19*(2), 313–330.

Marwick, B. (2013). Discovery of emergent issues and controversies in anthropology using text mining, topic modeling, and social network analysis of microblog content. In C. Yonghua & Y. Zhao (Eds.), *Data mining applications with R,* 63–93. Cambridge, England: Academic Press.

Mason, Z. J. (2004). Cormet: A computational, corpus-based conventional metaphor extraction system. *Computational Linguistics, 30*(1), 23–44.

Mathews, A. S. (2005). Power/knowledge, Power/ignorance: Forest fires and the state in Mexico. *Human Ecology, 33*(6), 795–820.

McCallum, A., & Li, W. (2003). Early results for named entity recognition with conditional random fields, feature induction and web-enhanced lexicons. *Proceedings of the Seventh Conference on Natural Language Learning.* Stroudsburg, PA: Association for Computational Linguistics.

McCallum, A., & Nigam, K. (1998). *A comparison of event models for Naive Bayes text classification.* Paper presented at the AAAI-98 Workshop on Learning for Text Categorization.

McFarland, D., Ramage, D., Chuang, J., Heer, J., Manning, C., & Jurafsky, D. (2013). Differentiating language usage through topic models. *Poetics, 41*(6), 607–625.

Merkl-Davies, D. M., & Koller, V. (2012). "Metaphoring" people out of this world: A critical discourse analysis of a chairman's statement of a UK defence firm. *Accounting Forum, 36*(3), 178–193.

Merton, R. K. (1949). On sociological theories of the middle range. In R. K. Merton, *Social theory and social structure* (pp. 39–53). New York, NY: Free Press.

Meyer, M. (2014, June 30). Everything you need to know about Facebook's controversial emotion experiment. *Wired.* Retrieved from http://www.wired.com/2014/06/everything-you-need-to-know-about-facebooks-manipulative-experiment

Mihalcea, R. (2007). Using Wikipedia for automatic word sense disambiguation. *Proceedings of NAACL HLT* (pp. 196–203). Retrieved June 27, 2015, from aclweb.org/anthology/N07-1025

Mihalcea, R., Banea, C., & Wiebe, J. (2007). *Learning multilingual subjective language via cross-lingual projections.* Paper presented at the Proceedings of the Association for Computational Linguistics, Prague, Czech Republic.

Mihalcea, R., & Strapparava, C. (2009). The lie detector: Explorations in the automatic recognition of deceptive language. *Proceedings of the ACL-IJCNLP 2009 Conference Short Papers* (pp. 309–312). Stroudsburg, PA: Association for Computational Linguistics.

Mikolov, T., Sutskever, I., Chen, K., Corrado, G., & Dean, J. (2013). Distributed representations of words and phrases and their compositionality. *Advances in neural information processing systems* (pp. 3111–3119).

Miles, M. B., & Huberman, A. M. (1994). *Data management and analysis methods.* Thousand Oaks, CA: Sage.

Miller, G. A. (1995). WordNet: A lexical database for English. *Communications of the ACM, 38*(11), 39–41.

Mische, A. (2014). Measuring futures in action: Projective grammars in the Rio+20 debates. *Theory & Society, 43*(3–4), 437–464.

Mohr, J. W., & Bogdanov, P. (2013). Introduction—Topic models: What they are and why they matter. *Poetics, 41*(6), 545–569.

Moser, K. (2000). Metaphor analysis in psychology—Method, theory, and fields of application. *Forum: Qualitative Social Research, 1*(2), Art. 21. Retrieved from http://nbn-resolving.de/urn:nbn:de:0114-fqs0002212

Mukherjee, A., & Liu, B. (2012). Aspect extraction through semi-supervised modeling. *Proceedings of the 50th Annual Meeting of the Association for Computational Linguistics.* (pp. 339–348). Stroudsburg, PA: Association for Computational Linguistics.

Mützel, S. (2015). Facing big data: Making sociology relevant. *Big Data & Society, 2*(2), 1–4.

Nakagawa, T., Inui, K., & Kurohashi, S. (2010). Dependency tree-based sentiment classification using CRFs with hidden variables. In *Human Language Technologies: The 2010 Annual Conference of the North American Chapter of the Association for Computational Linguistics* (pp. 786–794). Stroudsburg, PA: Association for Computational Linguistics.

Narayanan, A., & Shmatikov, V. (2008). Robust de-anonymization of large sparse datasets (How to break anonymity of the Netflix prize dataset). *IEEE Symposium on Security & Privacy*, Oakland, CA. Retrieved from http://arxiv.org/pdf/cs/0610105v2

Narayanan, A., & Shmatikov, V. (2009). De-anonymizing social networks. *IEEE Symposium on Security & Privacy*, Oakland, CA. Retrieved from http://www.cs.utexas.edu/~shmat/shmat_oak09.pdf

Navigli, R., & Ponzetto, S. (2012). *Artificial Intelligence, 193*, 217–250.

Neuman, Y., Assaf, D., Cohen, Y., Last, M., Argamon, S., Newton, H., & Frieder, O. (2013). Metaphor identification in large texts corpora. *PLOS ONE, 8*(4), 1–9.

Newman, M. L., Pennebaker, J. W., Berry, D. S., & Richards, J. M. (2003). Lying words: Predicting deception from linguistic styles. *Personality and Social Psychology Bulletin, 29*(5), 665–675.

Noel-Jorand, M.-C., Reinert, M., Bonnon, M., & Therme, P. (1995). Discourse analysis and psychological adaptation to high altitude hypoxia. *Stress Medicine, 11*(1), 27–39.

O'Halloran, K., & Coffin, C. (2004). Checking over-interpretation and under-interpretation: Help from corpora in critical linguistics. *Text and Texture: Systemic Functional Viewpoints on the Nature and Structure of Text*, 275–297.

O'Keefe, A., & Walsh, S. (2012). Applying corpus linguistics and conversation analysis in the investigation of small group teaching in higher education. *Corpus Linguistics and Linguistic Theory, 8*(1), 159–181.

Olthouse, J. (2014). How do preservice teachers conceptualize giftedness? A metaphor analysis. *Roeper Review, 36*(2), 122–132.

O'Mara-Shimek, M., Guillén-Parra, M., & Ortega-Larrea, A. (2015). Stop the bleeding or weather the storm? Crisis solution marketing and the ideological use of metaphor in online financial reporting of the stock market crash of 2008 at the New York Stock Exchange. *Discourse & Communication, 9*(1), 103–123.

Ortony, A., Clore, G. L., & Collins, A. (1990). *The cognitive structure of emotions*. New York, NY: Cambridge University Press.

Osmond, A. (2016). *Academic writing and grammar for students*. Thousand Oaks, CA: Sage.

Ott, M., Choi, Y., Cardie, C., & Hancock, J. T. (2011). Finding deceptive opinion spam by any stretch of the imagination. *Proceedings of the Forty-Ninth Annual Meeting of the Association for Computational Linguistics: Human Language Technologies—Volume 1 Association for Computational Linguistics* (pp. 309–319). Stroudsburg, PA: Association for Computational Linguistics.

Pang, B., & Lee, L. (2004). A sentimental education: Sentiment analysis using subjectivity summarization based on minimum cuts. *Proceedings of the Forty-Second Annual Meeting on Association for Computational Linguistics.* (pp. 271–278). Stroudsburg, PA: Association for Computational Linguistics.

Pang, B., & Lee, L. (2008). Opinion mining and sentiment analysis. *Foundations and Trends in Information Retrieval, 2*(1–2), 1–35.

Parker, I. (1992). *Discourse dynamics: Critical analysis for social and individual psychology.* London, England: Routledge.

Patton, M. Q. (1990). *Qualitative evaluation and research methods.* Thousand Oaks, CA: Sage.

Patton, M. Q. (2014). *Qualitative research & evaluation methods: Integrating theory and practice* (4th ed.). Thousand Oaks, CA: Sage.

Pauca, V. P., Shahnaz, F., Berry, M. W., & Plemmons, R. J. (2004). Text mining using non-negative matrix factorizations. *Proceedings of the Fourth SIAM International Conference on Data Mining.* Retrieved June 27, 2015, from epubs.siam.org/doi/pdf/10.1137/1.9781611972740.45

Peirce, C. S. (1901). Truth and falsity and error. *Dictionary of Philosophy and Psychology, 2,* 716–720.

Pennebaker, J. W., Francis, M., & Booth, R. J. (2001). *Linguistic Inquiry and Word Count (LIWC): A computerized text analysis program.* Mahwah, NJ: Lawrence Erlbaum.

Pennebaker, J. W., & King, L. (1999). Linguistic styles: Language use as an individual difference. *Journal of Personality and Social Psychology, 77,* 1296–1312.

Phillips, N., & Hardy, C. (2002). *Discourse analysis: Investigating processes of social construction.* Thousand Oaks, CA: Sage.

Plummer, K. (1995). *Telling sexual stories: Power, change and social worlds.* London, England: Routledge.

Popping, R. (1997). Computer programs for the analysis of texts and transcripts. In *Text analysis for the social sciences: Methods for drawing statistical inferences from texts and transcripts* (pp. 209–221). Mahwah, NJ: Lawrence Erlbaum.

Potter, J., & Wetherell, M. (1987). *Discourse and social psychology: Beyond attitudes and behavior.* Newbury Park, CA: Sage.

Propp, V. (1968). *Morphology of the folktale.* Austin: University of Texas Press.

Puschmann, C., & Burgess, J. (2014). Big data, big questions: Metaphors of big data. *International Journal of Communication, 8,* 1690–1709.

Quinlan, J. (1993). *C4.5: Programs for machine learning.* San Francisco, CA: Morgan Kaufmann.

Quinn, K. M., Monroe, B. L., Colaresi, M., Crespin, M. H., & Radev, D. R. (2010). How to analyze political attention with minimal assumptions and costs. *American Journal of Political Science, 54*(1), 209–228.

Ratnaparkhi, A. (1996, May). A maximum entropy model for part-of-speech tagging. *Proceedings of the Conference on Empirical Methods in Natural Language Processing* (Vol. 1., pp. 133–142).

Ravitch, S. M., & Riggan, J. M. (2016). *Reason & rigor: How conceptual frameworks guide research.* Thousand Oaks, CA: Sage.

Rees, C. E., Knight, L. V., & Wilkinson, C. E. (2007). Doctors being up there and we being down here: A metaphorical analysis of talk about student/doctor–patient relationships. *Social Science and Medicine, 65*(4), 725–737.

Resnik, P., Garron, A., & Resnik, R. (2013). Using topic modeling to improve prediction of neuroticism and depression in college students. *Proceedings of the 2013 Conference on Empirical Methods in Natural Language Processing* (pp. 1348–1353). Stroudsburg, PA: Association for Computational Linguistics.

Richards, L., & Morse, J. (2013). *README FIRST for a user's guide to qualitative methods.* Thousand Oaks, CA: Sage.

Richardson, D. C., Spivey, M. J., Barsalou, L. W., & McRae, K. (2003). Spatial representations activated during real-time comprehension of verbs. *Cognitive Science, 27*(5), 767–780.

Ricoeur, P. (1991). Narrative identity. *Philosophy Today, 35*(1), 73–81.

Riloff, E., & Jones, R. (1999). Learning dictionaries for information extraction by multi-level bootstrapping. *Proceedings of the Sixteenth National Conference on Artificial Intelligence and the Eleventh Innovative Applications of Artificial Intelligence Conference Innovative Applications of Artificial Intelligence* (pp. 474–479). Menlo Park, CA: American Association for Artificial Intelligence.

Roberts, C. W. (1997). *Text analysis for the social sciences: Methods for drawing statistical inferences from texts and transcripts*. Mahwah, NJ: Lawrence Erlbaum.

Roberts, C. W. (2008). *The fifth modality: On languages that shape our motivations and cultures*. Leiden, Netherlands: Brill Publishers.

Roberts, C. W., Zuell, C., Landmann, J., & Wang, Y. (2010). Modality analysis: A semantic grammar for imputations of intentionality in texts. *Quality & Quanitity, 44*(2), 239–257.

Roberts, C. W., Popping, R., & Pan, Y. (2009). Modalities of democratic transformation forms of public discourse in Hungary's latest newspaper, 1990–1997. *International Sociology, 24*(4), 498–525.

Roberts, M., Stewart, B., & Airoldi, E. (2016). A model of text for experimentation in the social sciences. *Journal of the American Statistical Association, 111*(515), 988–1003.

Roderburg, S. (1998). *Sprachliche konstruktion der wirklichkeit. Metaphern in therapiegesprächen*. Wiesbaden, Germany: Deutscher Universitäts Verlag.

Roget, P. (1987). *Roget's thesaurus of English words and phrases*. New York, NY: Longman. (Original work published 1911)

Rosenwald, G. C., & Ochberg, R. L. (1992). *Storied lives: The cultural politics of self-understanding*. New Haven, CT: Yale University Press.

Rousselière, D., & Vézina, M. (2009). Constructing the legitimacy of a financial cooperative in the cultural sector: A case study using textual analysis. *International Review of Sociology: Revue Internationale de Sociologie, 19*(2), 241–261.

Ruan, X., Wilson, S., & Mihalcea, R. (2016, August 7–12). Finding optimists and pessimists on Twitter. *Proceedings of the 54th Annual Meeting of the Association for Computational Linguistics* (pp. 320–325). Berlin, Germany.

Ruiz Ruiz, J. (2009). Sociological discourse analysis: Methods and logic. *Forum: Qualitative Social Research, 10*(2). Retrieved June 27, 2015, from qualitative-research.net/index.php/fqs/article/view/1298/2882

Ryan, G. W., & Bernard, H. R. (2010). *Analyzing qualitative data: Systematic approaches*. Thousand Oaks, CA: Sage.

Sahpazia, P., & Balamoutsoua, S. (2015). Therapists' accounts of relationship breakup experiences: A narrative analysis. *European Journal of Psychotherapy & Counselling, 17*(3), 258–276.

Salganik, M. (in press). *Bit by bit: Social research in the digital age*. Retrieved from http://www.bitbybitbook.com

Salmons, J. (2014). *Qualitative online interviews*. Thousand Oaks, CA: Sage.

Salton, G. (1989). *Automatic text processing: The transformation, analysis, and retrieval of information by computer*. Reading, PA: Addison-Wesley.

Santa Ana, O. (2002). *Brown tide rising metaphors of Latinos in contemporary American public discourse*. Austin: University of Texas Press.

Sapir, J., & Crocker, J. (Eds.). (1977). *The social use of metaphor: Essays on the anthropology of rhetoric*. Philadelphia: University of Pennsylvania Press.

Saussure, de, F. (1959). *Course in general linguistics*. New York, NY: The Philosophical Library.

Schmidt, B. M. (2012). Words alone: Dismantling topic models in the humanities. *Journal of Digital Humanities, 2*(1).

Schmitt, R. (2000). Notes towards the analysis of metaphor. *Forum Qualitative Social Research, 1*(1).

Schmitt, R. (2005). Systematic metaphor analysis as a method of qualitative research. *The Qualitative Report, 10*(2), 358–394.

Schonhardt-Bailey, C. (2013). *Deliberating American monetary policy: A textual analysis*. London, England: MIT Press.

Schuster, J., Beune, E., & Stronks, K. (2011). Metaphorical constructions of hypertension among three ethnic groups in the Netherlands. *Ethnicity and Health, 16*(6), 583–600.

Schwandt, T. A. (2001). *Dictionary of qualitative research*. Thousand Oaks, CA: Sage.

Shaw, C., & Nerlich, B. (2015). Metaphor as a mechanism of global climate change governance: A study of international policies, 1992–2012. *Ecological Economics, 109*, 34–40.

Shepherd, A., Sanders, C., Doyle, M., & Shaw, J. (2015). Using social media for support and feedback by mental health service users: Thematic analysis of a Twitter conversation. *BMC Psychiatry, 15*(29).

Silverman, D. (1993). *Interpreting qualitative data: Methods for analyzing talk, text and interaction*. Newbury Park, CA: Sage.

Silverman, D. (Ed.). (2016). *Qualitative research*. Thousand Oaks, CA: Sage.

Snow C. P. (2013). *The two cultures and the scientific revolution*. London, England: Martino Fine Books. (Original work published 1959)

Socher, R., Perelygin, A., Wu, J. Y., Chuang, J., Manning, C. D., Ng, A. Y., & Potts, C. (2013). Recursive deep models for semantic compositionality over a sentiment treebank. *Proceedings of the Conference on Empirical Methods in Natural Language Processing.*

Soroka, S., Stecula, D., & Wlezien, C. (2015). It's (change in) the (future) economy, stupid: Economic indicators, the media, and public opinion. *American Journal of Political Science, 59*(2), 457–474.

Speed, G. J. (1893). Do newspapers now give the news? *Forum, 15*, 705–711.

Spradley, J. P. (1972). Adaptive strategies of urban nomads: The ethnoscience of tramp culture. In T. Weaver & D. J. White (Eds.), *The anthropology of urban environments*. Boulder, CO: Society for Applied Anthropology.

Stark, A., Shafran, I., & Kaye, J. (2012). Hello, who is calling?: Can words reveal the social nature of conversations? *Proceedings of the 2012 Conference of the North American Chapters of the Association for Computational Linguistics: Human Language Technologies* (pp. 112–119).

Stone, P. J., Dunphry, D., Smith, M. S., & Ogilvie, D. M. (1966). *The General Inquirer: A computer approach to content analysis*. Cambridge, MA: MIT Press.

Stone, P. J., & Hunt, E. B. (1963). A computer approach to content analysis: Studies using the General Inquirer system. *AFIPS '63 (Spring) Proceedings of the May 21–23, 1963, Spring Joint Computer Conference* (pp. 241–256). doi:10.1145/1461551.1461583

Strachan, J., Yellowlees, G., & Quigley, A. (2015). General practitioners' assessment of, and treatment decisions regarding, common mental disorder in older adults: Thematic analysis of interview data. *Ageing and Society, 35*(1), 150–168.

Strapparava, C., & Mihalcea, R. (2007). SemEval-2007 task 14: Affective text. *Proceedings of the Fourth International Workshop on the Semantic Evaluations, Prague, Czech Republic* (pp. 70–74). Stroudsburg, PA: Association for Computational Linguistics.

Strapparava, C., & Valitutti, A. (2004). WordNet-Affect: An affective extension of WordNet. *Proceedings of the 4th International Conference on Language Resources and Evaluation*, Lisbon, Portugal.

Strauss, C. (1992). What makes Tony run? Schemas as motives reconsidered. In R. D'Andrade & C. Strauss (Eds.), *Human motives and cultural models* (pp. 191–224). Cambridge, England: Cambridge University Press.

Stroet, K., Opdenakker, M.-C., & Minnaert, A. (2015). Need supportive teaching in practice: A narrative analysis in schools with contrasting educational approaches. *Social Psychology of Education, 18*(3), 585–613.

Strunk, W., & White, E. B. (1999). *The elements of style* (4th ed.). New York, NY: Pearson.

Stubbs, M. (1994). Grammar, text, and ideology: Computer-assisted methods in the linguistics of representation. *Applied Linguistics, 15*(2), 201–223.

Sudhahar, S., Franzosi, R., & Cristianini, N. (2011). Automating quantitative narrative analysis of news data. *JMLR: Workshop and Conference Proceedings, 17*, 63–71.

Sudweeks, F., & Rafaeli, S. (1996). How do you get a hundred strangers to agree: Computer mediated communication and collaboration. In T. M. Harrison & T. D. Stephen (Eds.), *Computer networking and scholarship in the 21st century university* (pp. 115–136). New York, NY: SUNY Press.

Sun, Y., & Jiang, J. (2014). Metaphor use in Chinese and US corporate mission statements: A cognitive sociolinguistic analysis. *English for Specific Purposes, 33*, 4–14.

Sveningsson, M. (2003). Ethics in Internet ethnography. *International Journal of Global Information Management*, *11*(3). Retrieved from http://www.irma-international.org/viewtitle/28292

Sweeney, L. (2003). Navigating computer science research through waves of privacy concerns: Discussions among computer scientists at Carnegie Mellon University. *Tech Report*, CMU CS 03-165, CMU-ISRI-03-102. Pittsburgh, PA.

Sweetser, E. (1990). *From etymology to pragmatics: The mind-body metaphor in semantic structure and semantic change.* Cambridge, England: Cambridge University Press.

Sword, H. (2012a). *Stylish academic writing.* Cambridge, MA: Harvard University Press.

Sword, H. (2012b, July 23). Zombie nouns. *New York Times.*

Takamura, H., Inui, T., & Okumura, M. (2006). Latent variable models for semantic orientations of phrases. *Proceedings of the Eleventh Meeting of the European Chapter of the Association for Computational Linguistics* (pp. 201–208). Trento, Italy.

Tashakkori, A. M., & Teddlie, C. B. (2010). *SAGE handbook of mixed methods in social & behavioral research* (2nd ed.). Thousand Oaks, CA: Sage.

Tausczik, Y. R., & Pennebaker, J. W. (2010). The psychological meaning of words: LIWC and computerized text analysis methods. *Journal of Language and Social Psychology*, *29*(1), 24–54.

Teddlie, C. B., & Tashakkori, A. M. (Eds.). (2008). *Foundations of mixed methods research: Integrating quantitative and qualitative approaches in the social and behavioral sciences.* Thousand Oaks, CA: Sage.

Toerien, M., & Wilkinson, S. (2004). Exploring the depilation norm: A qualitative questionnaire study of women's body hair removal. *Qualitative Research in Psychology*, *1*(1), 69–92.

Toor, R. (2012, July 2). Becoming a "stylish" writer. *Chronicle of Higher Education*. Retrieved from http://chronicle.com/article/Becoming-a-Stylish-Writer/132677

Törnberg, A., & Törnberg, P. (2016). Combining CDA and topic modeling: Analyzing discursive connections between Islamophobia and anti-feminism on an online forum. *Discourse & Society*, *27*(4), 401–422.

Toutanova, K., Klein, D., Manning, C. D., & Singer, Y. (2003, May). Feature-rich part-of-speech tagging with a cyclic dependency network. *Proceedings of the 2003 Conference of the North American Chapter of the Association for Computational Linguistics on Human Technology—Volume 1* (pp. 173–180). Stroudsburg, PA: Association for Computational Linguistics.

Trappey, C., Wu, H., Liu, K., & Lin, F. (2013, September 11–13). Knowledge discovery of service satisfaction based on text analysis of critical incident dialogues and clustering methods. *2013 IEEE 10th International Conference on e-Business Engineering* (pp. 265–270). Coventry, United Kingdom: ICEBE 2013.

Trochim, W. M. K. (1989). Concept mapping: Soft science or hard art? *Science Direct*, *12*(1), 87–110.

Trochim, W. M. K., Cook, J. A., & Setze, R. (1994). Using concept mapping to develop a conceptual framework of staff's views of a supported employment program for individuals with severe mental illness. *Journal of Consulting and Clinical Psychology*, *62*(4), 766–775.

Turney, P. D. (2001). Mining the web for synonyms: PMI-IR versus LSA on TOEFL. *Proceedings of the Twelfth European Conference on Machine Learning (ECML-2001)* (pp. 491–502). Freiburg, Germany. NRC 44893.

Turney, P. D. (2002). Thumbs up or thumbs down? Semantic orientation applied to unsupervised classification of reviews. *Proceedings of the Fortieth Annual Meeting on Association for Computational Linguistics* (pp. 417–424). Stroudsburg, PA: Association for Computational Linguistics.

Turney, P. D., Neuman, Y., Assaf, D., & Cohen, Y. (2011). Literal and metaphorical sense identification through concrete and abstract context. *Proceedings of the Conference on Empirical Methods in Natural Language Processing* (pp. 680–690). Stroudsburg, PA: Association for Computational Linguistics.

Uprichard, E. (2012). Describing description (and keeping causality): The case of academic articles on food and eating. *Sociology*, *47*(2), 368–382.

Van Dijk, T. A. (1993). Principles of critical discourse analysis. *Discourse & Society*, *4*(2), 249–283.

van Ham, F., Wattenberg, M., & Viégas, F. (2009). Mapping text with phrase nets. *IEEE Transactions on Visualization and*

*Computer Graphics, 15*(6). Retrieved from http://ieeexplore .ieee.org/abstract/document/5290726

Van Herzele, A. (2006). A forest for each city and town: Story lines in the policy debate for urban forests in Flanders. *Urban Studies, 43*(3), 673–696. doi:10.1080/00420980500534651

van Meter, K. M., & de Saint Léger, M. (2014). American, French & German sociologies compared through link analysis of conference abstracts. *Bulletin of Sociological Methodology, 122*(1), 26–45.

Vapnik, V. (1995). *The nature of statistical learning theory.* New York, NY: Springer.

Viégas, F. B., & Wattenberg, M. (2008). TIMELINES: Tag clouds and the case for vernacular visualization. *Interactions, 15*(4), 49–52. doi:10.1145/1374489.1374501

Walejko, G. (2009). Online survey: Instant publication, instant mistake, all of the above. In E. Hargittai (Ed.), *Research confidential: Solutions to problems most social scientists pretend they never have* (pp. 101–115). Ann Arbor: University of Michigan Press.

Watson, M., Jones, D., & Burns, L. (2007). Internet research and informed consent: An ethical model for using archived emails. *International Journal of Therapy & Rehabilitation, 14*(9), 396–403.

Weale, A. Bicquelet, A., & Bara, J. (2012). Debating abortion, deliberative reciprocity and parliamentary advocacy. *Political Studies, 60*(3), 643–667.

Weisgerber, C., & Butler, S. H. (2009). Visualizing the future of interaction studies: Data visualization applications as a research, pedagogical, and presentational tool for interaction scholars. *The Electronic Journal of Communication, 19*(1–2). Retrieved June 26, 2015, from http://www.cios.org/ejcpublic/ 019/1/019125.HTML

Wertsch, J. V. (1985). *Vygotsky and the social formation of mind.* Cambridge, MA: Harvard University Press.

Wetherell, M., & Edley, N. (1999). Negotiating hegemonic masculinity: Imaginary positions and psycho-discursive practices. *Feminism and Psychology, 9*(3), 335–356.

Wheeldon, J., & Ahlberg, M. (2012). *Visualizing social science research: Maps, methods, & meaning.* Thousand Oaks, CA: Sage.

Wheeldon, J., & Faubert, J. (2009). Framing experience: Concept maps, mind maps, and data collection in qualitative research. *International Journal of Qualitative Methods, 8*(3), 68–83.

White, H. (1978). *Tropics of discourse: Essays in cultural criticism.* Baltimore, MD: Johns Hopkins University Press.

White, P. W. (1924). Quarter century survey of press content shows demand for facts. *Editor and Publisher, 57.*

Wiebe, J., Bruce, R., & O'Hara, T. (1999). Development and use of a gold-standard data set for subjectivity classifications. *Proceedings of the Thirty-Seventh Annual Meeting of the Association for Computational Linguistics* (pp. 246–253). Stroudsburg, PA: Association for Computational Linguistics.

Wiebe, J., & Mihalcea, R. (2006). *Word sense and subjectivity.* Paper presented at the Fourty-Fourth Annual Meeting of the Association for Computational Linguistics, Sydney, Australia.

Wiebe, J., Wilson, T., & Cardie, C. (2005). Annotating expressions of opinions and emotions in language. *Language Resources and Evaluation, 39*(2–3), 165–210.

Wilcox, D. F. (1900). The American newspaper: A study in social psychology. *The ANNALS of the American Academy of Political and Social Science, 16*(1), 56–92. doi:10.1177/000271620001600104

Wilkinson, L., & Friendly, M. (2009). The history of the cluster heat map. *The American Statistician, 63*(9), 179–184.

Wilson, T. (2008). *Fine-grained subjectivity and sentiment analysis: Recognizing the intensity, polarity, and attitudes of private states* (PhD thesis, University of Pittsburgh).

Windelband, W. (1998). On history and natural science. *History and Theory, 19,* 165–185. (Original work published 1894)

Windelband, W. (2001). *A history of philosophy.* Cresskill, NJ: The Paper Tiger. (Original work published 1901)

Winkel, G. (2012). Foucault in the forests—A review of the use of "Foucauldian" concepts in forest policy analysis. *Forest Policy and Economics, 16,* 81–92.

Wofford, T. (2014, July 28). OkCupid co-founder: "We experiment on human beings . . . that's how websites work."

*Newsweek*. Retrieved from http://www.newsweek.com/okcupid-founder-we-experiment-human-beingsthats-how-websites-work-261741

Woodwell, D. (2014). *Research foundations: How do we know what we know?* Thousand Oaks, CA: Sage.

Wu, H., Liu, K., & Trappey, C. (2014). Understanding customers using Facebook pages: Data mining users feedback using text analysis. *IEEE*, 346–350.

Yarowsky, D. (2000). Hierarchical decision lists for word sense disambiguation. *Computers and the Humanities*, *34*(1), 179–186.

Yu, H., & Hatzivassiloglou, V. (2003). *Towards answering opinion questions: Separating facts from opinions and identifying the polarity of opinion sentences*. Paper presented at the Conference on Empirical Methods in Natural Language Processing, Sapporo, Japan.

Yun, G. W., & Trumbo, C. W. (2000). Comparative response to a survey executed by post, e-mail, & web form. *Journal of Computer-Mediated Communication*, *6*(1).

Zagibalov, T., & Carroll, J. (2008). Automatic seed word selection for unsupervised sentiment classification of Chinese text. *Proceedings of the Twenty-Second International Conference on Computational Linguistics* (pp. 1073–1080). Stroudsburg, PA: Association for Computational Linguistics.

# INDEX

Note: Page references in italics refer to boxes, figures, and tables.